DEWEY'S
METAPHYSICS

DEWEY'S
METAPHYSICS

RAYMOND D. BOISVERT

FORDHAM UNIVERSITY PRESS
New York
1988

Printed in the United States of America

À MES CHERS PARENTS

DONAT ET IRÈNE

ACKNOWLEDGMENTS

John Dewey consistently stressed the importance, for humans, of associated activity. Genuine freedom, for him, was to be understood, not as autonomy, but as growing with the powers, the actual capacities, that resulted from the proper sorts of interaction with others. My own project underscores the correctness of this view. This work would never have been undertaken, much less completed, without the inspiration, encouragement, and assistance of numerous individuals.

John Anton and Jim Gouinlock deserve special mention in this regard: the former for suggesting to a reluctant graduate student, who had never turned a page of Dewey, that, for someone interested in traditional issues, reading Dewey would repay the effort; and the latter whose wide and sensitive understanding of Dewey has served as a model for my work and has saved me from many an egregious interpretive error. For conversations that have furthered my understanding of metaphysical issues, I am indebted to Paul Kuntz, Tom Alexander, Pete Gunter, Lillian Webb, and Sylvia Walsh. Rose Bode gave me crucial advice when I needed it. My wife, Jayne, the family grammarian, not only smoothed out many a convoluted passage but also provided constant encouragement—not to mention a cheerful willingness to share in the typing of the manuscript.

Several awards have supported this research in various stages. I wish to thank the United Negro College Fund for two grants: a Faculty Improvement Fellowship, and a fellowship through their Strengthening the Humanities Program. I am also grateful to the Mellon Foundation for a grant to the humanities division of Clark College in Atlanta while I was a faculty member there.

Dewey scholarship in general is indebted to two recent works: Ralph Sleeper's *The Necessity of Pragmatism* (New Haven: Yale University Press, 1987) and Thomas Alexander's *The Horizons of Feeling* (Albany: State University of New York Press, 1987). I was fortunate to have seen the latter in a pre-publication form, but Sleeper's book, unfortunately, I did not come upon until this manuscript had been completed. Both are important complements to the present study: Alexander's emphasizing Dewey's aesthetics, and Sleeper's, his logic and philosophy of language.

In dedicating this text to my parents, I express my gratitude for pro-

viding a home where intellectual discussion was nurtured and, what was more significant, for encouraging their children to choose their own way of life, even when the calling came from so unusual a direction as philosophy.

Siena College

CONTENTS

ABBREVIATIONS

Citations of Dewey's works appear, for the most part, as listed here. For complete bibliographical information, see the Bibliography.

AE	*Art as Experience.*
EEL	*Essays in Experimental Logic.*
EN	*Experience and Nature.*
ENF	*On Experience, Nature, and Freedom.*
EW I	*The Early Works*, volume 1.
HNC	*Human Nature and Conduct.*
LTI	*Logic: The Theory of Inquiry.*
LW V	*The Later Works*, volume 5.
MW II	*The Middle Works*, volume 2.
MW IV	*The Middle Works*, volume 4.
MW X	*The Middle Works*, volume 10.
PSY	*Psychology.*
QC	*The Quest for Certainty.*
RP	*Reconstruction in Philosophy.*

INTRODUCTION

1. Preliminary Remarks

There is a growing interest in the philosophy of John Dewey. This is due to a variety of factors: the existence of a vigorous Society for the Advancement of American Philosophy, the publication of Dewey's collected works by Southern Illinois University Press, a renewed concern with social and political issues, and the proselytizing of Richard Rorty, who enlists Dewey in the crusade against foundationalism.[1] This book seeks to contribute to this growing interest.

Locating Dewey as one in a long line of thinkers who recognized the importance of ontological considerations, it examines in particular the way Dewey dealt with the perennial issue of permanence and change. Since the time of Plato, this topic has been discussed within the context of "forms." As we shall see, Dewey's own reflections bring him to a revised understanding of this venerable philosophical term. While rejecting much that was in the tradition, Dewey nonetheless continued to ask questions and to suggest answers that place him at the level of classical metaphysicians. The aim of this book is to examine, explain, and interpret his questions and answers pertaining to the issue of change and permanence.

To avoid confusion in terminology, I shall specify the way in which two prominent terms, "ontology" and "form," are used in the text. "Ontology" is the etymologically more suitable word for the discipline known, prior to the eighteenth century, as "metaphysics." The most accurate description for this study was provided by Aristotle when he characterized it as the study of being *qua* being. Ontology deals with beings—that is, with things that exist—and it deals with them only insofar as they exist. Further specifications of beings (as animate, chemical, inanimate, etc.) circumscribe the subject matters of the special sciences, and do not concern the ontologist as such. Ontology seeks what is common to all entities. Dewey uses "ontology" and "metaphysics" interchangeably, and I follow him in this. I also employ various synonyms for "being." "Entity," "thing," and "existent" are so used, and in each case indicate *that which is*.

1

"Form" is both a venerable philosophical concept and a term commonly used in ordinary discourse. Because of this, it has acquired a variety of meanings. My usage of "form" follows that of a contemporary leader in the study of the topic, Lancelot Law Whyte. What is central to the many meanings of "form," according to Whyte, is the "notion of an ordered complexity."[2] When some elaboration of this compact formulation is provided, certain characterizations of form become evident. (*a*) Form always involves a blend of *unity* and *multiplicity*; sheer multiplicity and sheer unity describe situations in which form is not a factor. (*b*) Since form implies that a complexity is organized in a certain way, a *structure* or determinateness of some sort is achieved. (*c*) Because the multiplicity or complexity may be ordered in a variety of ways, form implies a *limitation* imposed upon the manifold.

Although not widely regarded as a metaphysician, Dewey explicitly recognized the significance of this discipline. He described philosophy as "a criticism of criticisms," meaning by the term "criticism" "discriminating judgment" or "careful appraisal" (EN 298). Such criticism is especially important and appropriate, Dewey insisted, where there is concern about "goods or values" (EN 298). But this kind of criticism would not provide the benefits of harmony and secured goods unless it had been developed in conjunction with an accurate metaphysics as "a statement of the generic traits manifested by existences of all kinds" (EN 308).

To grasp the connection between concern with metaphysics and concern with values, we must understand that for Dewey metaphysics involves more than the mere enumeration of generic traits. This discipline does not find its work exhausted when a list of characteristics such as individuality, multiplicity, process, contingency, and stability has been recited. Such an enumeration, as Dewey insisted, would have "nothing to do with wisdom" (EN 309). The importance of metaphysics is that it attempts to go further and to ascertain with respect to the general traits of nature "their degrees and the ratios they sustain to one another" (EN 309); it seeks, in other words, to articulate "the nature of the existential world in which we live" (EN 45).

Any attempt to consolidate and enhance values will be based, according to Dewey, on just such a vision of what the world is like. "The more sure one is that the world which encompasses human

life is of such and such a character (no matter what his definition), the more one is committed to try to direct the conduct of life, that of others as well as of himself, upon the basis of the character assigned to the world" (EN 309). For Dewey, philosophy's primary role was always the concern with values, but such concern, as he well recognized, does not exist in a vacuum. The human situation "falls wholly within nature" and "reflects the traits of nature" (EN 314). Because of this, the study of metaphysics as an examination of these traits assumes a fundamental significance. I am hopeful that the text which follows will both substantiate these views and provide an accurate presentation of Dewey's metaphysics.

2. THE NEED FOR SUCH A STUDY

This book was written in response to two major problems in Deweyan scholarship and to a third issue of a more purely theoretical character. (*a*) To begin with, there are scholars who dismiss the Deweyan attempt at formulating a metaphysics as superficial, irrelevant, and contradictory. (*b*) There are others who provide a caricature of Deweyan metaphysics as describing a natural world given over solely to flux, process, and change. (*c*) Finally, there is a general need, occasioned by developments in the sciences, for contemporary philosophers to deal with the issues encapsulated in the term "form."

(*a*) Freud complained that one bane of any thinker is to have too many friends or followers. It would not be long, Freud knew, before his name would be uttered in support of positions worlds apart from those he actually held. This was certainly true for a philosopher like Hegel, whose thought was led in conflicting and diametrically opposed directions by his followers. It is also true for Dewey in reference to interpretations of his metaphysics. Two commentators in particular, Richard Rorty and Sidney Hook, both avowed admirers of Dewey, fail to recognize the importance of the naturalistic metaphysics he developed.

Rorty claims that it is easier to think of *Experience and Nature*, Dewey's fundamental statement of metaphysics, "as an explanation of why nobody needs a metaphysics, rather than as itself a metaphysical system."[3] It is hard to see, Rorty claims, how Dewey's displaying of generic traits "could either avoid banality or dissolve

traditional philosophical problems."⁴ Hook's criticisms of the meta-physical dimension in Dewey's work comes at a surprising place, his introduction to the definitive edition of *Experience and Nature* published in 1981. Hook introduces Dewey's most articulate effort at formulating a metaphysics by denying any importance to that discipline as Dewey understood it. He claims that Dewey would have done well to revise the text by abandoning the enterprise of gaining knowledge about generic traits. He doubts that such traits exist and asserts that Dewey's philosophical outlook does not re-quire "that he interpret traits in this way" (EN xiv).

The major difficulty with the interpretations of these two men is that they begin by imputing to Dewey a position that only approx-imates the one he actually held: metaphysics is merely the ticking off of traits. It is quite probable that this sort of endeavor could not avoid banality (Rorty) or should be abandoned (Hook), but this is not what Dewey meant by metaphysics. As I pointed out earlier, Dewey does not conceive of metaphysics as the simple recitation of traits. It is true that at times he does provide this sort of list, but he is quick to append qualifications. Near the end of *Experience and Nature* he claims that only if the "general traits of nature existed in water-tight compartments" would it be enough "to sort out the objects and interests of experience among them" (EN 309). The mere listing of generic traits is not sufficient. The real work of meta-physics involves the examination of how these traits are implicated in actual existents and events. Typical metaphysical assertions in Dewey do not take the form suggested by Hook: "individuality and continuity, unity and multiplicity, the novel and the familiar, the clear and the obscure, the distant and at hand, and a host of other polarities" (EN xv). Such a collection of polarities would indeed be sterile and readily discarded, and would hardly distinguish Dewey's philosophy from that of other thinkers.

But Hook's list is misleading. A more accurate selection of meta-physical statements in Dewey would include the following: "Every existence is an event" (EN 63); "interaction is the one unescapable trait of every human concern" (EN 324); "all natural existences are histories" (EN 129; emphasis deleted); "esthetic quality, immedi-ate, final or self-enclosed, indubitably characterizes natural situa-tions as they empirically occur" (EN 82). These are important fun-

damental descriptive statements, quite different from alternative metaphysical theories. Dewey is saying that existents and events must not be viewed as static, isolated, or separate from values. Once ontological assertions are established, the work of developing philosophical analyses in fields such as education, politics, aesthetics, or ethics will move in a certain direction. The real issue is, not that of metaphysics *vs.* no metaphysics, but that of alternative metaphysical positions. Dewey was keenly aware of his need to articulate a metaphysics consistent with the discoveries of modern science, and he attempted to elaborate it in *Experience and Nature*. Scholars like Rorty and Hook who reject this attempt as trivial or misguided are actually overlooking the central import of that text. Their appreciation of Dewey can then be only partial and truncated.

(*b*) Yet the need for a careful examination of Dewey's metaphysics arises not only because of prominent scholars who judge his metaphysical enterprise not to be especially significant, but also because of those, equally prominent, who have misrepresented the positions Dewey held in his naturalistic metaphysics. Richard Bernstein has called attention to what he calls "the Dewey legend" (ENF ix–xi), the outcome of scholarship that has significantly misunderstood and consequently misrepresented Dewey's philosophical positions. Bernstein gives examples of what he considers to be "caricatures" of Dewey's views in the fields of epistemology, philosophy of education, and ethics. He might also have added the caricature of Dewey as the consummate metaphysician of flux, a new Cratylus preaching that nature is all change and process. This charge is refuted in the chapters that follow.

A typical articulation of this interpretation can be found in Jacques Maritain's description of Dewey's philosophy as one in which "there is no nature, there is only process."[5] Other commentators have expressed similar views. David Bowers, for instance, has linked Dewey's metaphysics of flux to an ethics of relativism, thus adding to the Dewey legend in two fields. "In short, by construing the conception of process in as extreme a form as possible, instrumentalism affirms the doctrine that nothing is permanent save change itself, and boldly accepts the relativistic implications of this view for human conduct."[6] Another scholar, Leo Ward, not satisfied with the role of pronouncing an interpretive judgment on

Dewey's philosophy, inaccurately paraphrases him so that Dewey himself appears to have publicly embraced the metaphysics of absolute flux: "He [Dewey] finally said that in his old Hegelian philosophy everything was form and structure, and that in his later development structure came to nearly nothing."[7] This book defends the thesis that, contrary to Ward's assertions, in his later thought Dewey recognized form and structure as significant, and incorporated them into a consistent ontological position. Some commentators, such as H. S. Thayer and Joseph Ratner, have argued for a more balanced view of Dewey, one in which elements of both change and permanence find their proper place.[8] Nonetheless, no one, so far as I can tell, has attempted to trace systematically, in Dewey's works, the development of the concept which he identified with the stable aspects of reality, that is to say, "form." This lacuna the present work hopes to fill.

(c) The final reason for undertaking the work presented here is the impetus given to metaphysical issues as a result of discoveries in the sciences. This is especially true with respect to the issue of "forms." The prominence of this topic stems principally from the growing impact of the biological sciences, but developments in physics have also brought out the need for philosophers to deal once again with the question of form or structure. The maturation of the biological sciences was given a great impetus with Darwin's publication of *The Origin of Species* in 1859. This maturation was certified nearly a hundred years later when Watson and Crick revealed the molecular structure of DNA in 1953. The great advances of biology have placed it in a special relationship to philosophy. Some commentators, like Henryk Skolimowski, have argued that biology has replaced physics as that science which primarily occasions and inspires philosophical speculation.[9] Even if this analysis is exaggerated, an important fact has to be admitted in the relationship of biology to philosophy: the data of the biological sciences can no longer be ignored or treated as special instances of chemistry and physics.

One very prominent datum biologists have focused on is form. D'Arcy Wentworth Thompson devoted two large volumes to a famous study entitled *On Growth and Form*.[10] The Nobel Prize–winning biologist Albert Szent-Györgyi emphasized the connection

between biology and form by arguing that life itself is impossible without form. "Life is made possible by order, structure, a pattern, which is the opposite of entropy."[11] Assertions like these, not uncommon among biologists, have helped to restore the issue of form to some of the prominence it held in pre-Cartesian philosophy.

Nor is biology alone in this respect. Between the publication of Darwin's *Origin* and the beginning of the twentieth century, an important discovery in physics had a direct bearing on the issue of form. Karl Popper has argued that the full impact of this discovery was not immediately felt, but that it was no less revolutionary than the work of Darwin and Copernicus. The discovery in question was the work of J. J. Thomson.

> J. J. Thomson's discovery (and theory) of the electron was also a major revolution. To overthrow the age-old theory of the indivisibility of the atom constituted a scientific revolution easily comparable to Copernicus' achievements: when Thomson announced it, physicists thought he was pulling their legs. . . . To assess the revolutionary significance of this breakthrough it will be sufficient to remind you that it introduced structure as well as electricity into the atom, and thus into the constitution of matter.[12]

Form, as I argued in Section 1, always involves unity and multiplicity. Classical atomistic theory, claiming a unity without parts for the atom, excluded the possibility of form on this level of analysis. The significance of Thomson's discovery is that the basis for this exclusion is no longer valid.

Of course, physicists have turned their attention to the search for an elementary particle more fundamental than the atom. As this search has progressed, a pattern analogous to the case of Thomson and the atom has materialized. As an article in a 1977 issue of *Science* reported, at each stage of this search what were once thought to be elementary particles "have successively been shown to be composites of more elementary particles."[13] Physics has, then, moved in a direction similar to that of biology. For the biologist, the study of life means the study of organized beings; for the physicist, the study of particles means the study of structured, composite entities. Because of these developments, the topic this book investigates is of interest not simply to Dewey scholars, but to the philosophical and scientific communities in general.

3. GENERAL OUTLINE

The approach I have taken in examining Dewey's metaphysics in this book is both theoretical and historical. The study is theoretical because it aims at *understanding* Dewey's metaphysics. It is not concerned with questions involving action or production. The possibility of associating theory with practice is not denied, but the topic dealt with is restricted to the search for accurate knowledge concerning Dewey's position.

To be thorough and accurate, I have traced Dewey's ontological analyses through each period of his lengthy philosophical career. Dewey was an active philosopher for seven decades, and one trait of this activity was an openness to novel and more effective approaches to philosophical issues. As a result, his writings are a living body of thought in which growth, modification, and development are evident. He has not left his interpreters a single position etched in stone. Dewey's opinions and formulations altered through time, and this book attempts to follow these alterations with respect to the issue of change and permanence.

The text is divided into three parts, Idealism, Experimentalism, and Naturalism, in accordance with the three major periods in Dewey's philosophical career. Part I, the shortest of the three, deals with questions of form and being in Dewey's writings during the last two decades of the nineteenth century. Part II takes up this topic in the context of the new "experimental logic" Dewey promulgated at the turn of the century. Part III, the lengthiest section of the book, is composed of four chapters that investigate ontological issues in the period beginning with the appearance of *Experience and Nature* in 1925. The concluding chapter reveals the ways in which Dewey's metaphysics can shed some light on a topic of contemporary significance, the foundationalist/anti-foundationalist controversy.

As we move into the post-modern world, leaving behind the epistemology-centered orientation that dominated during the period between Descartes and Nietzsche, we can benefit from Dewey's guidance. He had both a sensitive historical sense and an original vision to promulgate. He did not treat the past as a package that could be sealed and disposed of. The tradition, it is true, was in many ways one-sided or worn out with usage. This did not mean for

Dewey what it does for some contemporary commentators: that we are entering a post-philosophical culture. It was, rather, a challenge to provide a network of generative ideas which would function as a successful framework within which we could better come to understand the world in which we live. Dewey is important as we move into the post-modern environment because he provided such a network of generative ideas. Metaphysics is the home of this novel vision in its starkest elaboration. If this study serves to offer one way in which we can come to a constructive interpretation of post-modernism in philosophy, then it will have been successful.

NOTES

1. Rorty praises Dewey both in his popular and provocative book *Philosophy and the Mirror of Nature* (Princeton: Princeton University Press, 1979) and in numerous essays that have been collected as *The Consequences of Pragmatism* (Minneapolis: The University of Minnesota Press, 1982). Further references to these texts will be abbreviated as MN and CP respectively.

2. "Introduction," in *Aspects of Form: A Symposium on Form in Nature and Art*, ed. Lancelot Law Whyte (Bloomington: Indiana University Press, 1951; repr. 1961), p. 2.

3. CP 72.

4. CP 74.

5. *Moral Philosophy: An Historical and Critical Survey of the Great Systems*, trans. Marshall Suther et al. (London: Bles; New York: Scribner's, 1964), p. 417.

6. "Hegel, Darwin, and the American Tradition," in *Foreign Influences in American Life: Essays and Critical Bibliographies*, ed. David F. Bowers (Princeton: Princeton University Press, 1944), p. 147. Still another commentator who supports this kind of interpretation is Woodbridge Riley in his *American Thought: From Puritanism to Pragmatism and Beyond* (New York: Smith, 1941), p. 297.

7. "John Dewey in Search of Himself," *The Review of Politics*, 19 (1957), 206. Ward gives no specific reference to the text he is paraphrasing. The context seems to indicate a passage from Dewey's autobiography in which Dewey explains how he "drifted" from Hegel. Dewey does discuss "form" in this regard, but what he has in mind is a formalism or schematism that forces data into a preconceived dialectical framework. This is the "form" that he rejects. In other respects, Dewey is quite explicit in admitting that Hegel "left a permanent deposit in my think-

ing." The passage is actually quite laudatory of Hegel, and ends with praise for a philosopher not unassociated with forms, Plato. "The form, the schematism, of his [Hegel's] system now seems to me artificial to the last degree. But in the content of his ideas there is often an extraordinary depth; in many of his analyses, taken out of their mechanical dialectical setting, an extraordinary acuteness. Were it possible for me to be a devotee of any system, I still should believe that there is greater richness and greater variety of insight in Hegel than in any other single systematic philosopher—though when I say this I exclude Plato, who still provides my favorite philosophic reading" ("From Absolutism to Experimentalism," LW V 154). This article was originally published in 1930, when Dewey was seventy-one years old.

8. See Thayer, *The Logic of Pragmatism: An Examination of John Dewey's Logic* (New York: Humanities Press, 1952), pp. 16–18; and Ratner's "Introduction to John Dewey's Philosophy," in *Intelligence in the Modern World: John Dewey's Philosophy*, ed. Joseph Ratner (New York: Modern Library, 1939), p. 155.

9. "Biology is nowadays a special science, for it has become a philosophical battlefield on which a new paradigm for all human knowledge is being established. The reign of physics as the universal paradigm is now over. Biology is aspiring to produce a new paradigm" ("Problems of Rationality in Biology," in *Studies in the Philosophy of Biology: Reduction and Related Problems*, edd. Francisco Jose Ayala and Theodosius Dobzhansky (Berkeley & Los Angeles: University of California Press, 1974), p. 205.

10. 2nd ed., 2 vols. (Cambridge: Cambridge University Press, 1942; repr. 1952). In Volume I, Thompson describes forms as involving an "intrinsic harmony," and in a note provides an explanation that is fully consistent with the characterization of form given in Section 1 of this Introduction. "What I understand by 'holism' is what the Greeks called ἁρμονία. This is something exhibited not only by a lyre in a tune, but by all the handiwork of craftsmen, and by all that is 'put together' by art or nature. It is the 'compositeness of any composite whole'; and, like the cognate terms κρᾶσις and σύνθεσις, implies a balance or attunement" (p. 10, note explaining "harmony").

11. *The Living State: with Observations on Cancer* (New York & London: Academic Press, 1972), p. 2. Some expressions of the fundamental significance of form or organization are more poetic, as in the following passage from Loren Eiseley. "Men talk much of matter and energy, of the struggle for existence that molds the shape of life. These things do exist, it is true, but more delicate, elusive, quicker than the fins in water, is that mysterious principle known as 'organization,' which leaves all

other mysteries concerned with life stale and insignificant by comparison. For that without organization life does not persist is obvious. Yet
this organization itself is not strictly the product of life, nor of selection.
Like some dark and passing shadow within matter, it cups out the eyes'
small windows or spaces the notes of a meadow lark's song in the interior
of a mottled egg. That principle—I am beginning to suspect—was there
before the living in the deeps of water" (*The Immense Journey*, repr.
ed. [New York: Time, Inc., 1962], p. 18).

12. "The Rationality of Scientific Revolutions," in *Problems of Scientific Revolution: Progress and Obstacles to Progress in the Sciences*, ed.
Rom Harré, The Herbert Spencer Lectures for 1973 (Oxford: Clarendon, 1975), p. 89.

13. Arthur L. Robinson, "High Energy Physics: A Proliferation of
Quarks and Leptons," *Science*, Nov. 4, 1977, p. 481. More recently, two
Canadian physicists who prepared a series of radio programs with prominent biologists and physicists expressed a similar sentiment in explaining how the topics for the interviews were selected. "In selecting topics
for discussion, we have betrayed our own prejudices. . . . We have concentrated on areas which, we feel, hint at the next scientific revolution.
Perhaps in this context we owe an apology to an important group of
scientists—those engaged in elementary particle research. Some physicists
feel that the search for the 'ultimate building-blocks of matter' is one of
the most promising modern areas of research. It was our belief, however,
that there are deeper questions to be explored, and that the goal of 'the
most fundamental particle' is somewhat of a throwback to the presuppositions of classical physics" (*A Question of Physics: Conversations in
Physics and Biology*, edd. Paul Buckley and David F. Peat [Toronto:
University of Toronto Press, 1979], pp. ix–x).

I
IDEALISM

1

Change and Permanence
in
Dewey's Idealistic Period

1. INTRODUCTION

JOHN DEWEY PUBLISHED his first philosophical article in 1882 when he was twenty-two years old. He spent the next seventy years of his life in active and copiously productive philosophical activity. Because of this lengthy and energetic career, any attempt to investigate a particular topic in Dewey's philosophy is bound to be selective with regard to texts chosen as the foci of attention. This selectivity must avoid two equally dangerous paths. It must be neither too narrow nor too broad. If the selection is too narrowly chosen, then the development and growth of Dewey's thought will be underemphasized, if not ignored outright. Yet so numerous are Dewey's writings that if too wide a selection is made, there will be no opportunity for in-depth textual analysis except in a book of unmanageable length.

In Dewey's case, combining an overview of development with precise textual study is especially important. His sources of inspiration were diverse and often incompatible; nonetheless he sought to mold the fruitful portions of these sources into a unique, novel synthesis.[1] When this fact is combined with the notoriously difficult mode of expression[2] which resulted from this attempted synthesis, it becomes imperative that the successful interpreter be familiar not only with the mature statement of a position, but with its history in Dewey's intellectual growth as well.

Richard Bernstein has accurately characterized Dewey's career as consisting of three periods, each lasting roughly twenty years.[3] The first is the *idealistic* phase, beginning with the article of 1882 and lasting until 1903.[4] At that time Dewey introduced his new methodology in *Studies in Logical Theory*. These studies inaugurate the

15

experimental phase in which Dewey developed a novel methodology for dealing with philosophical issues. The successes of the scientific method, together with the impact of evolutionary thought, made evident, Dewey believed, the need to revise logical theory. The third phase, the *naturalistic*, is one in which Dewey attempted to present a coherent articulation of a naturalistic ontology. This period was announced in 1925 with the publication of *Experience and Nature*. Dewey was already sixty-five but his philosophical production remained as energetic as it had been.

If the ontological issue of "form," as that concept which embodies the permanent aspects of nature, is to be investigated successfully in Dewey's thought, all three of these periods will have to be studied, with special emphasis on the third one. During this phase, in a variety of important works, including some of his most famous (*The Quest for Certainty, Art as Experience, Logic: The Theory of Inquiry*), Dewey provided the most detailed development of ontology to be found in his writings. Accordingly, the three phases will not be equally represented here. I shall survey ontological topics as they were articulated during the idealistic and experimental periods in the first three chapters. The following four will be devoted to an examination of the final phase.

2. DEWEY'S IDEALISTIC YEARS

The idealistic period in Dewey's career, which the present chapter will investigate, can be divided into two sub-periods of unequal duration and importance. This division rests on the two main pillars of German idealistic thought, Kant and Hegel. Dewey's earliest philosophical orientation was heavily influenced by his exposure to Kant as an undergraduate and in the years of study immediately following his graduation.[5] In this earliest phase, which lasted from his final years as an undergraduate at the University of Vermont to his first years as a graduate student at Johns Hopkins, 1878–1884, Dewey can be considered a Kantian. This is especially true in relation to his interpretation of consciousness in terms of activity rather than passivity.

The second stage, 1884–1903, is dominated by Dewey's graduate teacher, George Sylvester Morris. Morris was a neo-Hegelian with a deep belief in the superiority of the idealistic tradition over the em-

piricist school of the British Isles. Hegelian philosophy as Morris interpreted it, "a logical and idealistic metaphysics with a realistic epistemology" (LW V 152), proved most congenial to Dewey, and he became a convert. This epoch of Hegelianism is by far the more significant of the two phases of his idealistic period. Most of his publications from this period were composed after his conversion to Hegelianism, and in these works the philosophical synthesis that he promulgated in the final decades of the nineteenth century is to a great degree worked out.

There are, however, a few articles that originated in the earlier period when, as Dewey admits, "of Hegel I was then ignorant" (LW V 150). I shall begin with these earliest articles. They are significant because the Kantian elements found in them not only describe Dewey's first philosophical allegiance but also reappear in various guises throughout his career.

2.1. Dewey's Kantian Phase

I cannot hope to provide a fully detailed account of the idealistic phase as a whole or even of the pre-Hegelian sub-period, which includes a very limited number of articles.[6] What I shall do is examine briefly Dewey's thinking on topics specifically relating to the questions of change and permanence. These issues will revolve around the dual axes of epistemology and ontology. The ontological discussions will focus on the nature of beings as such; the epistemological discussions, on the manner in which beings are known. In this pre-Hegelian period, Dewey's analyses tend to emphasize epistemological considerations, whereas the Hegelian period is marked by a decidedly ontological turn.

The Kantian bias of the earliest articles is the obvious source of Dewey's recognition of the primacy of epistemology. In his first article, "The Metaphysical Assumptions of Materialism," despite its deceptive title, the arguments against materialism are based, not on an analysis of being, but on an analysis of knowing. Dewey claims that materialists hold two inconsistent positions. They claim to possess a certain kind of knowledge, but are unable to explain the derivation of that knowledge on a strictly materialistic basis. This general transformation of metaphysical issues into epistemological ones applies equally well to the specific question of form. In this

article, Dewey offers what appears to be an ontological clue with respect to the issue of form when he distinguishes between "substance" and "mere succession of phenomena" (EW I 4). Such a negative description of substance opens the way for a positive characterization of it as formed or structured. But rather than interpret his assertion ontologically, Dewey reverts to epistemological considerations once again, arguing that mind is what provides the continuities, the sense of abiding, which any understanding of substance involves.

This reversion is not yet evident in the statement with which Dewey begins his explanation: "To have real knowledge of real being, there must be something which abides through the successive states" (EW I 5). Such an analysis is open-ended in the sense that the ingredients for a solution are introduced with no indication of the manner in which they are to be continued. The ontological and epistemological elements, "being" and "knowledge," are introduced immediately and equivalently. No suggestion is provided as to which will be given primacy. The third ingredient, the "something which abides," so crucial to the analysis of substance, could easily be interpreted in terms of either being or knowing. If Dewey wished to emphasize the sense of *abiding in nature*, then the solution would be provided in fundamentally ontological terms. If, on the other hand, abiding involves primarily noetic considerations, then substance is justified and explained epistemologically.

Dewey leaves no doubt as to his orientation during this period in his development. He continues the above quotation by arguing that the "something which abides through the successive states" also "*perceives* their relations to that being and to itself" (EW I 5–6; emphasis added). Dewey's choice is made. Abiding could have been associated primarily with either knowing or being. He categorically associates it with knowing. What differentiates substance from mere phenomena is not something that is a trait of beings themselves. There is being, as succession of phenomena, but substance requires the sense of permanence, of abiding, which can be attributed only through the mind.

This sort of analysis, which claims, not that being is mind-dependent, but that substance is thus dependent, forces Dewey to admit a radical distinction between mind and being. It is mind that provides the continuities that matter lacks. "To know substance,

matter, is required substance, mind" (EW I 5). This assertion, admitting, as it does, a dualistic analysis, Dewey will later vehemently reject. Nonetheless, it remains an accurate representation of his earliest philosophical outlook. The organization, or sense of abiding necessary to any account of form, resides, for Dewey at this stage, within mind. While undertaking this line of argument, Dewey makes two admissions about the nature of knowing which will stay with him even after he has rejected the dualistic analysis of his pre-Hegelian period: the first is his consistent assertion that knowledge always involves *mediation* of some sort; the second deals with the kind of contribution the intellect makes in knowing. Dewey admits the influence of Kant here, and argues that the primary task of the intellect is *synthesis*.

2.11. Knowledge as Mediated and Synthetic • These two closely related issues directly touch the question of formed entities. Dewey's distinction between substance and mere phenomena is his version of the form/matter distinction. But in this case substance is not a given of existence. It is mind-dependent. Without mediation, which Dewey interprets in terms of synthesis, substance will neither be perceived nor be. Mediation and synthesis make the very existence of structures possible at all. We already know that forms are mind-dependent, and when we search Dewey's text for an elaboration of this doctrine, we are led to mediation and synthesis.

Dewey's claim that knowledge must involve mediation can best be understood through reference to the topic of substance discussed above. A requisite condition for the knowledge of substance, Dewey argued, is the necessary existence of "something which abides through successive states." Non-mediated apprehension would result only in the recognition of a perpetual flux of phenomena. Since Dewey doubts neither that existence in itself is simply this flux of "mere" phenomena nor that there is knowledge of substance, non-mediated knowledge cannot provide a full explanation of our actual noetic experience. The "mere phenomena" must thus be mediated via the mental substance before the possibility of ascertaining material substance can be realized. In his second published work, "The Pantheism of Spinoza," Dewey reveals how important he considered knowledge as mediated to be. According to him, Spinoza's failure to grasp the fact of mediation is the foundation on which the incon-

sistencies in his system are based; Spinoza's system, he claims, "rests on the basis that the only real knowledge is immediate knowledge" (EW I 17).

Although Dewey's allegiance to idealism was to wane, his rejection of any doctrine that suggests immediate or non-mediated knowledge remains a constant trait of his thought. Mind is not a mere receptacle or mirror that passively reflects the order it finds in existence. Dewey's articulations of this view change, however, in each period of his development. The exact role played by mediation alters as his orientation is modified. The fact that Dewey considers mediation to be of such significance makes it important that it be properly understood. What exactly is the nature of mediation? What is involved in this activity? It is in answering these questions that Dewey's dependence on Kant is most prominently felt.

Dewey's doctoral dissertation at Johns Hopkins had as its subject "Kant's Psychology."[7] That text is lost, but an article published soon afterward, "Kant and Philosophic Method," was, according to Dewey, " 'in somewhat the same line [as the dissertation].' "[8] Though the article was written after his immersion in Hegelian philosophy, the text is, in fact, a transitional one, showing both the positive lessons Dewey had learned from Kant and the limitations that led him away from this thinker to Hegel. Dewey's analysis in "Kant and Philosophic Method" brings him back, once again, to the issue of substance. Building on the very schematic, tentative assertions about substance in his first article, he now deals, in more Kantian terms, with the conditions, not for knowing substance, but of "experience" and of "objects." Mediation is still important, and the debt philosophy owes Kant is his recognition of the nature of mediation: the work of synthesizing disconnected sensations.

Consciousness does not simply receive and record these impressions; it acts upon them, and this activity is synthetic. "The material, the manifold, the particulars, are furnished by Sense in perception; the conceptions, the synthetic functions from Reason itself, and the union of these two elements are required, as well for the formation of the object known, as for its knowing" (EW I 37). This is the most concise statement of Dewey's own position regarding form in his pre-Hegelian phase. The synthetic work of the conceptions results not only in knowledge, but, more important, in the *formation* "of the object known." Consciousness must be inter-

preted as both passive and active. Perceptions and conceptions must work together, but the syntheses provided by conceptions are the "*sine qua non*" (EW I 36) in the process of formation.

Formed entities do have some sort of objective status, but this status is a derivative one, one not originally given in the disconnected sensations of perception. In this pre-Hegelian phase, formed beings, as either substances or objects, cannot be understood apart from mind and its inherent activity. There are no structures apart from mind. "To know substance, matter, is required substance, mind" best encapsulates Dewey's thinking at this time.

2.12. The Transition to Hegelianism • This solution, which required that mind be set over against matter, was soon to be drastically revised. The occasion for this revision was Dewey's discovery of Hegel through George Sylvester Morris, his professor at Johns Hopkins. Dewey's allegiance so readily shifted from Kant to Hegel that one is led to question the depth of conviction with which he held the positions described in his first articles. Certainly, the fact that he was a very young man still trying to formulate a defensible synthesis had much to do with his ready change of allegiance. But there was another reason, one associated with his very decision to undertake the study of philosophy as a life's work.

Dewey tells us in his autobiography that this decision was made on the basis of the intellectual stimulation he received in a physiology course in which the text was Thomas H. Huxley's *Lessons in Elementary Physiology*. This course suggested to Dewey a vision of organic unity which could provide a paradigm for natural and social contexts alike, and gave direction to his thinking by supplying a "model" to which "material in any field ought to conform." "Subconsciously," he said, "I was led to desire a world and a life that would have the same properties as had the human organism in the picture of it derived from study of Huxley's treatment" (LW V 147–48). The Kantian position Dewey elaborated in his earliest writings required a dualistic analysis that violated this Huxleyan vision. This "subconscious" vision had been effectively held in check by both the influence of Dewey's teacher at Vermont, H. A. P. Torrey, and the power of Kant's philosophy. But once Morris introduced his student to Hegel, Dewey found a philosopher whose position dovetailed nicely with the Huxleyan model of organic unity.

2.2. Dewey's Hegelian Phase

The descriptive label "Hegelian," used to characterize this phase of Dewey's career, although accurate, must not be misinterpreted. There is no doubt that Dewey was deeply influenced by the thought of Hegel, but we must not make the mistake of fully identifying his thought with Hegel's. No great thinker appropriates the entire doctrine of a predecessor. Dewey was even less likely than most to engage in the wholesale absorption of Hegel's thought, since the Hegelianism he was taught had already been filtered twice through original and fertile minds. Dewey's immediate link to Hegel was, as we have seen, George Sylvester Morris. He, in turn, had studied in Germany with the Aristotelian scholar Friedrich Adolph Trendelenburg. Both teachers were greatly impressed with Hegelian philosophy, yet each added his own modifications to the master's thought. Some of these innovations are significant, and will help us to understand Dewey's ontological positions in both his idealistic and his later periods.

2.21. The Influence of Trendelenburg • Friedrich Adolph Trendelenburg (1802–1872) is remembered chiefly as the man most responsible for the revival of Aristotelian philosophy in mid-nineteenth-century Germany. He was, in addition, an original thinker and an influential teacher. Besides Morris, his pupils included Kierkegaard and Dilthey, both of whom spoke highly of their mentor.[9] Morris thought enough of his German teacher to insert a lengthy discussion of him in his translation of Ueberweg's *History of Philosophy*.[10] The best label for Trendelenburg's philosophy as it had an impact on Morris was fashioned by the French Deweyan scholar Gérard Deledalle: "an Aristotlelized Hegelianism."[11] The dominant force in German philosophy during the time of Trendelenburg's studies was, of course, Hegel, but Trendelenburg's considerable skill in philology had led to an interest in Greek thinkers, especially Aristotle.[12]

Trendelenburg treated the meeting of Hegel and Aristotle, not as a clash, but as an opportunity for synthesis, and in general sought to explain Hegelian insights within an Aristotelian framework. He was reinforced in this by an abiding interest in science which led him to integrate the discoveries of Darwin into his philosophy.[13]

The overall result was an Hegelianism without the dialectic of Spirit.[14] Nature was still viewed as dynamic, but this dynamism was given a fully naturalistic expression. "Subject" and "object," terms inherited from epistemology-centered philosophy, were no longer to be understood in the traditional manner. Instead of a subject as spectator examining the realm of objects, there was now the biological environment which involved the participation of organisms in their surroundings. The environment or situation provided the dynamic unity of interacting entities. No longer was the higher category of Spirit needed to embrace the artificially separated subjects and objects of post-Cartesian philosophy.

On the one hand, then, Trendelenburg left Morris a negative legacy: Hegel without the dialectic. On the other, the absence of the dialectic demanded some positive contributions from Trendelenburg. Specifically, how were the issues of motion and teleology to be construed apart from a dialectical framework? Trendelenburg was equal to the task. His most important contribution is the doctrine of constructive movement, *konstructive Bewegung*. Thought and being, subject and object, do not stand unalterably opposed to one another. Instead of a barrier between them, there is a mediator, common to both, which is motion. Constructive motion is a basic trait of nature and of thought, and Trendelenburg attempted to erect an alternative to dualism based on this mediating element.[15]

The important fact to grasp about this motion is that Trendelenburg interprets it in Aristotelian terms as the transition from potentiality to actuality.[16] It is this transition which defines motion in its most fundamental sense. Motion, understood in this manner, Trendelenburg argues, is common to thought and things. The alternative to a dialectical interpretation of motion becomes, then, a revised application of Aristotle's teaching on potentiality and actuality. A similar sort of transformation occurs to the notion of *telos* or end. Cut off from the progressive realization of *Geist* when Trendelenburg jettisoned the dialectic, *telos* nonetheless retained a place of prominence in his analysis.

The full force of Trendelenburg's naturalism is felt here. End (*Zweck*) must be understood in the context of organisms. *Telos* implies, not an outside directing force, but one of the factors necessarily bound together in an organism: " 'In the organism, matter, form, efficient causation and purpose are, as it were, with one an-

other and through one another. Purpose as the indwelling principle
constructs the body. Matter is assimilated in such a unique fashion
so that even chemically it possesses a specific character of its own.
Form is not imposed upon matter from without but created from
within.' "[17]

In such a biological context, forms are understood to emerge from,
rather than pre-exist, the context in which they are found. At the
same time, end ("purpose," *Zweck*),[18] as the directionality involved
in the process of organic development, is closely associated with
form. The intersection of this interpretation of teleology with Trendelenburg's doctrine of constructive movement now becomes evident. In an organism the movement from potentiality to actuality
is in the direction of an end. This end is the mature form of a particular being.[19] Morris interpreted motion and end as the two guid-
ing principles in Trendelenburg's philosophy,[20] and fastened on the
teleological dimension to emphasize Trendelenburg's commitment
to idealism. But this may have been a reflection more of his own
views than of Trendelenburg's. Whatever the case may be, Trendelenburg's American pupil was a convinced idealist, and he had a
direct and lasting impact on Dewey.

2.22. The Influence of George Sylvester Morris · Dewey's expression to describe Morris' thought, " 'substantial idealism,' "[21]
accurately characterizes his position in two respects: first of all, it
places him quite properly within the general framework of the German idealistic tradition; and, secondly, the qualifier "substantial"
indicates the uniqueness of his analysis within that tradition. Although Morris owed a great debt to Hegel, and although he was
deeply inspired by his classes with Trendelenburg, his own position
was an original one.

Unlike many idealists, Morris never felt that questions about the
possibility of knowledge or the existence of the external world were
burning philosophical issues. Dewey tells us, in fact, that Morris
used to ridicule philosophers who considered it their obligation to
investigate such questions. Instead of questioning the very existence
of the world, Morris sought to explore the *meaning* of that existence
(LW V 152). This quest for meaning appears to be the source for,
and to define the extent of, Morris' idealism. When Morris uses ex-

pressions like " 'universal self' " or " 'universal consciousness,' "[22] he
does not wish to indicate that matter is unreal or that behind the
material appearances there lurks a spiritual reality. Rather, he is
emphasizing, by using the philosophical tools available in the nineteenth century, that existence is meaningful.

To understand Morris accurately, we must recall the context in
which he did his philosophizing. Two great traditions dominated
philosophy, the empiricist and the idealist, and they appeared to
exhaust the alternatives. A philosopher had to choose, had to de-
clare his allegiance with, one or the other camp. Morris was familiar
with the British empiricist tradition, one that, as Dewey says, is
congenital to English-speaking thinkers (EW I 300). But this tradition, with its distinction between primary and secondary qualities,
provides us with a world that, in itself, is meaningless, a neutral
world of matter in motion.[23] The only possible source of meaning,
once such assumptions are accepted, is the individual consciousness
of a thinking being. Morris finds this less than satisfactory because
it eventually leads, as the British tradition from Hobbes to Berkeley
shows, to doubting the very existence of the external world.[24] For
Morris, this conclusion is a *reductio ad absurdum* and points to the
need for alternative solutions to those of empiricism.

Since the only viable alternative presenting itself at the time was
idealism, it is not surprising to find Morris embracing it as a " 'dem-
onstrated' truth" (LW V 152) and referring to the empiricist tradition as "superficial."[25] Nonetheless, if we are to understand the kind
of idealism taught Dewey at Johns Hopkins, we must not classify
Morris according to preconceived ideas of what an idealist is, but understand him instead in the manner just presented. When Morris
speaks of a "universal consciousness," he is saying that all existence
is meaningful. The alternatives are set down before him by the philosophical tradition. Either existence is radically bifurcated into a
meaningless matter and a meaning-endowing mind, or existence is a
non-bifurcated, unified network of meanings. Morris, believing that
the former led to unacceptable conclusions, chose the latter. In so
doing, he employed the only vocabulary at his disposal. Since meanings are associated with consciousness, all existence must be described in terms of consciousness.

Trendelenburg, it is interesting to note, had provided Morris

with the tools to break free from the either/or dilemma of empiricism *vs.* idealism. By avoiding the extension of either matter or mind to all of existence, and concentrating instead on potentiality and actuality in his doctrine of constructive movement, Trendelenburg had suggested a solution outside the dominant traditions. Morris seems not to have followed him on this point. But Dewey, as we shall see, was to revive this Trendelenburg type of emphasis on potentiality and actuality most prominently in his final "naturalistic" phase.[26]

In this first period, however, Dewey adheres rather closely to the teachings of his master. Morris was not only his teacher, but also his colleague later at the University of Michigan, and their relationship was the main force in shaping the first fifteen years of Dewey's philosophical career.[27] Besides the positive doctrine of "substantial idealism," Morris bequeathed a negative, polemical legacy to his pupil. If Morris was an adherent of the idealistic tradition, he was also, of necessity, an opponent of the empiricist tradition. Morris' opposition to empiricism manifested itself especially in two areas, both of which were to remain with Dewey well after he had grown out of idealism.

The first involved the empiricist theory of mind. In this tradition, subject and object are seen as in a mechanical relationship. Impressions come from an outer world and affect a passive mind. Morris considered this view to be wholly inadequate and, following Trendelenburg, stressed the necessity of recognizing both passivity and activity on the part of mind. The idealist doctrine of innate ideas was fruitful in one outstanding sense: it kept the activity of mind in prominence. Morris considered the expression "innate ideas" unfortunate, but he saw it as serving an important function in emphasizing that the mind not only receives impressions but also acts on them.[28]

Morris complemented this anti-passive approach to consciousness with a veritable crusade against dualisms. Dualisms, he claimed, had erected impenetrable barriers between the knower and the things to be known, and led philosophy in one direction: the gradual dissolution of the object of knowledge into an "unknowable substrate."[29] This in turn led, as the British tradition revealed, either to a form of subjectivism or to a form of skepticism. Morris

believed that such results were unacceptable and, more important, unnecessary. A properly understood idealism could resolve the difficulties.

After his studies with Morris, Dewey did not hesitate to use the term "Hegelianism" to describe his own philosophical allegiance. Nor did he hesitate, many years later, to pay the highest tribute to the genius of Hegel (LW V 152–54). But it must be understood that it was to *Hegelianism*, the movement, that Dewey attached himself, not to a comprehensive, thorough assimilation of Hegel, the individual philosopher. I have focused on the two men who mediated Hegel for Dewey to indicate the particular brand of Hegelianism to which he was exposed. It was sufficiently different from textbook versions of Hegel's doctrines for Deledalle to ask whether it was Hegelianism at all. "Trendelenburg had dealt a death-blow to the dialectic. Hegelianism seemed doomed. Aristotle rescued it. Was it still Hegelianism?"[30] Deledalle does not answer his own question. Nor does he pursue the implication that Hegelianism had been transformed into Aristotelianism. The best response to the question "Was it still Hegelianism?" is a less-than-categorical "yes and no." In terms of Dewey's development, the answer differs in each of the three major periods.

During the idealistic phase, while he was still under Morris' influence, Dewey's answer is "Yes, it is Hegelianism." In the experimental phase, which is the result of his "drifting" (LW V 154) from Hegel, he would give a negative response. The positive accomplishments of idealism are assimilated here into an experimental philosophy that rejects idealism outright. In his third phase, having moved beyond Morris and Hegel, Dewey reverts to Trendelenburg and Aristotle. An interpreter who favors eponyms could describe this naturalistic phase as "Aristotelian" with as much warrant as Dewey himself had in labeling his idealist phase "Hegelian."[31]

Deledalle's question thus provides the boundaries within which Dewey's philosophical growth occurs. The elaborations on this schematic outline will have to await later chapters. At this point we are still concerned with the Hegelian period. We have already seen that before his courses with Morris Dewey held a position that was greatly inspired by Kant. We also know something about the teaching lineage that reaches from Trendelenburg through Morris to

Dewey. What is necessary now is an analysis of Dewey's writings during this period to grasp what his position concerning form and being entails.

2.23. Dewey's Writings During His Hegelian Phase • Between 1884 and 1903, Dewey wrote eight books and more than one hundred articles and reviews. There is, obviously, enough material in this phase of his life to occupy many Dewey scholars. My aim here is a modest one: to provide a representative analysis of Dewey's position with respect to the question of form. Since I believe that he is to be taken literally when he says that he gradually "drifted" from Hegelianism, I have decided to focus on some of these earliest writings. They present a doctrine typical of his Hegelianism.

The main text on which my interpretation will be based is Dewey's second book, *Leibniz's New Essays Concerning Human Understanding*, published in 1888. Morris had conceived of a series on German philosophy, which would not only introduce German thinkers to Americans, but also serve as a polemical vehicle for illustrating the superiority of the idealistic over the empiricist tradition. Morris wrote some of the first books on the philosophies of Kant and Hegel; Dewey was charged with producing a study on the philosophy of Leibniz.[32] For a variety of reasons, the Leibniz book provides a good opportunity for investigating Dewey's metaphysics in his Hegelian phase. (*a*) An accurate reflection of his thought during this period, it not only is an early work, but one conceived by, and written under the influence of, Morris, the direct source of Dewey's Hegelianism. (*b*) Since the subject of the study was an outstanding ontologist, Dewey's interpretation, especially his emphases, will allow some insight into his own ontological position. (*c*) Finally, because of the polemical nature of the series in which the book appeared, Dewey felt called upon to add his own comments to the exposition of Leibniz' philosophy.[33]

2.24. Dewey on Leibniz • To reconstruct Dewey's ontological doctrine in this period of Hegelianism, we must be clear as to the kind of idealism he professed. Dewey's allegiance to the idealistic tradition cannot be questioned. In an article published in 1886 entitled "The Psychological Standpoint," he asserted that "Absolute Idealism (to which I hardly need say this article has been constantly

pointing) is assumed" (EW 1 35). What can be questioned is the meaning of the term when Dewey uses it. I have already indicated in my discussion of Morris' philosophy that idealism, as he understood it, did not stand opposed to a realistic epistemology, but was rather rigidly defined in opposition to the empiricist tradition. Morris had fastened on idealism as the doctrine which rejected (among other things) the ontology of primary and secondary qualities developed by the empiricist school.

The idealism Dewey adopted followed that of his teacher quite closely. In no way, for example, is Bertrand Russell's claim that idealists are those for whom "matter is an evil dream"[34] implied in Dewey's idealism. Morris and Dewey rejected both the empiricist tradition and the subjectivistic strain within the idealistic movement.[35] It is the view that idealism answers the insufficiencies of empiricism that made Leibniz such an attractive figure for the two of them. His *New Essays* offer the first sustained (and in their eyes accurate) criticism of one *magnum opus* in the tradition of empiricism, Locke's *Essay Concerning Human Understanding*.

When we turn to this book on Leibniz with the aim of extracting a metaphysical analysis, four topics stand out. (*a*) The most important one, to which all others are subordinated, is the question of *relations*. The way Dewey treats this issue reveals his shift from the epistemological emphasis of his earlier Kantianism to the ontological emphasis typical of his Hegelianism. (*b*) The ontological position, fully in line with his idealism, is expressed by generalizing the meaning of *intelligence*. (*c*) True to the intellectual heritage of Hegel, Trendelenburg, and Morris, Dewey articulates a *dynamic interpretation of existence*. (*d*) Finally, Dewey interprets Leibniz as resembling no philosopher more than Aristotle, and in so doing reveals as much about his position as he does about Leibniz'. In relation to the question of formed existents, three Aristotelian themes, already familiar from our analysis of Trendelenburg, prove to be especially important: *potentiality*, *actuality*, and *end*. No discussion of metaphysics in Dewey's Hegelian period would be complete without the inclusion of these Aristotelian elements.

2.241. Relations   The series of works in which the Leibniz book appeared had, as we have seen, a twofold purpose. It was to be both expository and disputatious. Its aim was, on the one hand,

to introduce German thinkers to an American audience, and, on the other, to demonstrate the superiority of those thinkers over their counterparts in the empiricist tradition. In the book on Leibniz, Dewey addresses a topic which will attain both these ends. By dealing with the issue of relations, he is able to explain Leibniz' position and to expose the insufficient way they are handled in Locke's writings.

Although both aims are carried out, the latter one, the criticism of Locke as a representative of the empiricist tradition, often seems to dominate. It is Locke's inconsistent and incorrect doctrine of relations which is at the root of his philosophical difficulties. "To Locke, as we have seen, knowledge is essentially a matter of relations or connections; but relations are 'superinduced' and 'extraneous' as regards the facts. Every act of knowledge constitutes, therefore, in some way a departure from the reality to be known. Knowledge and fact are, by their very definition, opposed to one another" (EW I 394). Dewey is continuing here a line of criticism, begun by Morris, which sought to show how it is empiricism, not idealism, which loses sight of the external world. Because an unmediated opposition between knowledge and facts is assumed, no opportunity is afforded for preserving the facts in knowledge.

Locke, by his own admission, grasps the necessity of relations in knowledge. Yet what is given to him as a knower is in itself unrelated. He is thus forced to hold that for knowledge to result "extraneous" relations have to be "superinduced" on the contents received by consciousness. The consequence of this position, as Dewey interprets it, is that knowledge (which includes relations), instead of adequately reflecting the facts of existence, actually falsifies them. Dewey extends his criticism by arguing that the Lockean position rests on the mistaken assumption that "reality is *mere* existence." By "mere existence" Dewey means that which allows of no characterization or determination; "it is something which is, and that is all" (EW I 374). Locke's idea of substance as that which "simply stands inactively, under phenomena" (EW I 374) reveals the unacceptable conclusions to which one is led by the consistent working out of a doctrine based on the assumption of "mere existence."

A similar theme appeared in Dewey's Kantian period,[36] when he distinguished "substance" from "mere succession of phenomena." The different ways these similar distinctions are treated during the

two idealistic phases is indicative of the complete shift in outlook which accompanied his conversion to Hegelianism. In the earlier phase Dewey dealt with the distinction in epistemological terms. Substance was subordinated to, made dependent on, the knowing faculty, which provided the sense of abiding inherent in any notion of substance. In the text now under consideration, Dewey's arguments have become ontological. The superiority of the idealistic tradition is viewed as based on that tradition's refusal to take seriously the ontology of "mere existence." Leibniz, according to Dewey, was a leader in this regard. He clearly saw that "facts" were not *mere* facts," but were instead manifestations, in Leibniz' own words, of a " 'determining reason and regulative principle' " (EW I 400).

The transition from epistemology to ontology can be exemplified by further exploring this analysis. Does an accurate description of existence in itself exclude relations, as Locke maintains, or must it include them, as Leibniz insists? Of course, Dewey sides with Leibniz. Now we can see how ontological considerations are fundamental in idealism's response to empiricism. We know that, for Dewey, the difficulty with empiricism is that knowledge and facts are admitted to be distinct and incompatible. This is based on the empiricist's combination of an ontology which claims that facts are devoid of relations and an epistemology which asserts that knowledge necessarily involves relations.

In response to this an idealist like Leibniz argues that the empiricist has caused his own difficulties by artificially emptying reality of its relations. Relations, Leibniz says, "are . . . not foreign to the material to be known, but are organic to it" (EW I 394). As a result, consciousness grasps the "real nature" of the objects known; it does not proceed by " 'superinducing' unreal ideas upon them" (EW I 395). The difficulties of the Lockean position are thus avoided. Dewey, true to the polemical intent of the series in which this book stands, complements his interpretation of Leibniz with the following editorial comment:

> The difficulty of Locke is the difficulty of every theory of knowledge that does not admit an organic unity of the knowing mind and the known universe. The theory is obliged to admit that all knowledge is in the form of relations which have their source in intelligence. But being tied to the view that reality is distinct from

intelligence, it is obliged to draw the conclusion that these relations are not to be found in actual existence, and hence that all
knowledge, whatever else it may be, is unreal in the sense that it
does not and cannot conform to actual fact [EW I 395].

The main outline of Dewey's own philosophical views is incorporated into this critical passage: reality and intelligence are not, as in
Locke, distinct from one another; there is an "organic unity" of the
knowing mind and the known universe.

One of the difficulties with assessing Dewey's position during this
phase is ascertaining just what "organic" means in the context of
the knower and the known. Organic unity, according to Dewey,
always involves the unification of a multiplicity. Yet just how this
biological model of unity is to apply to cognitive situations is not
really worked out in the book on Leibniz. "Organism" appears to
be a term used as a weapon of combat. It signifies a rejection of the
dualistic ontology espoused by the empiricist tradition, but the precise reasons why "organic" best expresses the alternative view are
not enumerated. In fact, "organic" seems to function as one of those
terms (like "logic" in the analytical tradition or "dialectic" in the
Marxist tradition) which are so utilized and so familiar to a particular group that they acquire a certain elasticity, along with a conviction that no explanation of them is necessary. We are in a more
favorable position with regard to "intelligence." Dewey argues, in
the above quotation, that reality is not distinct from intelligence.
By examining what is implied in the term "intelligence" we can
come to understand Dewey's idealistic ontology.

2.242. Intelligence   When Dewey asserts, as opposed to
Locke, that reality is intelligence, he is arguing nothing more than
that existence can be characterized as a system of interrelated, interconnected entities. Though both he and Locke agree that intelligence involves relations, Dewey differs in attributing relations and,
therefore, intelligence to the whole of reality.[37]

In rejecting the ontology of mere existence, Dewey is declaring
his allegiance to some version of a doctrine that interprets reality in
terms of formed entities. One difficulty in reconstructing such a
doctrine in Dewey's writings of this period is that he never uses the
word "form" to describe his own position, though he does use the
word in varying senses. Sometimes it refers to an individual being

(EW I 178); at other times, it is synonymous with "figure" (EW I 359).[38] Nevertheless, a careful examination of the term "intelligence" will reveal the implications of Dewey's usage and identify the elements that make up his version of an ontology of formed entities. The progressive unpacking of "intelligence" will lead to (a) structure, (b) unity, and (c) relations.

Dewey's assertion that intelligence "has a structure" (EW I 307) provides only the first step in unraveling his idealistic ontology: namely, the substitution of "structured" existence for the "mere" existence of the empiricists. Intelligence, he says elsewhere, is not meant to convey something empty or formal. It has a content, "the organic unity of a system of relations" (EW I 418). But the unity Dewey is speaking of is not the simple unity without parts of the Neoplatonic tradition. It is always a unity in multiplicity, and as such always involves relations. "Harmony, in short, means relation, means connection, means subordination and co-ordination, means adjustment, means a variety, which yet is one" (EW I 297).

Relations thus become, not unexpectedly, the pivot on which Dewey's ontological description of reality revolves. His position may be summarized in the following manner. (a) Reality is most accurately described in idealistic terms as intelligence. (b) This means that existence is structured existence. (c) Structured existence, in turn, implies an organic unity held together by a system of relations. The terms "structure," "unity," and "relations," while providing a fuller idea of what Dewey means when he says that reality and intelligence are not distinct, nonetheless remain a possible source of misinterpretation. For each of those terms may be viewed as indicating a philosophical position that is ultimately static. Interpreted on the model of geometry, for instance, structures, unities, and the relations constituting them, can be viewed as timeless, changeless figures and arrangements in space. But Dewey is quite clear that geometry is not the model through which the fruitful analyses of idealism are to be interpreted. The model on which Leibniz constructed his world view was, according to Dewey, not geometry but biology. "But it is the idea of organism, of life, which is radical to the thought of Leibniz" (EW I 277).

2.243. The Dynamic Interpretation of Existence   Dewey offers this interpretation not only as one which accurately describes

Leibniz' philosophical attitude, but also as one which is commendable. Dewey claims that this biology-inspired approach is what makes Leibniz still a sympathetic figure. He even compliments Leibniz for being the "first of that now long line of modern philosophers to be profoundly influenced by the conception of life and the categories of organic growth" (EW I 276–77).

In so doing Leibniz turned back a formidable adversary in the person of Descartes. According to Dewey, there are "two typical ways of regarding nature." One, the Cartesian, views it as "something essentially rigid and static" (EW I 279). The other, that taken by Leibniz, describes it as "something essentially dynamic and active. Change according to law is its very essence" (EW I 279). This dynamic interpretation of existence adds another dimension to Dewey's idealistic metaphysics. The structures and unities that make up the realm of intelligence are fluid rather than rigid, dynamic rather than static. In fact, Dewey describes as Leibniz' "greatest glory" his conjunction of unity and activity. "The unity, whose discovery constitutes Leibniz's great glory as a philosopher, is a unity of activity, a dynamic process" (EW I 415).

Now Dewey's reluctance to use the word "form" as a descriptive term for his position becomes understandable. In his eyes, "form" stands for the static and the unchanging. The view that opposes a dynamic interpretation of existence is, Dewey believes, dominated by the categories of "formal" logic. "The unity of formal logic is exclusive of any mediation or process, and is essentially rigid and lifeless" (EW I 415). Since the "formal" stands for the schematic, the static, and the lifeless, it can find no place in a system of dynamic idealism. Here, in this opposition between a dynamic idealism and the methodology of formal logic, Dewey finds something to criticize in Leibniz. Leibniz' major failing was that he never reworked the logic he had inherited so that it could be synchronized with his novel philosophical approach (EW I 414). His dynamic ontology offers an exciting breakthrough, according to Dewey, but it is limited by being "fettered by the scholastic method—that is, the method of formal logic" (EW I 417).[39]

2.244. Potentiality, Actuality, and End   Despite Leibniz' adherence to an overly formal methodology, Dewey finds much of

lasting significance in the German thinker: "Such thoughts as that substance is activity; that its process is measured by its end, its idea; that the universe is an inter-related unit; the thoughts of continuity, of uniformity of law,—introduced and treated as Leibniz treated them,—are imperishable" (EW I 435).

Here Dewey adds a new dimension to the dynamic interpretation of existence, the teleological. Thus far we have seen that intelligence is to be understood in terms of structure, which, in turn, is to be interpreted as the harmonization of interrelated processes. Now he says process "is measured by its end." Including teleological considerations in a proper understanding of structure is an element of Dewey's Hegelian phase that will remain a constant theme as his development progresses. It also introduces the name of Aristotle into the discussion. We have seen how Morris, under the influence of Trendelenburg, had brought back from Germany an appreciation for both Hegel and Aristotle. Dewey had even commented that Morris "had no difficulty in uniting Aristoteleanism and Hegelianism" (LW V 153). The same may be said of Dewey in relation to Leibniz with Aristotle.

The single philosopher to whom Dewey most compares Leibniz is Aristotle.[40] Among the many terms Dewey uses to express the active dimension of existence, "change," "process," "activity," "motion," and "movement" are the most prominent. Through each of these terms, however, there runs a common thread which has its roots in the Greek thinker. By relating Leibniz to Aristotle, Dewey is able to explain more fully his understanding of activity in Leibniz, and in so doing, provide a threefold foundation common to all kinds of processes: potentiality, actuality, and end. In the most generalized sense, then, when Dewey speaks of "activity," "change," "motion," or any of the other synonymous terms he uses, he means to indicate a passage from potentiality to actuality that is guided by an end.

> The name of Aristotle suggests the principles which guided Leibniz in his interpretation of the fact of motion. The thought of Aristotle moves about the two poles of potentiality and actuality. . . . Now, movement, or change in its most general sense, is that by which the potential comes to the realization of its nature, and functions as an activity. Motion, then, is not an ultimate fact, but is subordinate. It exists for an end [EW I 280].

Dewey's own organicism, as well as his sympathetic interpretation of Leibniz' philosophy, are obvious here. The implications for the issue of form are direct. The most important sentence in this respect is the one asserting that motion is "subordinate." Dewey is arguing against any philosophy which would view motion or change as an end in itself, as purely blind activity. When he denies that motion is an "ultimate fact," he is not intimating that motion is unreal. He is saying that motion is never *merely* motion; it is always motion *from* and motion *toward*. It is always motion within certain boundaries. This is precisely where the greatness of Aristotle and Leibniz can be found. The first set down the boundaries of potentiality, actuality, and end; the latter revived his approach some two thousand years later.

Form enters into consideration when Dewey clarifies what he means by saying that motion is subordinate to an end. That end, as Leibniz saw, involves existence realizing its "idea; that is, its proper type of action" (EW I 280). In the words "idea" and "type," we are presented with alternatives to the discredited term "form." Motion is the transition in existence from potentiality to actuality. This actuality involves the activity proper to a certain kind of existence. Such a "proper type of action" then becomes a dynamic philosophy's version of "form," a term which Dewey associated with a prescientific and thus a static world-view. Dewey's alternative expressions for "form" are not limited to "type" or "idea," both of which are derived from Leibniz; he also uses "structure" and the one which is perhaps his favorite since it is biologically inspired, "organism." Once these terms are seen as occupying in a philosophy of process the place of form in a static philosophy, Dewey's reworking of that doctrine as an idealist can be appreciated. There is, in the Dewey of this period, strictly speaking, no "problem" of form. Structure and organism are pervasive and evident. The entire universe, in fact, "is an organism" (EW I 296).

3. SUMMARY

Perhaps the most significant point about this phase of idealism is its dual character. Dewey's allegiance went first to Kant and then to Hegel. Although the Hegelian period was more prominent in terms

of duration and quantity of publications, the pre-Hegelian phase is important as well because of its lasting impact on Dewey. This was not made fully clear in the body of the chapter, and a few words of explanation are in order.

This earliest phase still haunted Dewey some forty-six years later when he wrote his autobiography. He admits there that his first articles were "highly schematic and formal" (LW V 150), terms we know to be pejorative. However, he claims after four and a half decades to suffer still from a "native inclination toward the schematic" (LW V 150), and because of it, he says, much of his later emphasis ("over-weighting" is the term he uses at one point) on the "concrete" and the " 'practical' " was a reaction to "what was more natural" (LW V 151). It was actually, he claims, a "protection against something in myself which, in the pressure of the weight of actual experiences, I knew to be a weakness" (LW V 151). Many of Dewey's critics, as we shall see in the next chapter, were to argue that he did not protect himself enough from this tendency. At any rate, this kind of testimony indicates the importance of this phase, which in terms of duration and publications would appear to be insignificant.

The two phases of idealism can, as we have seen, be roughly distinguished in the following manner. In the first, Dewey's thinking somewhat echoes Kant's. As a result, epistemological considerations are the most important, and he is forced to admit a dualistic interpretation of matter and mind. The second phase is dominated by the influence of Hegel. The primary concerns at this time become ontological, with mind and matter described as existing in an "organic unity." Both periods share the belief that knowledge necessarily involves mediation.

As far as the ontological analysis of form is concerned, in the first phase it is considered as mind-dependent, but it is a trait of existence in the second. In both, intelligence and structure are closely related. The innovation of the Hegelian phase is the generalizing of the meaning of intelligence. It now applies not only to a knowing being, but also to the universe at large. A detailed analysis of form or structure is provided only in the writings of the Hegelian phase. There, the following elucidations are provided. (a) Relations provide the key for understanding structure. (b) Structure, far from being op-

posed to process, actually involves motion or activity. (*c*) This motion must be interpreted as the transition from potentiality to actuality in light of an end.

NOTES

1. Dewey expresses the point this way in his autobiography. "I envy, up to a certain point, those who can write their intellectual biography in a unified pattern, woven out of a few distinctly discernible strands of interest and influence. By contrast, I seem to be unstable, chameleon-like, yielding one after another to many diverse and even incompatible influences; struggling to assimilate something from each and yet striving to carry it forward in a way that is logically consistent with what has been learned from its predecessors" (LW V 155).

2. According to Harold Larrabee, William James referred to Dewey's prose as " 'damnable, you might even say God-damnable' " ("John Dewey as Teacher," *School and Society*, 86 [1959], 379). Patrick Suppes justifies his publication of Nagel's lecture notes on Dewey by arguing that they might be "of some service" in understanding Dewey, "for Dewey has possibly the most impenetrable prose style of any serious philosopher since Hegel" ("Nagel's Lectures on Dewey's Logic," in *Philosophy, Science, and Method: Essays in Honor of Ernest Nagel*, edd. Sidney Morgenbesser, Patrick Suppes, and Morton White [New York: St. Martin's, 1969], pp. 24–25).

3. "Introduction" in ENF xix–xx.

4. Bernstein labels this period the "formative" years. While such a description has the virtue of emphasizing the continuous development of Dewey's thought, it does not provide any indication as to the position taken by Dewey during this time. At this point, Dewey held a coherent and well worked-out idealistic view. Because of this, I prefer the descriptive label "idealistic" to the chronologically-oriented "formative." Actually, while I am following Bernstein's threefold division in outline, the labels for the different periods and their characterizations are my own.

5. See, on this point, the discussion by Gérard Deledalle in *L'Idée d'expérience dans la philosophie de John Dewey* (Paris: Presses Universitaires de France, 1967), p. 22. George Dykhuizen's biography of Dewey also attests his early interest in Kant: "Henry Torrey's [Dewey's teacher] own deep interest in Kant, on whose *Critique of Pure Reason* he had cut his philosophical teeth, kept the author of the *Critiques* constantly in the foreground of his classroom discussions. Dewey acknowledges the influence on him of Torrey's lectures on Kant. 'Thanks to my intro-

duction under your auspices to Kant at the beginning of my studies,'
he wrote to Torrey, 'I think I have had a much better introduction
into phil. than I could have had any other way. . . . It certainly introduced a revolution into all my thought, and at the same time gave
me a basis for my other reading and thinking'" (*The Life and Mind of
John Dewey* [Carbondale: Southern Illinois University Press, 1973], pp.
15–16; the letter from Dewey is dated November 17, 1883).

6. Only four articles are included in this pre-Hegelian phase: (*a*)
"The Materialistic Assumptions of Materialism," published in 1882; (*b*)
"The Pantheism of Spinoza," also in 1882; (*c*) "Knowledge and the Rel-
ativity of Feeling," 1883; and (*d*) "Kant and Philosophic Method," 1884.
Each of these articles, originally published in the *Journal of Speculative
Philosophy*, has been reprinted in EW I.

7. Dykhuizen, *Life and Mind of John Dewey*, p. 37.

8. Ibid.

9. The comments of Dilthey and Kierkegaard in reference to Trende-
lenburg are cited in Gershon George Rosenstock, *F. A. Trendelenburg:
Forerunner to John Dewey* (Carbondale: Southern Illinois University
Press, 1964), p. 11.

10. Morris added six pages of text explicating Trendelenburg's philosophy. This addition was occasioned by Ueberweg's failure to include
any discussion of Trendelenburg in the first two editions of his work.
The third edition did contain a short (one-page) summation, but Morris
did not consider that brief analysis to be satisfactory. See Friedrich
Ueberweg, *History of Philosophy*. II. *History of Modern Philosophy*,
trans. George S. Morris (New York: Scribner's, 1873), pp. 324–30.

11. *L'Idée d'expérience*, p. 39. The expression does not sound nearly
so stilted in French: "l'hégélianisme aristotelisé de Trendelenburg."

12. His doctoral dissertation was entitled *Platonis de ideis et numeris
doctrina ex Aristotele illustrata*. See Rosenstock, *Trendelenburg*, p. 6.

13. Ibid., pp. 5, 78. See also Deledalle, *L'Idée d'expérience*, p. 37.

14. Rosenstock, *Trendelenburg*, p. 49.

15. Ibid., pp. 46–47.

16. Deledalle, *L'Idée d'expérience*, p. 37.

17. Quoted in Rosenstock, *Trendelenburg*, p. 59.

18. " 'Inherent end' " is the way Morris expressed his teacher's position. See the article entitled "Friedrich Adolph Trendelenburg" which
originally appeared in *The New Englander* in April 1874, and was reprinted in Marc Edmund Jones, *George Sylvester Morris: His Philosophical Career and Theistic Idealism* (Philadelphia: McKay, 1948), pp.
335–84. The discussion of "inherent end" is on p. 372.

19. Morris describes Trendelenburg's teaching that forms are results

in the following manner. "Looking now at the world of things, we find all activity connected with motion. All processes, mechanical, chemical, organic, are inconceivable without the idea of motion in space. All forms are the results of motion controlling matter" (Ueberweg, *History of Modern Philosophy*, trans. Morris, p. 326).

20. Jones, *Morris*, p. 372.

21. Dewey uses this expression in a letter to his former professor H. A. P. Torrey dated October 5, 1882. The letter is quoted in Dykhuizen, *Life and Mind of John Dewey*, p. 33.

22. See Dewey's letter to Torrey cited in note 21. See also Morton White, *The Origin of Dewey's Instrumentalism* (New York: Columbia University Press, 1943), p. 31.

23. Compare Whitehead's comment concerning the world of primary qualities: "Nature is a dull affair, soundless, scentless, colorless; merely the hurrying of material, endlessly, meaninglessly" (Alfred North Whitehead, *Science and the Modern World* [New York: Macmillan, 1926], pp. 79–80).

24. White, *Origin of Dewey's Instrumentalism*, p. 29.

25. Jones, *Morris*, p. 377.

26. "When men ceased to interpret and explain facts in terms of potentiality and actuality, and resorted to that of causality, mind and matter stood over against one another in stark unlikeness; there were no intermediates to shade gradually the black of body into the white of spirit" (EN 193).

27. White, *Origin of Dewey's Instrumentalism*, p. 7.

28. Ibid., pp. 17–18.

29. See the passage from Morris quoted at length in Herbert W. Schneider, *A History of American Philosophy*, 2nd ed. (New York: Columbia University Press, 1963), p. 409.

30. *L'Idée d'expérience*, p. 39.

31. Joseph Ratner has described Dewey's changing focus of attention in the following manner. "Forty and thirty years ago the Hegelian and Kantian philosophies and their derivatives were the main objects of his critical attention; thirty and twenty years ago, it was the then contemporary realisms of all varieties, American and English. But with *Experience and Nature* (1925), a great, though not unheralded, change took place: the foregoing receded into the background while into the focus of critical examination were placed the philosophies of Plato and Aristotle; and this interchange of position between modern and ancient philosophies has become more and not less marked with each succeeding volume" ("Introduction to John Dewey's Philosophy," p. 15).

32. White, *Origin of Dewey's Instrumentalism*, pp. 59–60.

33. Morton White also thinks that Dewey's book on Leibniz typifies his philosophical position at this time: "Because of its more general character, Dewey's work on Leibniz is an even better index of his position at that time than his *Psychology*" (ibid., p. 60).

34. *Bertrand Russell's Dictionary of Mind, Matter, and Morals*, ed. Lester E. Denonn (New York: Philosophical Library, 1952), p. 98.

35. Dewey criticizes subjective idealism in "The Psychological Standpoint" (EW I 135). Both Hume and Kant are judged as presenting inadequate analyses in "Kant and Philosophic Method" (EW I 34).

36. See above, sect. 2.1.

37. Dewey's position (as well as Leibniz' on his view) does not therefore assert that only consciousness exists and that all else is shadow or appearance. Bertrand Russell has characterized the German idealistic tradition as putting "an emphasis upon mind as opposed to matter, which leads in the end to the assertion that only mind exists." In the sense in which Russell means this—namely, that the extra-mental is unreal—the description has nothing in common with the type of idealism espoused by Dewey. Russell's comment is from *A History of Western Philosophy* (New York: Simon & Schuster, 1945), p. 704.

38. See also PSY 142.

39. We now know that Dewey could not have been more mistaken in his estimation of Leibniz' logical method. Far from being simply a follower of scholastic logic, Leibniz was "one of the greatest logicians of all time." He was an innovative logician who not only originated mathematical logic, centuries before its introduction by other thinkers, but also "introduced many new, or newly developed features" to the standard Aristotelian syllogistic. See I. M. Bocheński, *A History of Formal Logic*, trans. and ed. Ivo Thomas (Notre Dame: University of Notre Dame Press, 1961), p. 258. In fairness to Dewey, it must be noted that, apart from manuscript sources, he had no way of knowing about Leibniz' logical discoveries. The first publication of those sources by Couturat came in 1901, thirteen years after the publication of Dewey's book.

40. Describing the origins of Leibniz' philosophy, Dewey writes: "Two causes above all others stand out with prominence,—one, the discoveries and principles of modern physical science; the other, that interpretation of experience which centuries before had been formulated by Aristotle" (EW I 270–71).

II
EXPERIMENTALISM

2

Darwin, Change, and the Transition to Experimentalism

1. A RENEWED EMPHASIS ON CHANGE

DEWEY'S TRANSFORMATION from an idealist to a philosopher of experimentalism was not the result of a sudden and thorough rejection of his earlier views. As we saw, Dewey's own formulation was that he "drifted" from Hegelianism. In fact, the transition from idealism to experimentalism stemmed from the isolation and elevation in significance of two topics that were components in his idealistic synthesis. We know that Dewey's idealism was a dynamic one that gave due recognition to the fact of change. We also know, from his book on Leibniz, of his tendency to assimilate this view to a biological model. He had inherited from Morris and Trendelenburg an appreciation for the achievements of science in general and the specific importance of integrating Darwin's theory of evolution into a philosophical analysis.[1] These two concerns were now separated from his idealism and became the main pillars on which his experimental phase was built.

The beginning of Dewey's experimental phase is marked by his first public presentation of a new logical position in *Studies in Logical Theory*, published in 1903. This is a logic based on the experimental methodology of the sciences, and as such is fully in line with the emphasis on change which dominates this period of his development. For Dewey, logic means essentially methodology. A method based on that of the sciences requires that the subject matter of investigation, far from being rigid and unchanging, be amenable to alterations and manipulations during the process of inquiry.

This recognition of the importance of change as crucial to a novel way of philosophizing was not a uniquely Deweyan insight. In this

respect, Dewey simply typifies a movement of early twentieth-century thought.[2] In Europe, for example, the French philosopher Julien Benda has spoken of the "hiatus" which separates earlier thinkers from their twentieth-century counterparts. This hiatus, he has argued, "consists of the fact that for the former the most honored mode of being was immutability, whereas for the latter it is movement, change."[3] Sterling Lamprecht, an American historian of philosophy, agrees, but goes further in stating that this attitude was especially prevalent in his home country. "In any case, and however the facts of history are arranged, the development of a deliberate emphasis upon process or becoming is characteristic of a considerable part of twentieth-century philosophy, especially, I believe, of twentieth-century philosophy in the United States."[4] Dewey was a leader in molding American philosophy in the manner Lamprecht describes. The present chapter examines Dewey's specific version of this general movement and sets forth the context in which his metaphysics in the post-idealistic writings can be discussed.

I begin by analyzing the impact of Darwin's theory of evolution on Dewey, for it was this theory which most influenced his view of change. Next, I touch on a matter pertinent to my interpretation of Dewey, the charge of many critics that he remained an idealist. I have argued that the idealistic period can be divided into two phases. The first of these, dominated by Kant and epistemological concerns, was antithetical to ontological considerations. On such a view, nothing can be said of beings as such; they remain an unknowable "x."[5] My whole endeavor in this work, to describe the kind of ontology Dewey developed, would fail if he had never really altered his original Kantian outlook. The matter I take up in a late portion of this chapter involves critics of Dewey who make this very claim. They argue that Dewey remained an idealist, and explicitly compare him to Kant.

2. Darwin's Impact on the Conception of Form

John Dewey was born one month before Darwin published *The Origin of Species*.[6] This fact is a mere historical curiosity, but Darwin's influence on Dewey is not. In 1909 Dewey delivered a famous lecture entitled "The Influence of Darwinism on Philosophy." Linking the new philosophical appreciation of change to the bio-

logical theory of evolution, he argued that until Darwin philosophy had been predisposed toward the permanent and the unchanging. Prior to Darwin, living beings were thought to manifest eternal types or species. The Greek predisposition toward the permanent and the unchanging appeared to be empirically verified in the flora and fauna found so abundantly throughout the world. Darwin challenged this kind of verification. "The influence of Darwin upon philosophy resides in his having conquered the phenomena of life for the principle of transition, and thereby freed the new logic for application to mind and morals" (MW IV 7–8). This quotation contains the major ingredients for Dewey's experimentalism. Darwin and transition (change) are the axes on which Dewey's thinking in this phase will revolve, while the most significant contribution of the period is his "new logic," which can be applied not only to mind but to morals as well.

To understand Dewey's position, it is important to pay attention to the attitude he believed Darwin's theory had overturned. It is an attitude summarized by the term *eidos*.

> The conception of εἶδος, species, a fixed form and final cause, was the central principle of knowledge as well as of nature. Upon it rested the logic of science. Change as change is mere flux and lapse; it insults intelligence. Genuinely to know is to grasp a permanent end that realizes itself through changes, holding them thereby within the metes and bounds of fixed truth. Completely to know is to relate all special forms to their one single end and good: pure contemplative intelligence. Since, however, the scene of nature which directly confronts us is in change, nature as directly and practically experienced does not satisfy the conditions of knowledge. Human experience is in flux, and hence the instrumentalities of sense-perception and of inference based upon observation are condemned in advance. Science is compelled to aim at realities lying behind and beyond the processes of nature, and to carry on its search for these realities by means of rational forms transcending ordinary modes of perception and inference [MW IV 6].

By a series of identifications, Dewey makes explicit what *eidos* means. He begins by offering translations of the term, first into Latin, *species*, and then into English, *form*, which he qualifies with the adjective "fixed." Now, this identification of *eidos* as species, as

form, is not at all unexpected from someone familiar with the history of thought. Nonetheless, since one aim of these chapters is to discover how Dewey revises the concept of form in his own thought, it is important to be clear about what he means when he refers to it with respect to antecedent thought.

In a step which reflects his accurate historical sense, Dewey goes on to link form with final cause. He does not refer to any specific thinkers in his analysis, but in this respect he is following the tradition of Aristotle, for whom form and end, as two of his four causes, are closely interrelated in just the sense Dewey describes. The end of a particular line of development is the mature form of an individual being.[7] Up to this point, there appears to be nothing objectionable in the position Dewey describes. This is especially true if we consider the embryo as our model of development. Here changes do occur, but these changes are not unguided. They are directed toward a certain preferred state.

But in Dewey's interpretation *eidos* means more than this, and in this additional meaning Dewey finds reason for criticism. *Eidos* is identified with a *fixed* form and involves a *permanent* end. Packed into these two adjectives are all the objections he will bring to bear on the classical conception of form. His major criticism is that the actual fact of change is underemphasized when the focus of philosophical attention is placed on the fixed and permanent. The fixed form and permanent end may have been brought about by a series of changes, but the changes involved in producing these results are secondary and negligible. As long as natural entities are seen as being merely the unfolding of a prearranged plan, the real occurrence of change and alteration will be interpreted as insignificant, as making no real difference in the production of a being that had its end-state absolutely fixed from the beginning of growth and development.

Knowledge, on the traditional view, seeks to go beyond the vagaries of opinion and belief, aiming at the fixed and the permanent. Thus, ontology and epistemology combine to reinforce the importance of permanence at the expense of change. Dewey is arguing that in the Greek view of nature change is not so much denied as minimized. It is seen as so secondary and unimportant that philosophers would betray their exalted stature by concentrating on

the changing aspect of reality. They ought instead to seek the permanent, the static, and the unchanging.

In another work, twenty years later, Dewey ascribes this predisposition toward the fixed to the hierarchical structure of Greek society, with its artistic and religious practices. Practical activity, the concern with the mundane, the ever changing, was for lesser mortals; intellectuals concerned themselves with theory. "They glorified the invariant at the expense of change, it being evident that all practical activity falls within the realm of change" (QC 14). From the Deweyan point of view, the difficulty with this attitude is that the world confronting us is continually in flux. If only the permanent will satisfy the conditions of knowledge, and if reality as we experience it is in a constant state of change, then knowledge and science cannot deal with the immediate, lived world given to the thinker in everyday experience. Characterized by flux, uncertainty, strivings, successes, and frustrations, this immediate, lived world can never qualify as a proper source of knowledge in the Greek understanding of that term. Knowledge, in this sense, if it is to be secure, sure, absolutely certain, must have for its corresponding object a reality that is permanent and fixed.

Since philosophy interpreted in this way must seek the stable, it searches for it in a realm separated from experienced reality. It then spends its time, as Dewey says, seeking the "realities lying behind and beyond the processes of nature." All this is significant because it follows from the acceptance of an ontology that posits forms and ends. If Dewey rejects such an ontology, it is because it has traditionally led away from the concerns of the here and now to a concern with a hidden stability, with an exalted world of *stasis* and permanence.

I should indicate at this point that quotations from Dewey must be approached guardedly whenever historical references are involved. This is an issue that will recur throughout the present book. Passages of this sort are of importance for clarifying Dewey's own doctrines, but they provide very little accurate information about the thinkers he is criticizing. Dewey's penchant for gliding over significant details in the positions of an individual thinker or movement is nowhere more prevalent than in his treatment of Greek philosophy. More often than not, he lumps Greek thinkers together

and attributes a single position to all of them. For example, the passage cited above, concerning "realities lying behind and beyond the processes of nature," applies more directly to Plato than to any other Greek thinker. Dewey nonetheless implies that *eidos* meant the same thing for all the Greek philosophers. This kind of over-simplification is especially disappointing in a thinker who, following the example of his teacher Morris, was well versed in the history of thought. One of Dewey's students, Walter Veazie, in commenting on this situation, could only come to the conclusion that there were two Deweys. One, the faculty member and teacher, was meticulous in his approach to the history of thought. "On one occasion a member of the faculty was outlining to us an article subsequently published. He summed up a paragraph of the 'Transcendental Dialectic' of Kant's *Critique of Pure Reason*. Dewey: 'Wait a minute. It's been 25 years since I have seen the *Critique of Pure Reason*, but if I remember rightly, the passage runs thusly,' and Dewey quoted the paragraph *verbatim*." Dewey, according to Veazie, insisted on the same kind of rigorous standards from his students, demanding that they be able to recall the *"exact* words" of an earlier thinker. In spite of this historical competence, Veazie readily admits that there was a second Dewey, the author. In his written works, Veazie says, Dewey would make statements for which "he would have flattened a student."[8] Since many of the passages I shall cite contain references to Greek thought, this frustrating habit of Dewey's will have to be constantly kept in mind.

Dewey's technique, although unsound from a scholarly point of view, is effective from a polemical one. Once he has established what the pre-Darwinian view with its Greek roots involved, the impact of Darwin's theory can by contrast be set forth clearly and decisively. Darwin's significance lies in the fact that he undercut the scientific basis for such an interpretation of nature and, in so doing, inaugurated a new era, one in which change (or process, or variation) was not interpreted as a defect or a mark of inferior being, but was now actually seen to characterize reality. "In laying hands upon the sacred ark of absolute permanency, in treating the forms that had been regarded as types of fixity and perfection as originating and passing away, the *Origin of Species* introduced a mode of thinking that in the end was bound to transform the logic of knowledge, and hence the treatment of morals, politics and reli-

gion" (MW IV 3). This mode of thinking was an exact reversal of the older one: "And change rather than fixity is now a measure of 'reality' or energy of being; change is omnipresent" (RP 114). Contemporary scientists are no longer concerned with essences, as the manifestations of the permanent. They attempt, rather, to discover correlations of changes. Unlike their Greek counterparts, they do "not try to define and delimit something remaining constant *in* change" (RP 114).

If anything can now be labeled all-encompassing, it is change. Dewey quite rightly recognized that this philosophical turnabout was to a large extent due to Darwin's work. In *Human Nature and Conduct*, published in 1922, he went so far as to define evolution strictly in terms of change. "In fact evolution means continuity of change; and the fact that change may take the form of present growth of complexity and interaction" (HNC 197). As late as 1948, however, after both he and the *Origin* had been around for eighty-nine years, Dewey noted that the implications of this view had not yet really taken hold. The new introduction written especially for the reprinting of *Reconstruction in Philosophy* repeated his analysis of the effect of the discoveries of science, and complained that not all philosophers had yet come to realize the full significance of the scientific advances. Once again he formulated the new position against the background of the philosophical search for "the immutable and ultimate."

> Into this state of affairs in natural science as well as in moral standards and principles, there recently entered the discovery that natural science is forced by its own development to abandon the assumption of fixity and to recognize that what for it is actually "universal" is *process*; but this fact of recent science still remains in philosophy, as in popular opinion up to the present time, a technical matter rather than what it is: namely, the most revolutionary discovery yet made [RP 260–61].

These are strong words, and they indicate the seriousness with which any interpreter must approach the issue of change and permanence. For Dewey the significance of this "most revolutionary discovery yet made" is that philosophy cannot turn to an analysis of contemporary issues without being forced into certain prejudged molds. A philosophy that sought ultimate Being, the really real, be-

hind or within reality was most unsuited for dealing with problems posed by changing circumstances. In these situations, which after all are the situations in which humans continually find themselves, it is not an antecedent fixity that must be resorted to, but a consequent readjustment. "Significant stages in change are found not in access of fixity of attainment but in those crises in which a seeming fixity of habits gives way to a release of capacities that have not previously functioned: in times that is of readjustment and redirection" (HNC 197).

2.1 Implications of the New View for Traditional Philosophical Problems

A philosophical position that admits change as not only real and pervasive but also as the proper object of intellectual scrutiny can deal successfully with these situations. Unlike ancient philosophy which sought to uncover the antecedently real, it tries to "gain the kind of understanding which is necessary to deal with problems as they arise" (QC 14). This emphasis on dealing with problems must be underscored if we are to understand Dewey correctly, for his concerns are never far removed from the moral sphere. Even in discussions of ontology, this concern for ethical issues, which pervades his works, is manifest.[9] For this reason he makes such a forceful point of criticizing the ancient tradition. An ontology of fixed forms and ends contributes to a stagnant social situation, one in which novelty and innovation are restricted. Once these fixed forms and ends are accepted as characterizing natural existence, the social realm remains immobile. These fixed forms and ends, Dewey claims, "paralyze constructive human inventions" and condemn them to failure because human activity can "conform only to ends already set by nature" (RP 119–20).

Although Dewey interpreted Darwin's thesis as the major force liberating philosophy to deal effectively with concrete problems, it is important to examine in just what manner Darwin's influence was felt in philosophy. A philosophical outlook that took change seriously would, Dewey believed, prove fruitful in a special sense: it would enable philosophers to resolve problems which had traditionally frustrated them, especially prominent among which were

those formulated as irreconcilable oppositions—those, for example, of subject *vs.* object, freedom *vs.* determinism, teleology *vs.* mechanism, and substance *vs.* accident. Dewey argued that an accurate description of the situation would emphasize the dissolution rather than the solution of difficulties. It is a misunderstanding to think that all problems are solved by choosing one of the two alternatives assumed in the very posing of the problems. "Old questions are solved by disappearing, evaporating, while new questions corresponding to the changed attitude of endeavor and preference take their place" (MV IV 14).

Recent discussions in philosophical biology serve as a good elucidation of the point Dewey is trying to make. During the latter part of the nineteenth century and in the early portion of this century, the mechanist–vitalist controversy was much debated. The controversy polarized opinions. If all entities, including living beings, are thought to be composed solely of matter arranged in a certain configuration, and if matter is interpreted as passive and inert, then the problem can be posed in terms of rigid alternatives. Given this foundation, certain properties of living organisms remain difficult to explain. Either these properties are ultimately to be explained in terms of the material constituents, which would mean explaining them away, or they are accepted as irreducible and underivable from matter, and thus the result of a vital force of some kind.

Both antagonists, the mechanists and the vitalists, can be interpreted as sharing a similar theory of matter. But both the emphasis on biology which resulted from Darwin's work and the new physics of the twentieth century have undercut the basis for this presupposition. Biologists were beginning to study life historically and to recognize the gradual development of increasingly complex forms of life. At the same time physicists were significantly altering their conception of matter, describing it now in terms of energy. These kinds of developments provided an entirely new framework for the discussion of mechanism and teleology. As a consequence, the problem is framed no longer in terms of mechanism *vs.* vitalism, but in terms of varying complexities of organized material.[10] The burning issue of a past age has been gotten over in the very sense Dewey suggested. Darwin's influence is seen as crucial to contemporary philosophizing because he, more than any other thinker,

provided the framework in which philosophical problems, formerly thought insoluble, can be dissolved.

2.2 Specific Implications of the New View for the Question of Change and Permanence

The basic ontological question of change and permanence is not to be studied in terms of opposing, incompatible alternatives—that kind of opposition is precisely what Darwin's theory has helped philosophy to overcome—rather, the problem is to discover how these two facets of existence are related. We have seen how Dewey was anxious to emphasize change and to criticize philosophies that do not pay enough attention to it. Nonetheless, in the works that followed his lecture on Darwin, he clearly indicates that his analysis was not to disregard every kind of permanence. In *Reconstruction in Philosophy*, published in 1920, he argues that continuity of organization must be recognized in even the simplest forms of organisms. "Some degree of organization is indispensable to even the lowest grade of life. Even an amoeba must have some continuity in time in its activity and some adaptation to its environment in space. Its life and experience cannot possibly consist in momentary, atomic, and self-enclosed sensations" (RP 132). *The Quest for Certainty* echoes this, and offers an explanation of how the new philosophical outlook overcame the fixed distinctions between change and permanence: "Constants and relative invariants figure, but they are relations between changes, not the constituents of a higher realm of Being. . . . Instead of there being a fixed difference between it and something higher—rational thought—there is a difference between two kinds of experience; one which is occupied with uncontrolled change and one concerned with directed and regulated change" (QC 67).

This mention of "directed and regulated change" suggests a model which will be helpful in specifying just what Dewey's own position entails: the model of embryological development. The growth of an embryo to maturity embodies the tension between permanence and change in a manner consistent with the kind of analysis Dewey articulated. To clarify this somewhat, let us recall that Dewey wishes to reject two tenets of an antiquated vision of nature. Evolutionary theory has taught him, first of all, that natural beings are

not rigidly preprogramed to develop toward a fixed, unchangeable end. Secondly, change and process, far from being of negligible significance, are crucial to any proper understanding of nature. The embryological model satisfies both these criteria.

The growth from seed to maturity does proceed, it is true, as if directed by a certain end, but this end is no longer viewed as rigidly fixed. A series of real changes or alterations may occur during the process of maturation which will lead to the production of a variation, or even (given enough time) of a new species. Novelty is always a possibility. It is not denied on *a priori* grounds. Change, on this view, thus gains stature as a factor leading to very real alterations of the living creature. But on the embryological model, changes gain significance in another sense as well. An organism does not grow from within as the isolated unfolding of a prearranged plan. To develop, it must interact successfully with its surroundings, gaining sustenance from this environment while avoiding its hazards, dangers, and diseases. Because of this, changes and alterations in either the organism or its environment cannot be viewed as of little importance. Rather they are seen as crucial in both cases referred to: that of normal development, and in instances resulting in a new form. Dewey, however, has identified form with *eidos*, that concept which expressed the permanent and fixed features of reality so prominent in Greek thought. Since his own doctrine does not deny permanence, but rather reinterprets it, it is necessary to examine just how the concept of form in his philosophy changes accordingly. This topic will be taken up in Chapter 3.

3. DEWEY: STILL A KANTIAN?

The lecture on Darwin clearly brings out the factors that helped draw Dewey away from idealism. Many critics, however, argue that with the exception of some superficial alterations, Dewey's position remained unchanged. The accuracy of these interpretations is not a subsidiary issue in relation to my undertaking. The kind of idealism Dewey is said to hold denies the very possibility of a descriptive ontology. He has been called a "subjectivist"[11] and a "subjective idealist";[12] it has even been suggested that his thought can be characterized as a "solipsism."[13] Each of these labels indicates a return to the earliest phase of his career, his period of Kantianism. The

criticisms claim, in effect, that although Dewey may have believed that he had outgrown his earliest phase, he had not really done so. My interpretation, by contrast, depends decisively on the fact that Dewey did change his philosophical orientation. As we saw in the previous chapter, a Kantian-type of analysis disallows the assertion that beings are formed. Form then is not a trait of beings themselves, but mind-dependent.[14] Such an idealism can make only negative assertions about beings as beings. It is limited to the claim that beings are unknowable and that intelligibility must come from some other source, conscious activity.

The position I am proposing argues, rather, that Dewey did develop a descriptive ontology. This ontology asserts that, given a new philosophical outlook, there is justifiable cause for speaking of entities and situations as formed. The two approaches, the Kantian and that of descriptive ontology, are widely divergent and incompatible. This incompatibility alone would make the interpretation that Dewey is an idealist significant for the central argument of this book. But that fact is buttressed by the prominence and quantity of commentators willing to interpret Dewey in this manner. The list of critics who place Dewey in the idealistic camp is impressive. For instance, George Santayana, Benedetto Croce, and Bertrand Russell have expressed criticisms that either suggest or claim outright that he is really an idealist who has restricted the real and the knowable to the experienced.[15] Other thinkers have made similar claims. These include Stephen Pepper, Evander Bradley McGilvary, Harry Todd Costello, Robert Dewey, Charles Bakewell, and John Edward Russell.[16] We could add as well Richard Rorty as the most recent interpreter to argue for a lasting kinship between Dewey and Kant's idealism.[17]

Though each of these thinkers charges that Dewey remained an adherent of idealism, Pepper and Croce form a sub-group interpreting him as an objective idealist, while all the others contend that he held some form of subjective idealism. The similarity of criticism is made all the more significant because of the ideological and chronological diversity among these men. Pepper, for instance, was a pragmatist, while Croce was a neo-Hegelian. Having studied with Dewey and Woodbridge, Costello considered himself to be a naturalist. McGilvary, on the other hand, attempted to develop a novel form

of realism, "perspective realism." Robert Dewey (no relation to John) was sympathetic to pragmatism but he claimed that John Dewey had not consistently maintained his own position. Rorty lists Dewey as one of his non-foundationalist heroes, but complains of certain untenable strains in his thought. Moreover, the chronology involved is not restricted to a particular stage in Deweyan scholarship. It spans the twentieth century. Bakewell and McGilvary framed their criticisms in its first decade; Rorty and Robert Dewey, in the middle of the eighth.

Because this interpretation is both prominent and a serious obstacle to my own reading of Dewey, I shall quote a few representative selections from these thinkers so that the general nature of their claim will be understood. The major focus of criticism in each case is the same: Dewey's seeming identification of existence and experience, with the consequent ambiguity about the status of beings not experienced. The three thinkers I shall cite, McGilvary, Robert Dewey, and Rorty, take up this line of argument in diverse but complementary ways.

McGilvary was perhaps the most persistent of the critics.[18] Two Deweyan terms especially trouble him, "experience" and "objects." The problem, as McGilvary conceives it, is that for Dewey objects do not exist unless they are experienced.

> The object as it existed before it was experienced, was not reality, but only a condition of reality, and the condition is not sufficient to produce reality. Only when the condition is supplemented by an experience which realizes the object does the object become real. . . . No thinker, no thought-object; no experience somewhere and somewhen, no meaningful reality anywhere and anytime. This is the truth which is contained in Professor Dewey's contention.[19]

There are two directions in which I want to develop the analysis of this quotation. The first is historical. I shall indicate the manner in which McGilvary's interpretation in effect argues that the Deweyan position has remained unchanged since his first, Kantian, phase. The second involves the term "object," one of the foci for his remarks. The manner in which this term is understood has a direct bearing on the ontological issue I am discussing in this book.

(*a*) We saw in the last chapter that in his Kantian period Dewey distinguished "substance" from "mere succession of phenomena," and argued that the guarantor of substance was the sense of abiding provided by the active mind. Substance, on this view, becomes subject-dependent, and Dewey's position is a subjective idealism. Although McGilvary does not frame his criticism in the context of Dewey's development, the similarity is evident to those familiar with that development. Dewey's terminology has changed, to be sure, but McGilvary interprets those changes in a way that exactly corresponds to the earlier, Kantian, phase. Whereas Dewey had spoken of "mere phenomena," "substance," and "mind," McGilvary's interpretation deals with "condition of reality," "object," and "experience." Dewey's new terminology is being used, but the conclusion remains the same. Objects are not realized, have no reality, prior to their being experienced. In the earlier phase, Dewey's presentation has described "substance" as mind-dependent. McGilvary argues that Dewey is now (1908) describing "objects" as experience-dependent.

(*b*) The nature of "objects," the second consideration I wish to take up, can thus be recognized as important for a proper understanding of Dewey's philosophy. McGilvary focuses here on a term that Dewey had made central and, unfortunately, ambiguous. The line of argument this critic developed is based on the assumption that "object" is synonymous with "thing" or "entity." "Object" must be understood in the literal sense of something which "thrusts out" apart from the observing individual. When Dewey's philosophy, according to McGilvary, makes objects dependent upon experience, it also makes the beings of the world dependent on that same experience. It is not surprising, therefore, to find McGilvary characterizing Dewey's philosophy as a "thoroughgoing idealism, and a subjective idealism at that."

The implications for ontology of such an interpretation are devastating. Since ontology is the subject that deals with beings insofar as they are beings, its sphere of study is, in this case, severely limited. The only permissible statement that could be made in ontology, if this interpretation were correct, would be the very one uttered by McGilvary. Of beings as such, that is, as independent of constitutive experience, one could assert only that they are "conditions of re-

ality." It certainly would not be possible to argue that beings are in some sense formed. Since objects apart from experience do not possess reality, any intelligible descriptive statement about them is effectively ruled out.

By differentiating between objects prior to experience and objects after experience, McGilvary suggests that the shadow of the first Kantian critique extends through Dewey's earliest logical works. The other two critics make the relationship to Kant even more explicit. Richard Rorty is a thinker who recognizes that much of what Dewey accomplished was anti-Kantian. He nonetheless argues that Dewey's solution to the mind–body problem seemed "like one more invocation of the transcendental ego" because in both Kant and Dewey "the model of knowledge is the same." This model is "the constitution of the knowable by the cooperation of two unknowables."[20] An object such as a table, Rorty asserts, is for Dewey "neither an ugly brown thing whose hard edges bumped people, nor yet a swirl of particles, but something common to both—sheer potentiality, ready to be transformed in a situation."[21]

This critic is suggesting that Dewey accepts some version of Kant's noumena. On such an interpretation Dewey is said to view the "really real," behind the common-sense and scientific views of things, as merely an undifferentiated noumenal realm. Like McGilvary, Rorty accuses Dewey of surreptitiously (by using novel terminology) reintroducing a Kantian noetic scheme. The reality beyond the common-sense and scientific views of things remains unformed, undefined, and unknowable for both Dewey and Kant. Dewey does not, Rorty admits, use the Kantian phrase "constitution of objects," but he does substitute a phrase of his own, "transaction with the environment."[22] Rorty stops short of explicitly identifying the Deweyan "unknowable" or "sheer potentiality" with Kant's *Ding-an-sich*, but Robert Dewey does not hesitate to do so.

> When Dewey asserts that events as such are not objects of knowing, they become his process philosophy's version of the unknown somewhats (or Kantian unknowable *Dinge-an-sich*) constituting nature beyond the data of immediate experience. It further follows from this view that the world as it is (a system of unknown events) must be distinguished from the world as it is known (a system of objects). This distinction introduces a dualism as sharp as any which Dewey

has critiqued—a dualism which separates reality and knowledge as completely as reality and appearance are separated by the most ardent Platonist.[23]

Just as McGilvary and Rorty were helpful in concentrating on the constitution of *objects* as a problem, so Robert Dewey's analysis focuses on the term *event*. To understand the quotation properly, some explantion of this word is necessary.

I shall deal with this topic more thoroughly when *Experience and Nature* is analyzed. For the moment, I need only note that "event" is a technical term Dewey used to describe beings. It is an ontological term, one of the widest generality, applying to all beings. In this respect, Dewey is similar to other philosophers who develop an ontology and who find it necessary to employ a term that best exemplifies their interpretation of beings. For Aristotle it was *ousia*; for Aquinas, *substantia*. Leibniz used monad; Dewey preferred event. It is thus a crucial term that must be understood properly in any attempt to grasp what Dewey is saying. Robert Dewey interprets it as signifying that beings apart from experience are indeterminate, and thus unknowable. Once this is established the next significant aspect of this analysis, the relationship with Kant, follows with no difficulty. Events correspond to the *Dinge-an-sich*, and known objects can only be the results of the interplay of these events with experience.

These three critics provide us with a good summary of the idealistic interpretation of Dewey. First of all, the basic issue is clear: Dewey's failure to distinguish between things as existents and things as experienced.[24] Secondly, such a confusion leads McGilvary to argue that, for Dewey, "objects" do not precede thought. Rorty is led to claim that prior to transactions there exists for Dewey only "sheer potentiality." Objects are results, requiring experience or transactions for full realization. Thirdly, the term in Dewey's writings used to contrast "object" as result is said to be "event" on Robert Dewey's analysis. Events represent the unknown things as *merely* existents. To become objects these undifferentiated, indeterminate events require the completion experience brings. These three moments—namely, the unknown somewhats, or "events" that precede knowledge, the experience of these events, and the resultant known "object"—form the skeletal framework on which the interpretation of Dewey as an idealist is constructed. Since this parallels the *Dinge-*

an-sich, unity of apperception, and known object of the Kantian schema, Dewey is seen specifically as not having moved beyond the position of the German thinker.[25]

One commentator who comes close to, but stops short of, interpreting Dewey as an idealist is Sterling Lamprecht. His interpretation helps to put the arguments of the critics mentioned above into proper perspective and indicates the approach I believe is a more accurate one. Lamprecht asserts that Dewey himself often phrases his position in such a way that an interpretation of the sort these critics developed is almost inevitable. Certain passages in which Dewey emphasizes that the object of knowledge is a result and not an antecedent especially bother Lamprecht. The language which Dewey chooses, according to Lamprecht, "suggests the strange and unusual positions that only the future, never the past, can be known, and that only the promotion of successful action, never the disclosure of theoretical truth, is the objective of cognitive operations. Dewey repudiates these positions, and it would be unjust to belabor him further along these lines." However, a few pages later, Lamprecht exclaims, almost as if in exasperation: "Yet I confess that at times I see no possible way of so interpreting his words as to acquit him of the unsound ideas his words easily suggest to many of his critics."[26] Exclamations of this kind from a careful historian of philosophy who knew Dewey well are significant in two ways: (*a*) they give some credence to the idealistic interpretation; and (*b*) they warn the reader that, although this view of Dewey's work has many texts to fall back on for support, it is, in the end, false. I am in full accord with Lamprecht on this matter, and shall develop my criticisms of Dewey's interpreters in the following chapter.

My approach in the next chapters will be to examine Dewey's works according to the periods of his development. Chapter 3 will continue the analysis of the present one, by studying a major text of the experimental phase, *Essays in Experimental Logic,* published in 1916. The next four chapters will deal with texts from the period of naturalistic ontology. Three of these, *Experience and Nature, Art as Experience,* and *The Quest for Certainty,* published between 1925 and 1934, contain the major elements for reconstructing Dewey's philosophy as it relates to ontological issues. Because of this, I will discuss these books in a systematic rather than a chronological manner. They will be analyzed in three chapters, each of

which will deal with the appropriate sections of all three books. Finally, *Logic: The Theory of Inquiry*, published in 1938, will be discussed in Chapter 7.

4. SUMMARY

Chapter 2 begins the examination of two topics that will be continued in later chapters: the impact of Darwin's theory on Dewey's thought, and the recurring criticism that Dewey had not really turned his back on a Kantian-type of idealism. The first issue is significant because Dewey's constructive ontological syntheses are influenced by evolutionary theory; the second, because, if the critics are correct, Dewey could not, except in a severely restricted sense, have articulated a descriptive naturalistic metaphysics.

We saw in this chapter that Darwin had a threefold impact on Dewey. (*a*) The greatest result of Darwin's theory of evolution was to bring the fact of process, flux, or change into prominence. (*b*) Grasping the significance of this doctrine immediately, Dewey used it to criticize classical metaphysics as not sufficiently sensitive to the pervasiveness of change. He singled out the term *eidos* as the distillation of a philosophical attitude that emphasized the fixed and permanent at the expense of the fluid and aleatory. (*c*) Evolutionary thought also helped reveal the manner in which philosophical problems could be overcome by being dissolved rather than solved. This means that for certain fundamental issues such as change and permanence or unity and multiplicity the very way of phrasing the problematic would have to be altered. No longer should these problems be framed in terms of such incompatibilities as change *vs.* permanence or unity *vs.* multiplicity. The new way of formulating the issues asks in what ways these dimensions mutually interpenetrate each other. Finally, this chapter surveyed a prominent line of criticism in Deweyan scholarship: interpreters who claim that Dewey's post-idealistic writings retain a Kantian distinction between unknowable somewhats and an object-constituting subject.

NOTES

1. See chap. 1 for the influence of Trendelenburg. Morris' intellectual biographer describes Darwin's influence on Morris in this way: "Morris

began his mature thinking under the impact of these widely ramifying influences. He had acquired a new responsibility with the Johns Hopkins opening, and he found the intellectual world considerably changed from the general aspect familiar to him in 1874, when the Ueberweg translation and the Trendelenburg article were completed. He was confronted now by a revivified Hegelianism, which had come forward to complement the Darwinian ferment and which comprised a fresh and highly alive body of thought" (Jones, *Morris*, pp. 241–42).

2. On the European continent, the undisputed leader of this movement was Henri Bergson. He explained succinctly the significance of this attitude toward change in a lecture "The Perception of Change" delivered at Oxford in 1911: "I have chosen it [the topic of change] because I consider it to be fundamental, and because I believe that, if we are convinced of the reality of change and if we make an effort to grasp it, everything would be simplified. Some philosophical difficulties which we now consider insurmountable would be overcome" ("La perception du changement," in *Oeuvres* [Paris: Presses Universitaires de France, 1959], p. 1366). Dewey, as we shall see, is in complete agreement that the real significance of the new emphasis on change is the pathway it opens for reformulating traditional philosophical difficulties.

3. *Trois Idoles romantiques: Le dynamisme, l'existentialisme, la dialectique matérialiste* (Paris: Mont Blanc, 1948), p. 15.

4. *The Metaphysics of Naturalism* (New York: Appleton-Century-Crofts, 1967), p. 112.

5. The Kantian threat to metaphysics is well described by Copleston: "The cognitive function of the categories lies in their application to objects as given in sense intuition, that is, to phenomena. Things-in-themselves are not, and cannot be, phenomena. And we possess no faculty of intellectual intuition which could supply objects for a metaphenomenal application of the categories. Hence metaphysics of the classical type is excluded, when it is considered as a possible source of objective knowledge" (Frederick Copleston, s.j., *A History of Philosophy*. VI. *Wolff to Kant* [London: Burns & Oates, 1960], p. 277).

6. Dewey's date of birth is October 20, 1859, and the *Origin* was published on November 27 of the same year.

7. "And since 'nature' means two things, the matter and the form, of which the latter is the end, and since all the rest is for the sake of the end, the form must be the cause in the sense of 'that for the sake of which'" (*Physics* 199A30–33, in *The Basic Works of Aristotle*, ed. Richard McKeon [New York: Random House, 1941], p. 250).

8. "John Dewey and the Revival of Greek Philosophy," *University of Colorado Studies in Philosophy*, 2 (1961), 1–3.

9. In his autobiography, Dewey suggests the fruitfulness of a " 'Back to Plato' movement" in philosophy. This kind of revival would be especially helpful, he states, if it focused on the early and middle dialogues, in which the "highest flight of metaphysics always terminated with a social and practical turn" (LW V 155). What Dewey says about Plato in this context is equally true of Dewey himself.

10. George Gaylord Simpson, for example, has argued that although biology requires "compositionist" (in essence teleological) as well as "reductionist" (physico-chemical, mechanical) types of explanation, this does not imply a return to vitalism. "Here I should briefly clarify a point of possible confusion. Insistence that the study of organisms requires principles additional to those of the physical sciences does not imply a dualistic or vitalistic view of nature" ("Biology and the Nature of Science," *Science*, January 11, 1963, p. 87). Ernst Mayr argues similarly and concludes: "Vitalism as a possible theory of biology has been dead for some 40 or 50 years, as has been the entire argument of mechanism versus vitalism" (*Evolution and the Diversity of Life: Selected Essays* [Cambridge: The Belknap Press of Harvard University Press, 1976], p. 374).

11. Harry Todd Costello, "Professor Dewey's 'Judgments of Practice,' " *The Journal of Philosophy*, 17 (1920), 450.

15. Santayana, "Dewey's Naturalistic Metaphysics," *The Journal of ibid.*, 5 (1908), 593.

13. Robert E. Dewey, *The Philosophy of John Dewey: A Critical Exposition of His Method, Metaphysics, and Theory of Knowledge* (The Hague: Nijhoff, 1977), p. 113.

14. See chap. 1, sect. 2.1 as well as the quotation from Copleston in note 5 above.

15. Santayana, "Dewey's Naturalistic Metaphysics," *The Journal of Philosophy*, 22 (1925), 673–88 (this article has been reprinted in *The Philosophy of John Dewey*, ed. Paul A. Schillp, The Library of Living Philosophers 1 [New York: Tudor, 1939], pp. 243–61); Croce, "On the Aesthetics of Dewey," trans. Katharine Gilbert, *The Journal of Aesthetics and Art Criticism*, 6 (1948), 203–207; Russell, "Dewey's New Logic," in *Philosophy of John Dewey*, ed. Schillp, pp. 135–56.

16. For Costello, McGilvary, and Robert Dewey, see notes 11, 12, 13 above. The criticisms of the others in this list are found in the following articles: Pepper, "Some Questions on Dewey's Esthetics," in *Philosophy of John Dewey*, ed. Schillp, pp. 369–89; Bakewell, "The Issue Between Idealism and Immediate Empiricism," *The Journal of Philosophy*, 2 (1905), 687–91; Russell, "Objective Idealism and Revised Empiricism," *The Philosophical Review*, 15 (1905), 627–33.

17. "There is obviously *some* sense in which Dewey agrees with Kant that only the transcendental idealist can be an empirical realist" (CP 83).

18. Besides the article cited in note 12, McGilvàry's criticisms of Dewey can be found in the following writings: "Pure Experience and Reality," *The Philosophical Review*, 16 (1907), 266–84; "Pure Experience and Reality: A Reassertion," ibid., 422–24; and "Professor Dewey's 'Brief Studies in Realism,'" *The Journal of Philosophy*, 9 (1912), 344–49.

19. "The Chicago Idea," 593.

20. CP 85.

21. CP 84.

22. CP 84.

23. R. Dewey, *Philosophy of John Dewey*, p. 117.

24. Another commentator who knew Dewey well, Harry Todd Costello, argues that it is this very failure which leads Dewey to be criticized as a subjectivist. Costello says that Dewey is "surprised when people interpret him in subjectivist terms. Yet one who fails to distinguish between what is and what he experiences, has no reason to be surprised at such an interpretation" ("Professor Dewey's 'Judgments of Practice,'" 449–50).

25. Those thinkers who interpret Dewey as still under the influence of Kant are probably thinking of selections such as the following from the first version of the transcendental deduction of the categories. "What then is to be understood when we speak of an object corresponding to, and consequently also distinct from, our knowledge? It is easily seen that this object must be thought only as something in general = x, since outside our knowledge we have nothing which could be set over against this knowledge as corresponding to it. . . . But it is clear that, since we have to deal only with the manifold of our representations and since that x (the object) which corresponds to them is nothing to us—being, as it is, something that has to be distinct from all our representations—the unity that the object makes necessary can be nothing else than the formal unity of consciousness in the synthesis of the manifold of representations. It is only when we have thus produced synthetic unity in the manifold of intuition that we are in a position to say that we know the object" (Immanuel Kant, *The Critique of Pure Reason*, trans. Norman Kemp Smith [London: Macmillan, 1929], pp. 134, 136).

These citations contain all the main elements on which Dewey's critics have built their interpretation of him as an idealist. There is, to begin with, an environment which is a manifold of representations, in other words, an "x," beyond or outside of our knowledge. Secondly, there is the possibility that this manifold may be synthesized by the

unity of consciousness. This results, thirdly, in a known object. In Deweyan terminology these three moments become: (a) unknown subject matter, (b) the activity of inquiry, and (c) the object of knowledge.

26. *Metaphysics of Naturalism*, pp. 47, 53.

3

Change and Permanence
in the
Experimental Logic

1. INTRODUCTION

IN CHAPTER 2 I emphasized three factors that were responsible for Dewey's transition to experimentalism: Darwin's theory of evolution, the concomitant emphasis upon change, and the search for a new logic. The first two, evolution and change, were discussed in that chapter; the third, Dewey's new logic, forms the subject matter of the present one. Dewey understands logic as involving especially the search for method. His earliest attempt at developing a methodology fully consistent with the advances of modern science is found in *Studies in Logical Theory*, published in 1903. This book includes articles by Dewey and some of his colleagues at The University of Chicago. Dewey's articles from that volume, along with additional material of his own, plus an introduction, were printed in 1916 as *Essays in Experimental Logic*. Dewey's views were not developed in isolation from the philosophical controversies of his day. The type of logic he espoused is presented as a response to the perceived insufficiencies of alternative positions. Thus the new book on logic, like the earlier one on Leibniz, has a polemical as well as a constructive dimension.

The body of this chapter will be divided along these polemical and constructive lines. Section 3 will examine Dewey's objections to the two traditions that dominated philosophical discussion, realism and idealism, and will deal in greater detail with his understanding of the term "object," a topic merely touched on in Chapter 2. Section 4 will discuss the constructive doctrine Dewey propounded in his experimental phase and in this connection will treat a variety of issues: (*a*) his suggestion of a novel starting point for philosophizing;

(*b*) the way one aspect of his theory of knowledge can be described in terms of "intentionality"; (*c*) a re-examination of the charges made by the critics listed in Chapter 2; and (*d*) the place of *eidos* in these logical works. Prior to these polemical and constructive analyses I shall review in Section 2 the main issues under consideration.

2. RESTATEMENT OF THE PROBLEM

As we saw in the examination of Dewey's article on the influence of Darwin, the term "species" is a translation of the Greek *eidos*, which we render in English as "form." Any investigation of the ontological problem of change and permanence will result in some conceptual articulation of the relationship between these two aspects of experienced fact. The concept of form has traditionally been associated with the stable or the permanent, signifying as it does a certain ordered, delimiting structure. For example, it played a significant role in the philosophy of Aristotle, which Dewey interpreted as an early representative of naturalism because it placed humans fully within the natural world.[1] The beings that populated the world were viewed as organized beings, formed in certain definite ways. Knowledge resulted when the form was intellectually grasped.

The renascent naturalism of the twentieth century owed a great deal to the biological theory of evolution. John Herman Randall, Jr., a pupil of Dewey's and one of the main interpreters and theoreticians of naturalism, has made this point quite explicitly.

"Naturalism" came into vogue as the name for a recognized philosophic position during the great scientific movement of the nineteenth century, which put man and his experience squarely into the Nature over against which he had hitherto been set. The obliteration of the gulf between the nature of the "natural scientist" and human life was then associated with the discovery of the facts of biological evolution and of the descent of man.[2]

In terms of content, then, naturalism stressed the *continuity* of humans and the natural world, and challenged the dualistic and anthropocentric bias prominent in philosophy since the time of Descartes. The new analysis typified by this term "continuity" was somewhat of a return to the cosmocentrism of Aristotle. The assumption of continuity is prevalent in Dewey's thought and critical

to a proper understanding of his position. In "The Need for a Recovery in Philosophy," he dealt with it in the following way:

> Can one deny that if we were to take our clue from the present empirical situation, including the scientific notion of evolution (biological continuity) and the existing arts of control of nature, subject and object would be treated as occupying the same natural world as unhesitatingly as we assume the natural conjunction of an animal and its food? Would it not follow that knowledge is one way in which natural energies cooperate [MW X 24]?

This passage, first published in 1917, presents a clear statement of two important and interrelated Deweyan themes. First of all, the dualism of subject and object is challenged. As we know, Dewey's opposition to dualisms can be traced back to his studies at Johns Hopkins with Morris.[3] In the notion of biological continuity, Dewey found a theoretical, non-idealistic, formulation for his opposition. The stress on the continuum between humans and nature also re-emphasizes the position Randall expresses on the relationship between evolutionary thought and the recognition of continuity. By linking evolution, rather than "universal consciousness" or "intelligence," with the non-dualistic doctrine of continuity, Dewey succeeds in modifying his idealism without sacrificing one of the main beliefs he had held during that phase in his career. This shift in position typifies the manner in which Dewey was able to preserve many of the positions from his idealistic period while finding non-idealistic ways of expressing them.

If the theory of evolution brought forth this emphasis on continuity, a revived naturalism, and cosmocentrism, it suggested a naturalism without the Aristotelian corollary of natural forms. In fact, Darwin's theory did much to undermine any philosophical position that would be based on such a doctrine. The resulting situation for the naturalists of the twentieth century was, then, that naturalism was renewed but the attendant essentialism it had been associated with earlier was now suspect. This situation led to the problem of developing a new vision of nature, one consistent with the new science yet capable of meeting the challenge of reductionism. In his early works on logic Dewey articulates this new vision as an alternative both to realism, in its ancient and contemporary forms, and to the idealisms of the immediately preceding centuries.

Obviously those critics who accuse him of a lingering subjectivism do not find the arguments used to support his new position convincing. In fact, it is in his very attempt to develop a path between the doctrines he refers to as realism and idealism that Dewey becomes vulnerable to this interpretation. Because he is not a realist (in the sense of positing an independent, knowing mind which merely contemplates nature as it is), he seems to some interpreters such as Richard Rorty and Robert Dewey to resemble Immanuel Kant. This interpretation, as I mentioned in the previous chapter, poses a serious challenge to my own analysis of Dewey.

3. DEWEY'S CRITICISMS OF ALTERNATIVE VIEWS

In this section I shall examine Dewey's position as found in the early logical works, and focus on the nature and description of the beings of the world as he conceived them. The result is an ontological analysis that asks both what kind of descriptive attributes can be said to belong to beings simply as beings and whether there is anything in these early works to indicate that Dewey is willing to recognize form as a trait of existence.

But first I must clarify an important matter of terminology. Both realism and idealism are complex movements of thought with many and diverse positions within the schools themselves. In his early works on logic, Dewey refers to idealistic and realistic philosophies as foils to his own constructive analysis. But since his main interest is to develop and defend a novel doctrine, his *Essays in Experimental Logic* cannot be read as scholarly analyses of the various undertakings that go by the names of realism and idealism.

While engaged in polemics, Dewey is inclined to deal chiefly with *types* rather than with actual individuals. By "type" I mean a composite picture reflecting the major characteristics of a position without necessarily being exemplified in any single thinker.[4] Dewey's analysis of realism in the *Essays* manifests this very tendency. He discusses and rejects three versions of realism, analytic, presentative, and epistemological. In none of these discussions does he name particular individuals as representatives of the criticized views. The treatment of idealism is better focused since in this case Dewey has chosen a typical thinker, Hermann Lotze.[5] But here, too, Lotze is

used as a springboard for an attack on varying sorts of idealisms. My own presentation will follow Dewey in this regard. I shall examine somewhat briefly the positions he considers to be antithetical to his own, in the hope of bringing his positive contributions into better relief. This kind of analysis will not do justice to the complex texture of the realisms and idealisms vying for adherents at the beginning of this century; yet, given the aim of my study, the exploration of these issues remains a subsidiary consideration, one that can be overlooked at this time.

As was noted earlier, Dewey presents his new logic, which he sometimes calls "instrumentalism,"[6] as a way of overcoming the polarization between realism and idealism. It shares characteristics with both, but avoids what Dewey considers to be their respective errors. Like the realists, Dewey does not give to the intellect the power of actually constituting reality. "In bare outline, it is obvious that the two latter [realism and instrumentalism] agree in regarding thinking as instrumental, not as constitutive" (MW X 338). Yet, as we saw in our discussion of Dewey's idealistic period, humans are not simply passive observers of the world. From Trendelenburg and Morris, Dewey learned that awareness of the world around us involves not only passivity, but activity on the part of individuals. This position remains unchanged in the *Essays*. "In so far as it is idealistic to hold that objects of knowledge *in their capacity of distinctive objects of knowledge* are determined by intelligence, it is idealistic" (MW X 338). Given the point of view of this inquiry, which is to ascertain just what Dewey allows in terms of an ontological description of entities, the expression *distinctive objects of knowledge* should be kept securely in mind.

As we saw in the previous chapter, McGilvary based much of his contention that Dewey is an idealist on the way Dewey deals with the concept of "object." In his analysis, Dewey is seen as distinguishing between objects simply as existents and objects as known, and as holding the doctrine that, although the very existence of an entity is not knowledge-dependent, its intelligibility is. Intelligibility, in other words, resides, not in beings themselves, but in some other source. The implication for the line of argument I am undertaking is direct: the structure or form of an entity is not an ontological given.

3.1 "Objects" in Dewey's Instrumentalism

McGilvary's position is based on the identification of objects with existents or things-in-the-world. These are seen as not having full reality or as needing the completion of experience. But Dewey rarely uses the word "object" in that sense.[7] For him, "object" has a special logical sense. It means the *result of an intellectual investigation.* "Object" for Dewey means knowledge-object, and is to be distinguished from the entities setting the context for the investigation that results in its (the object's) discovery. It indicates the end aimed at in the process of investigation or experimentation. The sense in which Dewey uses this term can best be exemplified in a question such as: What is the object of your inquiry? The term "object," as used in this type of question, indicates what is sought after or looked for.

Dewey's favorite example to illustrate this point is a physician. When patients visit a doctor, they present a series of symptoms to which the doctor brings training and expertise. The physician's task is to discern the illness and prescribe a remedy. As Dewey explains this situation in logical terms, the descriptions of the patient, together with the competence of the physician, are *means* to secure the object which is not yet given, not yet known.

> Now, in the degree to which the physician comes to the examination of what is there with a large and comprehensive stock of such possibilities or meanings in mind, he will be intellectually resourceful in dealing with a particular case. They (the concepts or universals of the situation) are (together with the sign-capacity of the data) the *means* of knowing the case in hand; they are the agencies of transforming it, through the actions which they call for, into an object—an object of knowledge, a truth to be stated in propositions [MW X 340–41].

The object, as Dewey expressed it earlier, is "suggested by what is given, but is no part of the given" (MW X 340). This understanding of what Dewey means by object may remove a possible source of misconstrual. Objects are the results of a line of investigation. They are to be expressed in propositions: "This person has an ulcer"; "Genes are discrete units which determine heredity"; "Your blood is type AB." In none of these cases could we say that the object was

given directly to the inquirer. It was actually what was not given, a missing piece of the puzzle that was sought out. If this fairly restricted meaning of object is kept in mind, it will be possible to understand how Dewey preserves some aspects of idealism, without committing himself fully to that doctrine. At the same time, by focusing on what an object is for Dewey, we will be able to understand his quarrel with some realistic philosophies.

3.2. Dewey and Realism

Dewey finds three types of realism unsatisfactory: analytic, presentative, and epistemological. These are described not so much as wholly distinct positions as various facets of a philosophical movement that is in some ways mistaken. His arguments against these positions must be viewed in light of two wider and, according to Dewey, erroneous assumptions. The first, a familiar Deweyan *bête noire*, is a dualistic ontology; the second, what Dewey calls the "ubiquity of the knowledge relation."

These realisms accentuate the dualistic attitude because they are products of that very doctrine. If one is willing to accept a Cartesian bifurcation into *res cogitans* and *res extensa,* then one consistent implication for epistemology is to accept a mental, cogitating power surveying from the outside the affairs of the material world. When, in addition, the rich complexity of experience is reduced to presentation of data to a knower (the ubiquity of the knowledge relation), certain difficulties follow.

Since this second assumption is basic to Dewey's analysis, it is important to understand exactly what he means by it. In ordinary parlance, Dewey argues, "knowledge" is a term employed to distinguish the settled outcome of a certain situation from one that remains indeterminate or ambiguous, and to contrast securely attained information "with ungrounded conviction, or with doubt and mere guesswork, or with the inexpertness that accompanies lack of familiarity" (EEL 264).

This common use of the term stands in sharp opposition to the "epistemological use" favored by professional thinkers and taken over, as Dewey asserts, by both the realists and the idealists. "In its epistemological use, the term 'knowledge' has a blanket value which is absolutely unknown in common life. It covers any and every

'presentation' of any and every thing to a knower, to an 'awarer,' if I may coin a word for the sake of avoiding some of the pitfalls of the term 'consciousness' " (EEL 264–65). One way of understanding what Dewey is saying is to see this particular argument as a continuation of the line of criticism directed against non-mediated, or "immediate," knowledge which is present in his earliest writings. The expression "ubiquity of the knowledge relation" is only an alternative way of indicating the confusion between mediated and non-mediated knowledge. The use of the term "knowledge" to indicate what is gained in immediate "presentation" to a knower—in other words, knowledge as ubiquitous or non-mediated—involves a misunderstanding of the actual cognitive situation, according to Dewey. As in his earlier phase, Dewey insists that there is a specific meaning for "knowledge," and that that meaning involves mediation of some sort. What is directly presented to an "awarer" is a complex situation that includes qualities as well as moral and aesthetic elements. The reductive assertion that what is directly presented is merely cognitive involves the oversimplification and falsification of experience typical of positivism.

The problems Dewey finds associated with analytic, presentative, and epistemological realism can now be dealt with in this context. The labels "analytic" and "presentative" are lucidly illustrative of the positions in question. Both share the view that thinkers are to *analyze* data *presented* to them. On this view, thinkers are passive onlookers. Data and knowledge are then overlapping terms because of the ubiquity of the knowledge relation. The individual knower is strictly a recipient, active in no significant way in determining the proper object of knowledge. The main difficulty which flows from this position, according to Dewey, is coordinating the data of common sense with that of the sciences. If both are treated equally as cases of knowledge, as cases of knowledge-objects given to an inquirer, then a conflict is inevitable.

In illustrating this point, Dewey uses the example of a star as both the light shining in the night sky and the actual physical object identified by astronomers and physicists. The conflict becomes one of adjudicating between two equally valid, but incompatible objects of knowledge (EEL 255). A solution may then be sought in one of two ways, both of which Dewey finds untenable. Either the common-sense world is accepted as the truly real, and science is denigrated;

or the scientific view is accepted, and the *really real* is said to be something behind the appearances of everyday existence.

We are here face to face with a crucial point in analytic realism. Realism argues that we have no alternative except either to regard analysis as falsifying (à la Bergson), and thus commit ourselves to distrust of science as an organ of knowledge, or else to admit that something eulogistically termed Reality (especially as *Existence*, Being as subject to space and time determinations) is but a complex made up of fixed, mutually independent simples: viz., that Reality is truly conceived only under the caption of whole and parts, where the parts are independent of each other and consequently of the whole [MW X 343].

In any case, realisms of this sort are led to ask about the possibility of knowledge in general, of the relation between mind and the objective world. Dewey pejoratively labels these questions "epistemological." The resulting realism is thus called "epistemological realism," and is an outgrowth of accepting the two leading assumptions of presentative and analytic realism.

Dewey wishes to distinguish this as a third erroneous aspect of realism because he finds here the locus of questions which have traditionally bothered epistemologists and for which there is no solution. The only path out of the dilemmas these kinds of questions engender is to reject the presuppositions on which these varieties of realism are based. Because both realism and idealism develop their views by assuming the ubiquity of the knowledge relation, both are challenged when this assumption is brought into question (EEL 266).

Besides dealing with both the ontological and the epistemological presuppositions and consequences of the three versions of realism, Dewey's line of argument once again reveals his preoccupation with ethical concerns and his awareness of the social consequences that follow from a theoretical analysis. In this respect, the failure to place human beings within nature has a practical corollary in allowing philosophers to stand aloof from the vexing practical problems that continually arise in the course of a human life. It makes them a special, privileged class, and this, as I suggested in the last chapter, is an equally serious reason for Dewey's rejection of realism. The moral tone of any theoretical analysis is never very distant for

Dewey. He argues that there are considerations which allow us to understand how such a social organization came about; but conditions have now changed, and so must the philosopher's orientation.

> I can see how specialists at any time, professional knowers, so to speak, find in this doctrine a salve for conscience—a solace which all thinkers need as long as an effective share in the conduct of affairs is not permitted them. Above all, I can see how seclusion and the absence of the pressure of immediate action developed a more varied curiosity, greater impartiality, and a more generous outlook. But all this is no reason for continuing the idealization of a remote and separate mind or knower now that the method of intelligence is perfected, and changed social conditions not only permit but demand that intelligence be placed within the procession of events [MW X 365].

Realism then is untenable for three reasons. (*a*) It is a product of two incorrect assumptions: the dualistic interpretation of mind and nature, and the ubiquity of the knowledge relation, both of which have been called into question by evolutionary biology. (*b*) The realist who takes his common-sense perceptions as reflecting the "really-real" world must inevitably fall into conflict with scientists whose methods of observation provide them with a different version of things. (*c*) Finally, the practical consequence of such a position, the remote, disinterested, aloof philosopher, involves an abdication of responsibility.

3.3. Dewey and Idealism

One of the most admirable aspects of Dewey's analyses of earlier positions is that, even in criticism, he seeks out the positive, the fertile, the fruitful. He rarely engages in wholesale condemnation. This is especially true in regard to idealism because of his own earlier allegiance to a version of it. His criticisms fall into two categories, following the two kinds of idealism to which he had once adhered. Both kinds are significant with respect to the question of forms. The first is "constitutive" idealism, which assumes a certain formlessness in external entities and argues that it is the mind that constructs or constitutes reality in a certain way. Dewey counters this theory by providing physical rather than psychical explanations

for the cases these idealists cite in support of their position. The second type, objective idealism, which argues for an "objective thought" or "Reason" as responsible for structuring or organizing the world, is shown to be involved in logical difficulties.

The thinker against whom Dewey specifically argues in these matters is Hermann Lotze. Dewey never labels the particular kind of idealism Lotze espoused, but his descriptions indicate that he considers it to be of a subjectivistic, Kantian kind. The two marks which allow Lotze to be classified in this manner are a radical separation of subject and object[8] and a distinction between mere existence and organized existence. These marks are reminiscent of those of a younger Dewey who differentiated between "mere succession of phenomena" and "substance." Later in his career, Dewey suggested that the use of the adjective "mere" offered a clear sign of a dualistic (anti-naturalistic) position.[9]

Using Lotze as a foil helps to connect the discussion of idealism with that of realism. As was mentioned in the previous section, Dewey conceives of both as dependent on a belief in the ubiquity of the knowledge relation and on a dualistic ontology. Because of these assumptions, the epistemological problem of the relation of thought in general to reality in general once again presents itself. The realistic option, as we have seen, recognizes a passive role alone for the mind in dealing with this difficulty. The idealistic solution, as embodied by Lotze, emphasizes an active role for the mind, independent of particular contents. "Lotze refers to 'universal forms and principles of thought which hold good everywhere both in judging of reality and in weighing possibility, *irrespective of any difference in the objects'* " (MW II 302).[10]

Dewey interprets this as Lotze's statement of one term in the epistemological problem, that of *thought as such*. The reason Dewey centers his attention on Lotze is that Lotze makes a conscious attempt to deal adequately with the other term as well, *subject matter as such*. "Then we have the question of 'how far the most complete structure of thought . . . can claim to be an adequate account of that which we seem compelled to assume as the object and occasion of our ideas.' This is clearly the question of the relation of thought at large to reality at large. It is epistemology" (MW II 302–303). We already know enough about Dewey to recognize that to label something "epistemology" is to mark it as tainted and defective. Episte-

mology as the inquiry which deals with the possibility of knowledge in general, and of the relationship between thought as such to subject matter as such, is, whether in realism or idealism, the result of an erroneous starting point.

If on these assumptions the crucial problem for the realist is to harmonize the contents of common-sense knowledge with those of scientific knowledge, the idealist, exemplified by Lotze, faces a different problem of harmonization. His self-contained activity of thinking cannot be consistently and organically connected with the external material conditions that occasion the thought and should ultimately justify it.

> In other words, *logically* speaking, we are at the end just exactly where we were at the beginning—in the sphere of ideas, and of ideas only, plus a consciousness of the necessity of referring these ideas to a reality which is beyond them, which is utterly inaccessible to them, which is out of reach of any influence which they may exercise, and which transcends any possible comparison with their results. . . . At the end, after all our maneuvering we are where we began:—with two separate disparates, one of meaning, but no existence, the other of existence, but no meaning [MW II 365–66].

The idealist who tries to solve the epistemological dilemma by emphasizing an active, self-contained thought-function thus fares no better than the realist with his passive, receptive view of knowing. Lotze's fate was sealed, on the Deweyan interpretation, as soon as he argued for forms and principles of thought that were applicable everywhere "irrespective of any difference in the objects." This non-temporal, non-relative, but absolutist interpretation of consciousness may safeguard the absolute certainty and security of thought, but it does so at the expense of severing its connections with the subject matter of which Lotze had hoped to give an account. That such an account cannot be given successfully is Dewey's major objection.

Another version of idealism is the objective kind, in which some "Absolute Thought," "consciousness," or "Reason" is actually regarded as the underlying reality. Here, once again, we are approaching the central question of this study, which may be phrased as seeking an accurate philosophical description of the entities that are

part of human experience. We are particularly concerned to discern whether one traditional articulation—that the beings of the world are formed entities—retains any validity in a post-Darwinian era. The idealism we are now dealing with argues that the beings of the world are the products of an Absolute Reason that guarantees their structural integrity and their intelligibility.

Dewey finds that, although this solution is attractive in some respects, it suffers from major flaws. When a distinction is made, as it has to be, between this constructive thought and the reflective thought the individual brings to inquiry, certain difficulties surface. The first and most serious problem is the supposed need for two kinds of thought. "For the more one insists that the antecedent situation is constituted by thought, the more one has to wonder why another type of thought is required; what need arouses it, and how it is possible for it to improve upon the work of previous constitutive thought" (MW II 334). This is the point, Dewey argues, at which the flight of idealistic metaphysics begins. "This difficulty at once forces idealists from a logic of experience as it is concretely experienced into a metaphysic of a purely hypothetical experience" (MW II 334).

Dewey may, in this passage, be arguing somewhat against his former self. He is assuredly continuing the criticism begun in his book on Leibniz. There he suggested the need for a new logic to complement the newer ontology. In the *Essays*, however, a new logic of experience is seen as displacing ontology. Once the experimental method is understood and applied, the need for the meta-empirical hypotheses of idealistic metaphysics is removed. The lasting insights of idealism can be secured without recourse to this hypothesis. The "hypothetical experience" is the need to posit an Absolute Reason of a sort that remains hidden to human awareness. From a Deweyan perspective what is given as an explanation in this idealistic position is an unnecessary and artificial construct. But even this construction itself is not free from difficulties. For why should this Thought call forth reflective inquiry? Why should it even occasion such inquiry if it has constructed the world successfully? "How does it happen that the absolute constitutive and intuitive Thought does such a poor and bungling job that it requires a finite discursive activity to patch up its products" (MW II 334)?

Dewey, in other words, is puzzled as to why any puzzling situa-

tions eliciting reflective thought should arise, given the pervasiveness of an Absolute Reason. There is, in the end, no real justification
for positing such an existence, for erecting such a metaphysics.

> If reflective thought is required because constitutive thought works
> under externally limiting conditions of sense, then we have some
> elements which are, after all, mere existences, events, etc. Or, if
> they have organization from some other source than thought, and
> induce reflective thought not as bare impressions, etc., but through
> their place in some whole, then we have admitted the possibility
> of organization in experience, apart from Reason, and the ground
> for assuming Pure Constitutive Thought is abandoned [MW II
> 335].

Dewey's objections to idealism, then, are threefold. (a) To begin
with, the idealist such as Lotze is not able to deal adequately with
the subject matter that occasions thinking. (b) Idealists who suggest
the necessity of a mentalistic constitution of objects are refuted
on the basis of physical explanations of the critical phenomena on
which they base their opinion. (c) Finally, the absolute idealist
is viewed as erecting an unnecessary and self-contradictory metaphysics.

In the context of his critical remarks about absolute idealism,
Dewey gives us a positive indication of his own position. He admits
that his criticisms of Lotze are not so different, after all, from those
that might be labeled "neo-Hegelian." But Dewey is not fully satisfied with this label, and he characterizes the position as one "developed by many writers in criticizing Kant" (MW II 333). Presumably
these "many writers" include George S. Morris and Dewey himself.
At any rate, in listing what the parallels rather than the differences
are, he makes some definitive ontological assertions. "They [Dewey's
position and the Neo-Hegelian] unite in denying that there is or can
be any such thing as *mere* existence—phenomenon unqualified as
respects organization and force, whether such phenomenon may be
psychic or cosmic. They agree that reflective thought grows organically out of an experience which is already organized, and that it
functions within such an organism" (MW II 333).

Dewey offers here a very important descriptive statement which
is central to the analysis I am undertaking. Once again the key term
is "mere." Dewey uses it to indicate the position he is arguing

against, claiming that there is no such thing as *"mere* existence."
He explains this by saying that mere existence would involve phenomena "unqualified as respects organization and force." I take this
to mean, translated into positive terms, that existences and situations are organized existences. It is too soon to construct an interpretation on an isolated quotation, but this excerpt does provide the
connection with the following section, which will be devoted to
Dewey's own theory. I shall be especially careful to note whether in
the logical works this concept of organization is elaborated or developed.

4. Dewey's Constructive Doctrine

Dewey not only criticizes the consequences and developed positions
of both realism and idealism; he also believes that they err in their
choice of a starting point. An accurate theory about thinking begins, quite naturally, with a proper beginning.

> Grant, for a moment, as a hypothesis, that thinking starts neither
> from an implicit force of rationality desiring to realize itself com-
> pletely in and through and against the limitations which are im-
> posed upon it by the conditions of our human experience (as all
> idealisms have taught), nor from the fact that in each human being
> is a "mind" whose business it is just to "know"—to theorize in the
> Aristotelian sense; but, rather, that it starts from an effort to get
> out of some trouble, actual or menacing [MW X 333].

Here we have the key to understanding the novel doctrine Dewey
expounds. Thinking is not primarily a detached appraisal of the
way things are; nor is it an attempt to reach an ultimate synthesis in
which difficulties will have disappeared. Rather it is the activity of
reflecting on a situation beset with some difficulties. It is significant
that in the *Essays in Experimental Logic,* Dewey prefers the terms
"reflection" and "thinking" to "knowing" because of the inherent
association of "knowing" with the realistic and idealistic positions
he considers untenable.

Naturalism, as John Herman Randall pointed out, owes much to
the doctrine of evolution. We saw in the last chapter how strongly
Dewey, in particular, felt the influence of Darwin. In the matter at
hand, Dewey's theory is merely the application to epistemological

problems of Darwin's teaching on adaptation. It may, therefore, be helpful in understanding what Dewey is saying to develop an analogy with this biological thesis.

Two facts struck Darwin as especially significant. The first was the careful adjustment of individual to environment; the second, the continuous production, within groups of similar creatures, of individual variations. When these two facts are combined with the reality of a continually changing environment, the force of Darwin's discovery can be appreciated. Since the surroundings in which a plant or animal finds itself do not remain constant, the equilibrium of adaptation will invariably be upset. But it may be that some of the individual differences continually produced in nature will provide advantages for their bearers in the new surroundings. Thus, the individuals carrying these changes will increase and multiply, while those in which these newly adaptive traits are absent will dwindle and eventually perish.

One of the many examples Darwin used is the discovery of a Mr. Wollaston. When studying beetles on the island of Madeira, he noted the surprising fact that many of them could not fly. This was the case in more than two-thirds of the species inhabiting the island.[11] Also significant was the almost total absence of certain genera of beetles which could not survive without flying. Darwin explains this condition by noting that the climate on the island, being very windy, presents a special and deadly problem for winged insects: the danger of being blown out to sea. Those insects that remained on the island and flourished there are those in which an alteration of behavior and structure favored the new conditions. "For during many successive generations each individual beetle which flew least, either from its wings having been so little less perfectly developed or from indolent habit, will have had the best chance of surviving from not being blown out to sea; and, on the other hand, those beetles which most readily took to flight would oftenest have been blown out to sea and thus destroyed."[12]

An important fact is underscored here: namely, that the same trait, such as strong wings and ability for flight, is not always a favorable one. Whether or not it is favorable depends on the conditions in which the individual exists. A situation that has remained stable for a long time may be altered, and organisms either adjust accord-

ingly or perish. This relational character of evolutionary biology
Dewey understood well.

> The significance of the evolutionary method in biology and social
> history is that every distinct organ, structure, or formation, every
> grouping of cells or elements, is to be treated as an instrument of
> adjustment or adaptation to a particular environing situation. Its
> meaning, its character, its force, is known when, and only when, it
> is considered as an arrangement for meeting the conditions in-
> volved in some specific situation [MW II 310].

Of course, beetles, along with other animals, do not think, and
any attempted analogy with the human situation will break down
on this point. Yet there are other elements in this description of
natural selection which will help us to understand Dewey's position.
The first is a recognition that an optimal state is one of equilibrium
or successful adaptation. This adaptation is the result of a relationship involving the individual and its environment. The second is
the realization that this environment is to some degree unstable and
changing. Thirdly, as a consequence, if the equilibrium is to be
maintained under these changing conditions, the creatures existing
in them will have to change themselves or alter the environment.

Thinking, for Dewey, has its roots in just such a troubling situation. It begins when the adaptive equilibrium has been upset, and
it has as its goal the institution of a new adaptive equilibrium. Like
the poor beetle buffeted by winds, whose wings, formerly so advan-
tageous, have become a liability, the human animal often finds itself
in a predicament requiring a solution.

The example of a physician treating an illness is helpful once
again for elucidating what Dewey is saying. A pain or a discomfort
of some kind disturbs the previously satisfactory state and arouses
reflective behavior that seeks to correct the situation. This reflection
is not that of a disinterested observer seeking to "know" what the
matter is, but that of an interested party seeking useful information.
Where is the pain located? What caused the discomfort: too much
food, a sudden increase in exercise, nervous tension, a virus? When
one of these is fastened on as the cause, then a solution related to
it—such as a reduced diet, programed exercising, a vacation, anti-
biotics—is suggested. The success of the solution reflects the accu-

racy of the analysis. Failure is merely a prod to attempt one of the other possible solutions. In these early logical works, Dewey calls the condition that provokes thought "tensional." "In other words, reflection appears as the dominant trait of a situation when there is something seriously the matter, some trouble, due to active discordance, dissentiency, conflict among the factors of a prior non-intellectual experience; when, in the phraseology of the essays, a situation becomes tensional" (MW X 326).

From this overview we can begin to piece together how the elements taken from evolutionary theory are forged into Dewey's own doctrine. (a) Thought always arises in a context that presents troublesome or "tensional" aspects. This means (b) that thought or reflection is not detached. It does not indifferently catalogue the facts. Rather, it is *attached* in a very significant sense as a participant in overcoming the difficulty. (c) The events or data of immediate experience serve as indications of what must be discovered. If they themselves were the objects of knowledge, the troublesome situation would not exist. A bodily ache, for instance, is a sign of something else, a something that has to be discerned (or "inferred," to use the word Dewey preferred) by investigation. (d) The success or failure in reaching a new optimal situation, or new equilibrium, is not strictly a theoretical matter, but a practical one as well. As a result, (e) *experimentation* with various possibilities is an indispensable ingredient in this analysis of thinking. Thinking and doing, in other words, are not antithetical activities. Dewey uses the term "instrumentalism" to indicate this intricate connection between knowing and doing.

When instrumentalism is developed in this manner, it becomes clear how much it owes to the positive recognition of change as a factor in experience. For intelligence is viewed as the means for bringing about a continually renewed stability out of a state of affairs constantly in flux. Although this may, to some degree, sound similar to idealism, it serves as one of Dewey's main objections to that doctrine. Idealism, Dewey argues, sets a limit on change. It has a fixed end in view, such as the Hegelian *Geist*, in which contradictions are harmoniously interwoven. Such an attitude, as far as Dewey is concerned, removes the conditions which occasion thinking. "For a theory which ends by declaring that everything is, really and eternally, thoroughly ideal and rational, cuts the nerve of the specific

demand and work of intelligence" (MW X 333). As a result of such considerations it is possible to appreciate the manner in which change is crucially interwoven into the fabric of Dewey's experimental phase.

Few people today would doubt that change is pervasive. But what about permanence? How does Dewey's scheme of thought provide for elements of stability? In a classical doctrine, such as Aristotle's, the permanent factors are to be found in the very character of the things which the world comprises and which consequently are the objects of knowledge.[13] The first point that must be noted in this very formulation of the issue is that Dewey's analysis will be misconstrued if the Aristotelian vocabulary is retained. I have already remarked that the term "object" is to be understood in a very restricted sense in the Deweyan corpus. Object means object of knowledge. As such, objects are precisely the things not given in experience. Atoms, genes, and sound waves, for instance, are all objects of knowledge because each was discovered by, and not given to, the investigators as an initial datum. If Dewey is to be viewed from the perspective of ontological considerations, his analysis of "objects" must be examined in greater detail.

4.1. Thought and Things

To borrow terminology from another tradition: for Dewey, thinking is, in the word reintroduced into philosophical discourse by Franz Bretano, "intentional." That is to say, thinking is relational, is directed toward phenomena that are outside of itself. Thinking is, in other words, thinking about something; knowing is knowledge of something.[14] This characterization of knowledge as intentional immediately leads to questions of ontology. If knowledge is *knowledge of* something, then one can expect that a theory of beings which would provide the generic characteristics of these "some-things" would be forthcoming. A minimal statement about them, for instance, would indicate that they are intelligible. It is precisely at this juncture, so critical to my reading of Dewey, that the confusions surrounding the word "object" can be most misleading. To understand Dewey accurately, the word "object" must not be used to indicate both "thing" and "result of inquiry." Its meaning is restricted strictly to the latter.

Dewey must be seen against the background of the realistic and idealistic theories which he seeks to avoid. He is attempting a formulation which does not interpret the intellectual capacities of human beings as the sheer passivity of the realist or the sheer activity of the idealist. Dewey wants to show that in the activity of investigation or inquiry not only does one receive data, one does something with them. He uses the word "object" to express the results of these investigations. As such, it is contrasted to thing/existent, and should in no way be confused with it. Data, in other words, include the *immediate* givens received by the individual. In contrast, "object" necessarily involves mediation. Dewey distinguishes between "objects" and "data" in the following manner. "We have stated that, strictly speaking, data (as the immediate considerations from which controlled inference proceeds) are not objects but means, instrumentalities, of knowledge: things by which we know rather than things known" (MW X 346). The data set the context for investigation, but only when results are obtained may the term "object" be used in its technical Deweyan sense.

Dewey's altered usage of "object" is not as incongruous as it may at first appear. Actually, the new usage reflects the considerable distance between Dewey and the epistemology-centered philosophies of modernity. What Dewey came to realize was that the terms "object" and "subject" form a correlative pair on the interpretive grid of post-Cartesian philosophy. In this view, "object" as thing-in-the-world is paired off against "subject" as spectator. Since one of Dewey's primary concerns is to overcome the dualistic bias of modern philosophy, "object" can no longer be a suitable term for the entities that populate our existential milieu. As soon as these entities are called "objects," inexpugnable epistemological connotations become associated with them. Dewey's distance from the Cartesian orientation can be measured by the way he modifies the inherited terminology. No longer are humans to be thought of as "subjects." Indeed, the "subjects" or subject matters are those events which constitute our milieu and, as problematic situations, occasion thinking. The "objects" become then, as we have seen, the objectives sought in the process of inquiry.

Dewey defends his analysis by contrasting it with Aristotle's, and supporting it with the authority of modern science.

Aristotle was not lacking in acuteness nor in learning. To him it was clear that objects of knowledge are the things of ordinary perception, so far as they are referred to a form which comparison of perceived things, in the light of a final cause, makes evident. If this view of the objects of knowledge has gone into the discard, if quite other objects of knowledge are now received and employed, it is because the methods of *getting* knowledge have been transformed, till, for the working scientist, "objects of knowledge" mean precisely the objects which have been obtained by approved processes of inquiry. To exclude consideration of these processes is thus to throw away the key to understanding knowledge and its objects [MW X 360].

What is obvious here is Dewey's belief that the decisive difference between the older and the newer version of objects is the methodology of the sciences. Science is not content to leave the objects of the world untouched. It manipulates them, testing and experimenting until a certain result is found.[15] Water is not simply accepted as such, but subjected to electrolysis, in order to break it down into its atomic constituents. This methodology, according to Dewey, has proven to be most effective. "For the world of science, especially of mathematical science, is the world of considerations which have approved themselves to be effectively regulative of the operations of inference" (EEL 434–35). This emphasis on signs and inference is crucial to Dewey's epistemology. Illness, as we have seen, is a popular Deweyan example. The ruptured appendix and the kidney stone are *objects* of knowledge which come as the result of inquiry. They are objects as "objectives" (MW X 329) of the inquiry. Likewise, we might argue that the molecular structure of DNA was not given to Watson and Crick as an initial datum, but was the outcome, the result, of a lengthy process of investigation and hypothecation.

Now we can come to a concrete appreciation of the confusion engendered by an improper understanding of the way the word "object" functions in Dewey's philosophy. For Dewey, this term grows out of a particular epistemic analysis and is employed in a very specific manner. But in common philosophical usage "object," as its etymology suggests, has primarily an ontological meaning. It refers to something there, a being or an existent given or cast up in the environment. A misrepresentation of Dewey will result if this

second sense is introduced into his texts. On a Deweyan interpretation, as we have already seen, the object is *not* given prior to inquiry. The object does not exist before the actual work of investigation. Object means precisely the result or objective of inquiry. Knowledge of the structure of DNA did not, could not, antedate the work of the experimenters who discovered it. It is in this sense, and in this sense alone, that a Deweyan analysis denies the pre-existence of an object.[16] Since object means knowledge-object, it is not possible that it could exist prior to inquiry. The very occasion for a particular inquiry is the fact that the object is unknown.

If this term is read in its etymological/ontological sense, Dewey's position will be misconstrued as an idealism. For now object (ontological sense) is said to be dependent for its existence on the procedures of intellectual investigation. Dewey's position, I maintain, is not that at all. Using the example of Watson and Crick, we can say that they may have discovered the molecular structure of DNA as the result of a lengthy process of inquiry, but that structure itself pre-existed the discovery. Nothing in Dewey's analysis, if properly understood, argues against this. The DNA molecule was intelligible, was organized in such a way that intellectual inquiry, given enough diligence and ability, was able to succeed in determining its structure. However, as a discovered object, the structure of the DNA molecule was new. Previously, it had been unknown, and so had not existed as the result of any of the feverish inquiries aiming at this end.[17] Only in this sense does Dewey's doctrine lead to the conclusion of an object's inexistence prior to inquiry.

If, however, the limited sense of "object" is not understood as Dewey meant it, then misinterpretations will follow, and the charge of idealism will be most prominent among them. The cases of Robert Dewey and Richard Rorty, quoted in the last chapter, offer examples of this misunderstanding. Robert Dewey says that "when Dewey asserts that events as such are not objects of knowing, they become his process philosophy's version of the unknown somewhats (or Kantian unknowable *Dinge-an-sich*) constituting nature beyond the data of immediate experience."[18] Rorty claims that Dewey's epistemology involves "the constitution of the knowable by the co-operation of two unknowables."[19]

The arguments of these critics are reduced here to their starkest

simplicity. Events (things in the environment) cannot be the objects of knowledge, so they are unknowable. They become simply unknown somethings, and the Kantian-type of idealism follows. But here precisely is where we find that the confusion surrounding the word "object" has led interpreters astray. The misrepresentation of John Dewey's position is most evident when these critics confuse "unknown" and "unknowable."

Events as "unknown somewhats" are compared to the "unknowable" things-in-themselves of the Kantian philosophy. But Dewey is not saying this at all. Events are eminently knowable; his books on logic are analyses of the methodologies best suited for securing knowledge. But knowable does not mean the same as known. There is no "constitution of the knowable by the cooperation of two unknowables." Rorty has misunderstood Dewey on this point. There is, instead, inquiry (research, experimentation) aimed at resolving a certain problem. The solution is not yet known but it is certainly knowable. Dewey can assert with perfect consistency that events or aspects of events are unknown, but that they are knowable. When he says that they (events) are not "objects of knowing," he is simply asserting that inquiry seeks to discover something about them which thus far has remained elusive, unknown. The object of knowledge cannot be identical with the thing in existence, the event, because inquiry would then not be necessary. Pasteur, for instance, knew what wine was and what an important role it played in French life. He also knew that fermentation was a chemical process in its production. What he did not know, what he sought as the object of his investigations, was the causal process through which fermentation occurred.

In such a case, an event, the fermentation of wine as it is given to the observer, is not the object of knowledge. The object is the "unknown somewhat" the investigator seeks to uncover. To make this distinction Dewey separates "event" and "object." I find Dewey's retention of the word "object" in his idiosyncratic sense to be a very poor choice. I am sympathetic to the ready misunderstandings that it occasions. But I do believe that it is possible by a careful reading of the texts to frame an accurate portrait of Dewey's position. When this position is understood, it may be seen as embodying certain flaws, but not that it is a thinly disguised idealism.

4.2. *Eidos*

But what about the concept of *eidos* or form? As presented thus far, my interpretation merely allows the possibility that Dewey could have developed a revised version of an ontology that recognizes forms-in-nature. Are there more constructive signs in these logical texts that Dewey did, in fact, carry out such an undertaking? By and large, the answer is that, in these middle works at least, he did not.

I pointed out earlier that in Dewey's analysis thinking is intentional. That is to say, thinking is always thinking of or about something. Thinking is a relational activity, with the data of thought accepted as a necessary ingredient. Dewey's position on this point was formulated in his earliest work on logic, *Studies in Logical Theory*, and reprinted in the *Essays in Experimental Logic*. "As we submit each characteristic function and situation of experience to our gaze, we find it has a dual aspect. Wherever there is striving there are obstacles; wherever there is affection there are persons who are attached; wherever there is doing there is accomplishment; wherever there is appreciation there is value; wherever there is thinking there is material-in-question" (MW II 311). Dewey's analysis here seems quite correct and well-founded. Thinking is always thinking about something. But now the question arises as to the nature of this something that is thought about. What, in other words, can be said about the "material-in-question" Dewey refers to? I contend that unless the situations that occasion thought are recognized as structured and organized in a certain way, no proper epistemology, save the idealistic, can accurately account for the fact of knowledge. What I am arguing is that the notion of *eidos* must be, not rejected, but reformulated in terms of structure and organization.

Dewey, as I have shown, appears to admit as much when he compares the neo-Hegelian position to his own. At that point, he says quite specifically that there cannot be "any such things as *mere* existence—phenomenon unqualified as respects organization and force, whether such phenomenon be psychic or cosmic."[20] Yet such an explicit ontological statement about existents as organized is the exception rather than the rule in these texts. While defending his experimental logic, Dewey is concerned with stressing the plasticity of existents more than their definiteness. The very success of the

experimental method depends on flexibility and changeableness. If this method is to be effective, beings must be such as to allow experimentation. This means that beings as subject matter must be capable of undergoing the kinds of alterations and manipulations demanded by successful experimentation.

Dewey is also heir to the philosophical legacy of Bacon and Descartes, both of whom rejected the formal causes of the Scholastics as trivial to the actual understanding of nature. He was born, as we saw, five weeks prior to the publication of Darwin's *Origin of Species*. This work carried the mechanistic plan set in motion by Descartes and Bacon into the biological realm which had heretofore been exempt.[21] Species, those last remnants of medieval essentialism, were now discarded under the impact of a powerful and well-documented biological thesis. It is not at all surprising, therefore, to find Dewey somewhat hesitant to portray beings as formed in certain characteristically determinate ways. This reluctance, it seems to me, make those few admissions all the more significant.

How, then, does he describe this "material-in-question"? What does he say about it? At this point we can recognize just how wary Dewey is of admitting forms-in-nature. The terminology he selects to describe the tensional situation that must be resolved is instructive in this respect. He speaks of "crude or raw data" (MW X 336), "means, instrumentalities" (MW X 346), "evidence" (MW X 347), "brute fact," "particulars (parts, fragments)" (MW X 334), and a material "alogical in character" (MW X 331). Each of these labels, it should be noted, indicates a situation that is ontologically indeterminate, that is, exists as inchoate. As is the case with much else in the way Dewey expresses himself, this could readily lead one to interpret him in a Kantian sense. If the material-in-question is ontologically indeterminate, then it could be argued that it needs completion of some sort, which, in this case, would be provided by the individual carrying out the inquiry.

Does Dewey mean to indicate a complete indeterminateness and malleability in existents? I do not think so. To understand what he is saying we need to place him in an historical context. As one deeply influenced by Darwin and the whole movement of post-medieval science, he is struck by the great improvements that came about when manipulation and experiment replaced contemplation as the noetic ideal. Were species fixed, final, and wholly unchange-

able, the work of knowledge and the appreciation of aesthetics might collapse into a single endeavor. But species are not fixed, and science has progressed by going beyond the limitations of presentative realism. Scientific facts, Dewey says, "are discovered facts, discovered by physical manipulations which detach them from their ordinary setting" (MW X 346). Since Dewey is attempting to develop a generalized theory of inquiry based on the model of scientific knowing, we should not be at all surprised that he would stress the amenability of the subject matter to this type of investigation. The terms he chooses to describe the material that is to be subjected to investigation, "means," "raw data," "instrumentalities," "evidence," are selected to emphasize that inquiry does not work on recalcitrant material. The process of inquiry does not of necessity result in frustration and failure. Insofar as some success is achieved, the material is capable of being manipulated to the degree necessary in the various sorts of inquiries. This necessary condition for inquiry, coupled with the theoretical support of evolutionary doctrine, allows Dewey to stress the malleable and plastic in the subject matter of research.

His expressions are not meant to deny entirely the organization or structure in existents. He does not mean to imply that the subject matter of inquiry is a wholly indeterminate "stuff" capable of being formed in any manner whatsoever because it has no form of its own. If his language tends to lead a reader to interpret him in that way, it is because he was anxious to set forth the conditions necessary for his own theory. The great enemy of his approach is the belief that beings are formed in rigid, fixed, absolutely determinate, unchangeable patterns. If this were true, then a procedure that would progress by experimenting, manipulating, introducing changes would be vitiated from the outset.

Since Dewey is concerned to reject this view, he tends to overstate his case somewhat by choosing terms that indicate an amorphous, malleable, subject matter. However, seen in the context of what he is trying to accomplish, he can be interpreted correctly. Structure or organization is not denied, only its rigidity, fixity, and utter unchangeableness. One way to characterize Dewey's thought during his experimental phase is to say of him in reference to form exactly what he said of the Greeks in reference to change. Form, for Dewey, is not denied, just minimized and viewed as not especially significant. This fact contrasts Dewey's experimental phase decisively with

his Hegelian period. In that earlier period, form, under various synonyms, was a prominent consideration. In the experimental phase, form receded quite dramatically into the background. Just what becomes of it in the next phase will be the subject of the following chapters.

5. SUMMARY

If we grasp the major lines of thought developed in these books on logic, a solid foundation can be built for the kind of interpretation I am suggesting. The details of this interpretation are still lacking, and will be taken up in later chapters. For the moment, it may be worthwhile to list in summary fashion some of the main concerns that have arisen in this chapter. I will divide these into two groups, the negative, those positions Dewey rejects, and the positive, the ones he embraces. On the negative side, we saw, to begin with, that Dewey rejects two assumptions he finds to be sources of many misconceptions in contemporary philosophy: dualism and the ubiquity of the knowledge relation. Secondly, he rejects certain tenets of both realism and idealism. This means, thirdly, that cognitive activity is neither purely passive nor purely active. Finally, he is hesitant to describe entities as formed because of the associations of this term with utter fixity.

On the positive side, this chapter gives us, first of all, an indication of the theoretical weapon, suggested by evolutionary theory, on which most of Dewey's arguments are based, that of *continuity*. Secondly, we find in the early logical books a very definitive statement from Dewey that entities must be recognized as being organized, although this insight is in no way pursued or developed. Thirdly, this organization cannot be absolutely rigid because the experimental method depends on some degree of plasticity in the materials being investigated. Finally, no proper understanding of Dewey is possible unless his very idiosyncratic and restricted meaning for "object" is grasped.

NOTES

1. "Philosophical naturalism has a more distinguished ancestry than is usually recognized; there are, for example, the names of Aristotle and

Spinoza" ("Antinaturalism *in Extremis,*" in *Naturalism and the Human Spirit,* ed. Yervant H. Krikorian, Columbia Studies in Philosophy 8 [New York: Columbia University Press, 1944], p. 1).

2. "Epilogue: The Nature of Naturalism," in ibid., p. 356.

3. See chap. 1, sect. 2.22.

4. The manner in which realists and idealists are treated offers but another example of Dewey's disregard for detail when he is engaged in critical evaluation of philosophies he considers to be mistaken. We have seen this already in relation to Greek philosophy in chap. 2. Bothersome as Dewey's procedure may seem, it is defended to some extent by no less a theoretician of methodology in the humanities than Ernst Cassirer. It is from Cassirer that I have borrowed the word "type." He argues that humanists deal in "types" and that Jacob Burckhardt's "Man of the Renaissance" offers a perfect example of this procedure. Burckhardt's description exemplified an era even though no single individual could actually be found who fit perfectly the traits of the "Man of the Renaissance" which he enunciated. Cassirer argues that what is attempted in cases such as these is the delineation of a "unity of *direction,* not a unity of *actualization.*" He goes on in the following way: "The particular individuals *belong together,* not because they are alike or resemble each other, but because they are *cooperating in a common task,* which, in contrast to the Middle Ages, we perceive to be new and to be the distinctive 'meaning' of the Renaissance" (*The Logic of the Humanities,* trans. Clarence Smith Howe [New Haven: Yale University Press, 1961], pp. 139–40). Cassirer's analysis offers a defense for Dewey's use of collective terms such as "Greeks," "realists," or "idealists" if it is argued that Dewey, like Burckhardt, sought to indicate a "unity of direction" or to deal with groups of individuals "cooperating in a common task."

5. Dewey asserts that Lotze has "well stated" the "various aspects of logical theory" which he, Dewey, is interested in pursuing (MW II 302).

6. Dewey defined "instrumentalism" in the following manner: "It means that knowing is literally something which we do; that analysis is ultimately physical and active; that meanings in their logical quality are standpoints, attitudes, and methods of behaving toward facts, and that active experimentation is essential to verification" (MW X 367).

7. The fact that he is not fully consistent in his usage adds to the difficulties of interpreting him accurately. For instance, in the following passage from EN 199, "object" is used in a manner synonymous with "thing," "existent." "For when, through language, sentience is taken up into a system of signs, when for example a certain quality of the active relationship of organism and environment is named hunger, it is seen as an organic demand for an extra-organic object."

8. "It is a total contrast of thought as such to something else as such that he [Lotze] requires, not a contrast within experience of one temporal phase of process, one period of a rhythm, from others. . . . This contrast arises because of the attempt to consider thought as an independent somewhat in general which nevertheless, in *our* experience, is dependent upon a raw material of mere impressions given to it" (MW II 330–31). Dewey's reading of Lotze, however, overly emphasizes the dualistic tendencies in this German thinker. Dewey had but to examine Morris' translation of Ueberweg in order to find a more balanced view (*History of Modern Philosophy*, pp. 314–15). Recently, Paul Kuntz has interpreted Lotze in terms of contemporary process philosophy. The Lotze Kuntz describes is actually in some crucial respects quite close to Dewey. Both Lotze and Dewey shared an admiration for Leibniz which is manifested in the centrality of relations in their respective philosophies. According to Kuntz, the main thread that runs through Lotze's metaphysics is the doctrine that " 'to be is to be related.' " We have already seen how Dewey focused on relations in his book on Leibniz (chap. 1, sect. 2.241). This emphasis will recur, especially in reference to the question of form, in his third phase. However, an expression such as Lotze used is not found anywhere in Dewey because he was most uncomfortable with the language of being. See George Santayana, *Lotze's System of Philosophy*, ed. Paul G. Kuntz (Bloomington: Indiana University Press, 1971). Kuntz discusses Lotze's philosophy in a lengthy introduction to this volume, pp. 3–87. The mention of Lotze's phrase " 'to be is to be related' " occurs on page 22.

9. "The word 'mere' plays a large role in antinaturalistic writings" ("Antinaturalism *in Extremis*," p. 2n1).

10. The underscoring has been added by Dewey. He is quoting from Lotze's *Logic* I, ed. and trans. Bernard Bosanquet (Oxford: Clarendon, 1888), pp. 10–11.

11. "Of twenty-nine endemic genera, no less than twenty-three have all their species in this condition" (Charles Darwin, *The Origin of Species and The Descent of Man* [New York: Modern Library, n.d.], p. 103).

12. Ibid., p. 104.

13. "Thinking, both speculative and practical, is regarded as akin to a form of perceiving; for in the one as well as in the other the soul discriminates and is cognizant of something which *is*" (*De anima* 427A18–21); "The thinking part of the soul must therefore be, while impassible, capable of receiving the form of an object; that is, must be potentially identical in character with its object without being the object. Mind must be related to what is thinkable, as sense is to what is sensible" (ibid. 429A14–17, in *Basic Works of Aristotle*, ed. McKeon, pp. 586 and 589).

14. Brentano described "intentionality" in the following manner: "Every mental phenomenon is characterized by what the Scholastics of the Middle Ages called the intentional (or mental) inexistence of an object, and what we might call, though not wholly unambiguously, reference to a content, direction toward an object (which is not to be understood here as meaning a thing), or immanent objectivity. Every mental phenomenon includes something as object within itself, although they do not all do so in the same way. In presentation something is presented, in judgement something is affirmed or denied, in love loved, in hate hated, in desire desired and so on" (*Psychology from an Empirical Standpoint*, trans. D. B. Terrell, Antos C. Rancurello, and Linda L. McAlister, ed. Linda L. McAlister [London & New York: Humanities Press, 1973], pp. 88–89). A recent author, comparing Dewey to the phenomenological tradition, has also noted the place of intentionality in Dewey's thought. "Implicit in Dewey's notions of interaction and transaction is a well-developed conception of intentionality" (Victor Kestenbaum, *The Phenomenological Sense of John Dewey: Habit and Meaning* [Atlantic Highlands, N.J.: Humanities Press, 1977], p. 1).

15. In fairness to Aristotle, it must be noted that he and the members of his school did actively engage in one form of experimentation: dissection. Contrary to what Dewey says about the objects of knowledge being for Aristotle the "things of ordinary perception, so far as they are referred to a form," Aristotle sought empirically to investigate what was not given in ordinary perception. This included embryological research on chickens, and perhaps even humans, and the investigation of the digestive tracts of various animals. See W. D. Ross, *Aristotle*, 5th ed. (New York: Barnes & Noble, 1964), p. 113. Dewey is following here the tradition of Aristotelian interpretation popularized by Francis Bacon in his *Novum Organum*. Bacon knew of Aristotle's experiments but refused to ascribe any importance to them. See *Novum Organum* 1.63, in *The English Philosophers from Bacon to Mill*, ed. Edwin A. Burtt (New York: Modern Library, 1939), pp. 43–44.

16. In a letter to James, Dewey asserted that his theory did not deny pre-existence in any other sense. He said that his " 'instrumental theory of knowledge is clearly self-contradictory unless there are independent existences of which ideas take account and for the transformation of which they function. . . . I have repeated *ad nauseam* that there are existences prior to and subsequent to cognitive states and purposes, and that *the whole meaning of the latter* is the way they intervene in the control and revaluation of the independent existence' " (quoted in Schneider, *History of American Philosophy*, p. 473).

17. Just as there undoubtedly remain many unresolved questions

about the DNA molecule today, Dewey realizes that success comes to an investigator after experimentation. This should not, however, be interpreted as indicating a belief on Dewey's part in the possibility of coming to a final, definitive solution that would make further reflection and inquiry unnecessary. Not only is further inquiry always a possibility, but the possibility also exists for revising previously held results.

18. *Philosophy of John Dewey*, p. 117.

19. CP 85.

20. See sect. 3.3.

21. One good article which deals with Darwin's philosophical inheritance is F. S. C. Northrop's "Evolution in Its Relation to the Philosophy of Nature and the Philosophy of Culture," in *Evolutionary Thought in America*, ed. Stow Person (New Haven: Yale University Press, 1950), pp. 44–84.

4

Dewey's Objections to Traditional Doctrines

1. Introduction

THE PREVIOUS CHAPTER dealt with works that, because of Dewey's exceptionally long career, represent only the middle stage in the development and exposition of his thought. He was already fifty-seven in 1916 when *Essays in Experimental Logic* appeared, but it was not until 1938, when he was seventy-nine, that *Logic: The Theory of Inquiry* was published. The next three chapters will deal with major works of his which appeared during the intervening years. These books include *Experience and Nature*, published in 1925, *The Quest for Certainty*, the Gifford Lectures of 1929, and *Art as Experience*, brought out in 1934. Together with *Logic: The Theory of Inquiry*, which will be studied separately in Chapter 7, they represent the most profound articulation of Dewey's naturalistic ontology.

Unlike Chapter 7, which will be devoted exclusively to one book, the following three chapters will not each be given over to the analysis of a single text. Instead, the three books published between 1925 and 1934 will be studied together, thematically. During the time he prepared these books, Dewey was attempting to work out a unified ontological position. Because of this, the texts complement each other, and Dewey can best be understood by examining certain issues as they are expressed in all three works. The focus of attention will remain the same as in the previous chapter. We shall be examining Dewey's writings to discern exactly what his position is with respect to an ontology of formed entities. A prominent characteristic of these books is the rejection of what he considers to be the traditional metaphysical view that recognizes the importance of forms. He realizes that the problem that occasioned the need to speak of forms is still a valid one, but disagrees with the kind of

solutions undertaken by traditional (i.e., Greek and medieval) thinkers.

Because of this sweeping opposition, an awareness of the weaknesses and errors Dewey finds in the traditional doctrines of this kind is crucial in piecing together the constructive doctrine he propounds. A major portion of this chapter, therefore, will be given over to examining the objections Dewey has to earlier ontologies. This examination will occupy the middle part of the chapter. I shall begin by reviewing a traditional distinction—that between *techne* and *physis*—which is essential to an understanding of Dewey, especially in relation to earlier naturalistic thinkers. Next, I shall examine his works to elucidate his objections to other theories of form. These will come mostly from *Experience and Nature* and *Art as Experience*. Finally, I shall deal with certain sections of *The Quest for Certainty* which provide a good link with both the discussions of idealism in the last chapter and the constructive analyses to come in subsequent chapters.

2. *Techne* and *Physis*

We saw in the previous chapter that, continuing an insight from his idealistic years, Dewey wishes to emphasize the active role of the individual in inquiries. Knowledge is something arrived at after investigation and experimentation.[1] The kinds of examples Dewey selects as illustrations are fully in line with such considerations. We know that the physician is a favorite of his, and examples from industry detailing the manufacturing of a certain product or artifact are also plentiful.[2] All these instances involve human participation as a factor effecting an alteration in the material being investigated. Dewey's model for his philosophical theory is human activity.

This distinguishes him immediately from a Greek thinker such as Aristotle, for whom "nature" and natural activity are paradigmatic. The traditional distinction between *techne* and *physis*—"art" and "nature," respectively—will be helpful in describing how different the two attitudes are. As major distinguishing characteristics, they divide all entities into two main groups: those that are produced by themselves (by their own kind) and those whose source of production is outside them (in other kinds of beings). Aristotle set forth the distinction in his *Metaphysics*: "For things come into being

either by art or by nature or by luck or by spontaneity. Now art is a principle of movement in something other than the thing moved, nature is a principle in the thing itself (for man begets man), and the other causes are privations of these two."[3] Not only does this type of classification allow us to provide an ontological organization into two sorts of beings, but it also provides the framework within which we can point to a decisive difference between Dewey and an earlier naturalistic view represented by Aristotle.

We know that there was a prominent current of Aristotelian thought in Dewey's philosophical formation at Johns Hopkins. Dewey's teacher George Morris, under the influence of Trendelenburg, had taught an "Aristotelized" Hegel.[4] Dewey, in his book on Leibniz, chose to compare Leibniz to Aristotle, and provided a favorable view of both thinkers. It is not surprising, considering this background, that there should be certain parallels between the positions of this Greek thinker and Dewey. I shall pursue some of these in the next chapters. In recognizing these similarities, however, an interpreter must be clear on just how the two thinkers are alike and how they are different. Unless the distinction between *techne* and *physis* is made explicit, and the implications for the two thinkers drawn out, an interpreter might forge a closer alliance between the two philosophers than actually existed. Broadly speaking, the differences between these two men can be characterized in the following manner: Aristotle tended to emphasize nature (*physis*), whereas Dewey tended to emphasize production (*techne*).

Aristotle's most basic philosophical category, *ousia*, a being or an entity, refers primarily to natural existents. For instance, the statement in the *Metaphysics* that "the something which they ["the natural comings to be"] come to be is a man or a plant or one of the things of this kind, which we say are substances [*ousiai*] if anything is . . ."[5] indicates that the fundamental model Aristotle is working with is based on nature as the source of its own being and development. Nonetheless, Aristotle does not overlook *techne*. In discussing knowledge, he argues that there are three kinds. The first, as might have been expected, is *theoretical*, and aims at understanding. The other kinds, *practical* and *productive*, deal with the important role of *techne* in human life. Practical knowledge involves activities concerned with doing; productive knowledge, those involving making.[6] Even though Aristotle admits these three kinds of knowledge, he

does not consider them to be of equal value. The most prominent good for man, according to Aristotle, is to be found, not in activity that transforms the world, but in contemplation aimed at understanding it.[7]

Dewey, on the other hand, builds his theory on a paradigm of productivity. It seems to me that he would not have any real quarrel with Aristotle's breakdown of knowledge into three kinds, but he would disagree about the subordination of productive to theoretical knowledge. Dewey does not deny the value of purely theoretical understanding,[8] but in his view the undue emphasis on that kind of knowledge too readily leads to the mistaken analysis that posits a passive knower who merely contemplates the spectacle of beings set before him. Against this view, Dewey stresses that knowledge is primarily productive knowledge because the subject matter investigated is manipulated so as to produce a certain result.

A good starting point for an understanding of the Deweyan approach is, not unexpectedly, Aristotle's analysis of art. In a detailed explanation of art, Aristotle stresses the importance of "making."

> Now since architecture is an art and is essentially a reasoned state of capacity to make, and there is neither any art that is not such a state nor any such state that is not an art, *art* is identical with a state of capacity to make, involving a true course of reasoning. All art is concerned with coming into being, i.e., with contriving and considering how something may come into being which is capable of either being or not being, and whose origin is in the maker and not in the thing made. . . . Making and acting being different, art must be a matter of making, not of acting.[9]

This description of the link between *techne* and productivity, especially since it focuses on the course of reasoning requisite for success, applies most accurately to Dewey's vision of philosophy. We have already seen that in his first works on logic one of his favorite examples was that of a doctor. Dewey's point was that the doctor is not satisfied with the simple contemplation of patients and their symptoms. Physicians must use their training and intelligence to alter the situation which confronts them. Even the very term "truth" undergoes a change of meaning within this theory. No longer is it the *adequatio intellectus ad rem* of the Aristotelian tradition; now it is contingent upon the results of the making or

transformation effected by the human agent.[10] Ideas are prospective; their validation depends on the consequences of the activities they engender. A physician's diagnosis is true if the regimen followed as a result of the diagnosis leads to the restored health of the patient.

Another of Dewey's illustrations comes from industrial production. In the *Essays in Experimental Logic,* through an example which quite clearly illustrates that contemplation of natural beings is in no sense an epistemological ideal for him, Dewey stresses that the object and objective of thought go together. "Let us take the sequence of mineral rock in place, pig iron and the manufactured article, comparing the raw material in its undisturbed place in nature to the original *res* of experience, compare the manufactured article to the objective and object of knowledge, and the brute datum to the metal undergoing extraction from raw ore for the sake of being wrought into a useful thing" (MW X 341). The object of knowledge in this case is clearly not the mineral in its natural state, but a product into which it has been transformed by human intervention, by art or *techne.*

Dewey explicitly recognizes the difference in emphasis between his own thought and that of the Greeks in *The Quest for Certainty.*

> When the things which exist around us, which we touch, see, hear and taste are regarded as interrogations for which an answer must be sought (and must be sought by means of deliberate introduction of changes till they are reshaped into something different), nature as it already exists ceases to be something which must be accepted and submitted to, endured or enjoyed, just as it is. It is now something to be modified, to be intentionally controlled. It is material to act upon so as to transform it into new objects which better answer our needs. Nature as it exists at any particular time is a challenge, rather than a completion; it provides possible starting points and opportunities rather than final ends.
>
> In short, there is a change from knowing as an esthetic enjoyment of the properties of nature regarded as a work of divine art, to knowing as a means of secular control—that is, a method of purposefully introducing changes which will alter the direction of the course of events [QC 80–81].

It is no small wonder that this attitude, emphasizing, as it does, the practical and the productive, led Santayana to suggest that if Sparta and Carthage had produced philosophies, they would have been

akin to Dewey's.[11] Nature, for Dewey, is a "challenge"; the natural beings which surround us are "interrogations." The key terms summarizing his position are "reshaping," "modification," and "control." Contemplation—"esthetic enjoyment," in Dewey's phraseology—is explicitly removed from its place as the single consummation of intellectual inquiry. In its stead, Dewey suggests the Baconian ideal of the modification and transformation of nature in order to subject it to human control. The emphasis on this ideal, on this attitude toward nature, is what decisively separates Dewey's thought from that of the earlier naturalist, Aristotle.

This point is the aim of the present section. I shall on many occasions compare the doctrines of Dewey and Aristotle. Each time a similarity is pointed out, it will be necessary to remember that the comparisons can go only a certain distance since one thinker will be referring basically to beings in their natural state and the other will be dealing with products of human craft.

3. CHANGE, PERMANENCE, AND THE NEED FOR PHILOSOPHY

No one who has studied the history of philosophy can fail to be impressed with the diversity of opinion with respect not only to established systems but even to so basic an issue as the meaning of philosophy itself. Beyond this diversity, however, there stands a similarity in the impetus to philosophize, in the source from which the need to think philosophically arises. Dewey recognizes this source, and gives expression to it in *Experience and Nature*. He says there that it is the "intricate mixture of the stable and the precarious, the fixed and the unpredictably novel, the assured and the uncertain, in existence which sets mankind upon that love of wisdom which forms philosophy" (EN 55). This quotation does not give us any indication as to how Dewey will resolve this rather vexing problem, which has been with philosophy since its inception. Yet, in the next few pages, and in *Art as Experience*, he is quite careful to point out that a great deal more than just philosophy itself depends on the "intricate mixture" of which he has just spoken. The very possibility of both moral and artistic experience is due to just such a complex state of affairs. "A purely stable world permits of no illusions, but neither is it clothed with ideals. It just exists. To be good is to be better than; and there can be no better

except where there is shock and discord combined with enough assured order to make attainment of harmony possible" (EN 57). Without thirst, we would not know the satisfaction of a refreshing drink, and without an ever-shifting human predicament, there would be no occasion for fastening onto the better conditions and relationships that are attainable within that predicament. As far as Dewey is concerned, change alone allows for no solutions, while permanence alone provides no problems.

A like situation obtains with regard to artistic considerations. In *Art as Experience* Dewey suggests that the denial of either the fluctuating or the stable elements of reality would be deadly for aesthetic experience.

> There are two sorts of possible worlds in which esthetic experience would not occur. In a world of mere flux, change would not be cumulative; it would not move toward a close. Stability and rest would have no being. Equally is it true, however, that a world that is finished, ended, would have no traits of suspense and crisis, and would offer no opportunity for resolution. . . . Because the actual world, that in which we live, is a combination of movement and culmination, of breaks and re-unions, the experience of a living creature is capable of esthetic quality [AE 22].

What Dewey is concerned with is providing a description of the actual world of human experience. It is a world in which the need for philosophy is evident, and one in which aesthetic and moral experience are obvious facts. In each case, Dewey's statements clearly acknowledge the presence of both change and permanence, though he does not provide any clues as to the relationship he sees as obtaining between them. He is careful to insist, as we have seen, that an accurate representation of existence will include both. In fact, if we refer to the quotation from *Experience and Nature* at the beginning of this section, and add the sentence which immediately follows it in the text, we get an explicit statement of a path Dewey wishes to avoid: "Yet too commonly, although in a great variety of technical modes, the result of the search is converted into a metaphysics which denies or conceals from acknowledgment the very characters of existence which initiated it, and which give significance to its conclusions" (EN 55).

This rejected approach denies one of the factors of existence at the expense of the other. Since Dewey argues that the factor denied

is most often change, flux, or contingency, he regards the ontology of form which results from such a denial as an especially common and serious error. If we are to reconstruct a theory of formed existents within his own philosophical horizons, we must take the preliminary step of examining what form is not.

Dewey's analysis of various theories of form asks the questions "how" and "why." How, or by what fallacious turn of reasoning, can certain thinkers fail to recognize the significance and pervasiveness of the changing aspects of reality? Why would anyone remain comfortable with an investigation that would lead to these conclusions? Let us begin with the question "why."

Dewey argues that the denial that process or change is of the same significance as the permanent stems from three causes. (*a*) To survive effectively humans need to control their environment. Control means the minimization of the haphazard, and the paying of maximum attention to the stable and the repetitive. (*b*) The analysis of the actual world has sometimes been based on an analogy that is not completely accurate, the analogy with art. This kind of undertaking was especially prominent in Greek thought. (*c*) Since Aristotle's approach was biological and grammatical, it was natural for him to recognize the obvious fact that natural beings fall into certain kinds or species. On this basis he erected an essentialism that was bequeathed to European philosophy by the thinkers of the Middle Ages.

3.1. Permanence and Social Need

Dewey does not argue that other, earlier, thinkers did not recognize the reality of change. Indeed, he suggests that the very fact of change, permeating so much of experience, was one important factor that led individuals to seek refuge in the permanent.

> If classic philosophy says so much about unity and so little about unreconciled diversity, so much about the eternal and permanent, and so little about change (save as something to be resolved into combinations of the permanent), so much about necessity and so little about contingency, so much about the comprehending universal and so little about the recalcitrant particular, it may well be because the ambiguousness and ambivalence of reality are actually so pervasive. Since these things form the problem, solution is more

apparent (although not more actual), in the degree in which whatever of stability and assurance the world presents is fastened upon
and asserted [EN 46].

Dewey does not mention agriculture, but this activity serves as a
good example to illustrate his position. A calendar that records the
recurrence of the seasons is essential to a successful harvest. Communities are dependent on the predictable sequence of spring, sum-
mer, fall, and winter, in order that they may prepare for planting
seeds at the most appropriate time. Although each day is unique,
and no two springs or summers exactly replicate each other, their
temporal relationship involves a certain kind of permanence. This
permanence must be recognized and fastened on if the community
is to produce enough food to ensure its survival.[12]
   But this fastening on one particular aspect of experience Dewey
considers to be the source of a serious philosophical error. It is not
an error in itself. It becomes one only when the context in which
the focusing occurs is forgotten. The result is that the permanent
aspects are isolated and accorded independent existence.

> But the demand and the response which meets it [the permanent]
> are empirically always found in a special context; they arise be-
> cause of a particular need and in order to effect specifiable conse-
> quences. Philosophy, thinking at large, allows itself to be diverted
> into absurd search for an intellectual philosopher's stone of abso-
> lutely wholesale generalizations, thus isolating that which is per-
> manent in a function and for a purpose, and converting it into the
> intrinsically eternal, conceived either (as Aristotle conceived it) as
> that which is the same at all times, or as that which is indifferent to
> time, out of time [EN 32–33].

Permanence, as in the case of a calendar predicting the return of
spring, is always a stable aspect of a world in flux, isolated because
of a certain "function" and for a definite "purpose." Viewing the
permanent outside of the needs which brought it forth and the situation in which it is discovered is, for Dewey, a philosophical sim-
plification (EN 33)—and a dangerous one because the actual circumstances in which humans find themselves and through which
further solutions to additional problems will be found are now
viewed inaccurately. Dewey's first point, then, is that it is quite easy
to understand why people chose to concentrate on the elements of

stability in experience. Such a choice, however understandable, incorporates a serious limitation: the removal of the permanent from the context that occasioned and suggested it.

3.2. Art and Forms

Dewey's second explanation deals with art. He suggests that one interpretive scheme the Greeks were very fond of using in dealing with nature was to compare it to an artistic creation. This kind of analogy led them so readily to accept form as the key concept in the understanding of nature, and acceptance of form in this context had certain important implications. First of all, form stood for the *fixed* aspects of nature, and, secondly, invention, novelty, and change were interpreted as of less importance than form. Just as Dewey claims that the permanent in general provided a refuge from the vagaries of actual experience, so he argues that the stable beauty of artistic creation offered a similar refuge on a different level.

> Greek philosophy as well as Greek art is a memorial of the joy in what is finished, when it is found amid a world of unrest, struggle, and uncertainty in what, since it is ended, does not commit us to the uncertain hazards of what is still going on. Without such experiences as those of Greek art it is hardly conceivable that the craving for the passage of change into rest, of the contingent, mixed and wandering into the composed and total, would have found a model after which to design a universe like the cosmos of Platonic and Aristotelian tradition [EN 77–78].

Dewey does not merely suggest that this emphasis on stability was common to both philosophy and art. He argues that there is a causal link between the two. Greek philosophy glorified form *because* Greek art did the same.

> Form was the first and last word of philosophy because it had been that of art; form is change arrested in a prerogative object. It conveys a sense of the imperishable and timeless, although the material in which it is exemplified is subject to decay and contingency. It thus conveys an intimation of potentialities completely actualized in a happier realm, where events are not events, but are arrested and brought to a close in an eternal self-sustaining activity [EN 78].

Dewey's second reason is not altogether different from his first. In both cases the motivating force is the need to escape contingency.

What has been presented are two varieties of escape. The former involved the need for controlling the environment, an attitude essential to survival. The second stressed the use of art as a solace from confusion and caprice.[13]

But a novel element is introduced in the discussion of this second reason. That new element has to do specifically with the characterization of form as a separate, unchanging pattern to which the entities of nature correspond. According to Dewey, the philosophers of nature in ancient Greece did not view forms as flexible and dependent on the actual course of natural events because in art the forms were not thought of as dependent on the inventiveness of the artist. They were models fixed by tradition. They were, Dewey argues, "objectively given" and had only to be "observed and followed" (EN 79).

What Dewey finds in Greek art is therefore not only a reason that explains the Greek fascination with the fixed and the final, but also the particular characterization of this fixed aspect of reality, which is form. Form is not malleable, flexible, or susceptible to any kind of alteration because it is independent in two senses: it is independent of the artist, and it is independent of nature. The artistic creation and the natural event stand as approximations of their fixed models. Any deviation from the model is discouraged in art and impossible in nature.

3.3. Biology and Language

The final reason in Dewey's explanation for the enduring allure of the permanent in philosophy deals specifically with Aristotle. Dewey is both attracted to and critical of the Greek thinker. He claims that more than any other philosopher of the classical era Aristotle approached the promulgation of a doctrine that would have avoided the kinds of errors we have just been discussing. However, Dewey is convinced that Aristotle did just that, merely came close to an accurate position. He did not, in Dewey's view, go far enough. Two factors contributed to the limitations inherent in Aristotle's analysis. One was his interest in biology; the other, the grammatical model on which his theory of being was based.

Dewey emphasizes again and again his own version of the coincidence of opposites, and bemoans the fact that any thinker would so

emphasize one side of an opposition that the other would be forgotten. "Qualities have defects as necessary conditions of their excellencies; the instrumentalities of truth are the causes of error; change gives meaning to permanence and recurrence makes novelty possible" (EN 47). This very tension between opposites is what characterizes the experience of being human in the world. For it is not a world of mere existence, which it would be if these tensions were to disappear. It is a world, rather, of satisfactions and disappointments, truth and error, recurrence and novelty. What Dewey is arguing is that these pairings are correlative. If one is present, then so must the other be (at least potentially). If, for example, one never utters a statement in the form of a proposition, then one will never be in error. But, at the same time, the possibility of truth is excluded. As Dewey points out, the very instrumentalities of truth are the sources of error. If the search for truth is undertaken, then the danger of error becomes real. The two are present together or not present at all. The fact of correlativity, which Dewey implies here, will be crucial in developing a defensible theory of formed entities.

These facts have not always been overlooked in the history of philosophy, but Dewey thinks that they had not always been accorded the kind of importance they should receive. It is in this context that Dewey admits some positive content in Aristotle's position. He thinks that the recognition of the interdependence of defect/excellence, truth/error, change/permanence, and recurrence/novelty should be regarded as "fundamentally significant for the formation of a naturalistic metaphysics." Dewey asserts that Aristotle's metaphysics came close to recognizing and developing this insight. However, to his discredit, Aristotle was unwilling to surrender his "bias in favor of the fixed, certain and finished" (EN 47). As we saw above, Dewey attributes this failure to Aristotle's preoccupation with biology and to his uncritical acceptance of a parallel between grammatical structure and ontological fact. I will deal with each of these explanations separately.

First of all, Aristotle was a student of nature, and, as such, had ample opportunity to examine the complexity and diversity of natural beings. But even with this kind of observation in the background, Dewey claims, Aristotle stuck fast to the type-form analysis, which was inherited from Greek art. "A type-form had no separate being; but, being embodied in particulars, it made them an intrin-

sically unified and marked out class, which as a class was ungenerated
and indestructible, perfect and complete" (EN 163). Dewey goes on
to say that Aristotle's theory of type-forms can no longer be valid in
the light of modern science, but in the Greek world it was natural
to interpret biological observations in this way.[14]

This kind of classificatory scheme, which Dewey explains as a
normal reaction to the immediate observation of nature, is viewed
as being buttressed in Aristotle by a doctrine of categories based on
the grammatical model. Dewey is referring here to the ten categories, the most fundamental of which is substance. It is a simple
matter to see how Aristotle's doctrine of categories can be blended
with the biological doctrine of type-forms. Just as the particular,
individual, characteristics of a living being are treated as secondary
and unimportant with regard to a scheme of classification, so the
system of categories stresses one as fundamental and the others as
"accidental." As far as Dewey is concerned, this means that although
Aristotle approached a pluralistic theory of existence, the positive
content of such a doctrine was mitigated by a rigid grammatical
organization.

> His [Aristotle's] philosophy was closer to empirical facts than most
> modern philosophies, in that it was neither monistic nor dualistic
> but openly pluralistic. His plurals fall however, within a gram-
> matical system, to each portion of which a corresponding cosmic
> status is allotted. Thus his pluralism solved the problem of how to
> have your cake and eat it too, for a classified and hierarchically
> ordered set of pluralities, of variants, has none of the sting of the
> miscellaneous and uncoordinated plurals of our actual world
> [EN 48].

The same theme is repeated again and again in Dewey. Aristotle
avoids some errors of modern, dualistically inclined, philosophers
because his methodology is empirical and his solution pluralistic.
Nonetheless, his tendency to emphasize the fixed and the final at the
expense of the truly flexible, the unchanging rather than the pro-
tean, remains a serious limitation for the Greek thinker. This evaluation notwithstanding, Dewey seeks to understand his position in
terms of cultural, temporal, and linguistic factors. He does not criticize Aristotle for not being ahead of his time, but rather shows how
easily one could develop a doctrine like Aristotle's if the context in
which the doctrine germinated is understood.

As I have attempted to demonstrate, this is Dewey's attitude toward the entire tradition which does not sufficiently emphasize the importance of flux. By referring either to cultural necessity or to artistic and scientific climates of opinion, Dewey is able to explain the extraordinary durability of the view he is seeking to modify. The third branch of this explanation, that dealing with Aristotle, is in a way a recapitulation of the other two. The first reason grew out of the need for control over the environment. The third reason develops from the need for intellectual control. Classification is necessary if one is to get beyond the immediate contact with facts. This realization was certainly well recognized by Aristotle, whether in biology or in language. In dealing with art, Dewey gave clear expression to the doctrine of form that he was rejecting. This was form as an independent and unchanging reality. In spite of Dewey's recognition that Aristotle's forms have no separate existence, the fact remains that he considers the Aristotelian forms as changeless and therefore unacceptable.

3.4. Selective Emphasis

This threefold exploration of reasons why philosophy followed a mistaken path does not make explicit the fallacy which Dewey believes was committed in each case. When Dewey analyzes the question "why" he is a most generous commentator, allowing his reader to understand the factors which led to the error. But when he turns to a discussion of the "how" he becomes a much sharper critic of this philosophical heritage, accusing other thinkers of engaging in an "absurd search" (EN 30), of exhibiting "cataleptic rigidity" (EN 31), and of committing "*the* philosophical fallacy" (EN 34).

What exactly does Dewey mean by these charges? Essentially, he believes that earlier philosophers fell into the error of hypostatizing partial aspects of analysis. He suggests that the results of intellectual abstraction were transformed into independent existents. This kind of procedure he calls *the* philosophic fallacy, and his understanding of it is framed within a discussion of what he labels "selective emphasis." We noted earlier how Dewey presents his own version of a coincidence of opposites. Selective emphasis is another instance of opposites bound together. Any intellectual operation uses this procedure, but it is at the same time a common source of error.

The world in which we live provides a dizzying array of phenomena on which we can focus our attention. Since our approach to any issue, as Dewey points out, is usually instigated by a problematic situation, and since not every element of experience is crucial to the particular problem at hand, some selection from the diversity is demanded. Oliver Wendell Holmes, Jr., in describing the facts a lawyer would want to present in court, provides a good illustration of the point Dewey is trying to make: "The reason why a lawyer does not mention that his client wore a white hat when he made a contract . . . is that he foresees that the public force will act in the same way whatever his client had upon his head."[15] The problematic situation in this instance is the need to make a judicial decision. To make that decision successfully, judges cannot allow themselves to be overwhelmed by a mountain of irrelevant, albeit real, detail. There must be some selection, or selective emphasis, if there is to be success in resolving the issue.

Dewey argues that this kind of selectivity is not only common but necessary in any intellectual endeavor. "Selective emphasis, with accompanying omission and rejection, is the heart-beat of mental life. To object to the operation is to discard all thinking" (EN 31). Selective emphasis is successful when the individual involved in the selection is mindful that the elements fastened on are not in themselves isolated. They are part of a greater context. In science as well as in ordinary life, the wider context is generally kept in mind. "But in ordinary matters and in scientific inquiries, we always retain the sense that the material chosen is selected for a purpose; there is no idea of denying what is left out, for what is omitted is merely that which is not relevant to the particular problem and purpose in hand" (EN 31). Philosophers, however, seem especially prone to let the context dissolve away as they focus on selected elements: "But in philosophies, this limiting condition is often wholly ignored. It is not noted and remembered that the favored subject-matter is chosen for a purpose and that what is left out is just as real and important in its own characteristic context. . . . It is natural to men to take that which is of chief value to them at the time as *the* real" (EN 31).

In this context Dewey speaks of a "fallacy of selective emphasis" rather than a "principle of selective emphasis." The isolation of certain elements from their context is the process Dewey believes re-

sponsible for the emphasis on permanence at the expense of change in traditional philosophy. This fallacy explains how philosophers, in the face of a complex, changing world, could nonetheless direct their attention to unchanging forms, unmoved movers, and permanent substances. The fallacy thus committed is common enough because it is the improper application of a necessary procedure in mental activity.

4. DEWEY AND KANT RE-EXAMINED

This fallacy of selective emphasis is applicable to a wider range of issues than simply that of change and permanence. The division between realistic and idealistic thinkers can also be viewed from the perspective of this fallacy. It is possible so to emphasize the dative character of the experienced world that the work of inquiry is reduced to a passive acceptance and cataloguing of presented facts. This is the realistic position as Dewey understands it. On the other hand, if the activity of the inquiring mind is overly emphasized, the idealistic analysis of knowing is the outcome. We have already examined Dewey's attempt to break free from both positions.[16] His own understanding of inquiry is that it involves both passivity and activity on the part of the individual undertaking an intellectual search. This median position, which stresses both receptivity and activity on the part of consciousness, is one of the reasons why Dewey has been compared to Kant.[17]

His relationship with Kant did not entirely escape Dewey's notice, and in *The Quest for Certainty*, published in 1929, he undertook to unravel the similarities and differences between them. Dewey readily admits that there is a "superficial resemblance" between his views and Kant's. "The element of similarity," he claims, "is suggested by Kant's well known saying that perception without conception is blind, conception without perception empty" (QC 137).[18] Dewey is restating here what we already know from our study of his development. Neither he nor Kant believes that consciousness, whether of the subjective sort or of the objective kind, constitutes beings. There is a passive, receptive dimension to consciousness which must be recognized in a proper interpretation of its function. But this passive dimension alone is not sufficient to provide knowledge. An active element, ideas, or concepts must interact with the data re-

ceived. Each doctrine shares a concern that both these dimensions be given their proper significance. Beyond this similarity, however, there is found a disparity that decisively separates the two thinkers.

There is accordingly opposition rather than agreement between the Kantian determination of objects by thought and the determination by thought that takes place in experimentation. There is nothing hypothetical or conditional about Kant's forms of perception and conception. They work uniformly and triumphantly; they need no differential testing by consequences. The reason Kant postulates them is to secure universality and necessity instead of the hypothetical and the probable. Nor is there anything overt, observable and temporal or historical in the Kantian machinery. Its work is done behind the scenes. Only the result is observed, and only an elaborate process of dialectic inference enables Kant to assert the existence of his apparatus of forms and categories [QC 231].

If we list the descriptive terms for the respective positions either included in or suggested by this passage, then the differences between Kant and Dewey begin to manifest themselves more clearly. Dewey's analysis stresses "experimentation" and "consequences." It is "probable" and "temporal." Kant's theory involves "necessity" and "universality" and is "atemporal" as well as "unobservable." Both, however, make use of the pivotal term "object." This troublesome word will serve as the focal point for unraveling the differences between these two thinkers.

For Dewey, an object is determined through a process of inquiry. It is not simply a matter of a consciousness applying categories to a manifold of sensation. The discrimination of an object involves manipulation, which means actual physical involvement with external materials. This involvement, as we have seen, results from the need to resolve a problematic situation. Because of this, the consequences of the physical experimentation are of the utmost importance, since they will decide whether the situation is resolved or not. In the medical kind of example favored by Dewey, the physician, after having engaged in inquiries, which include such processes as examining blood samples and taking blood pressure, offers a suggested remedy. Only the consequences of using that remedy will allow the doctor to realize whether a particular diagnosis was accurate. There is never any question of absolute necessity or certainty.

Suggested solutions are only probable, and they must always be tested in terms of consequences. Accordingly, the whole process of inquiry is historical. That is to say, it occurs as a temporal sequence of interactions between the investigator and the subject matter undergoing inquiry.

This *public* aspect of experimentation is what Dewey most wishes to stress as differentiating his position from Kant's. The object is determined, not within consciousness, but in the process of actually doing something to the entities or events in question. This is a significant difference from the point of view of my own study. Whereas the Kantian doctrine is oriented inward, toward the subject, and away from the physical things-in-the-world, Dewey's position is outward-looking. As such, it suggests the need for an ontology, for a general theory of those things-in-the-world.

4.1. Takens or Givens?

Dewey argues that much could be gained in terms of clarity if philosophical discourse would substitute "takens" for "data" or "givens" when dealing with the subject matter of inquiry.

> The history of the theory of knowledge or epistemology would have been very different if instead of the word "data" or "givens," it had happened to start with calling the qualities in question "takens." Not that the data are not existential and qualities of the ultimately "given"—that is, the total subject-matter which is had in non-cognitive experiences. But *as* data they are *selected* from this total original subject-matter which gives the impetus to knowing; they are discriminated for a purpose:—that, namely, of affording signs or evidence to define and locate a problem, and thus give a clew to its resolution [QC 142–43].

The emendation from "given" to "taken" is in several respects an indication of the kind of ontological analysis Dewey will undertake. (*a*) Being and knowing are not co-extensive. Beings, taken as total possible subject matters, offer too vast an area for the limited scope of human cognitive power. (*b*) These beings are given originally in "non-cognitive experiences." This is but another way in which Dewey denies the ubiquity of the knowledge relation. Existents are appreciated, feared, preferred, and used. These are examples of the non-cognitive experiences Dewey is referring to. (*c*) They present

themselves as capable of being known. (*d*) This knowledge results only after they have been experimented on or manipulated in some way.

These indications do not allow us to argue that Dewey has developed a revised ontology which recognizes forms-in-nature. What they offer is a context in which such a doctrine can emerge. If inquiry involves irreducibly a material that is subjected to experimentation, then certain traits of that material must make it susceptible to this kind of investigation. To admit this much is to begin engaging in ontology. The implications derived from Dewey's preference for "takens" instead of "givens" lead directly to another terminological modification that is introduced in *The Quest for Certainty*. He suggests that in his philosophical framework "intelligence" plays the role that "reason" did in earlier theories.

4.2. Reason and Intelligence

Dewey argues that "reason" is a word overlaid with the significance of sheer passivity or receptivity. Since his theory stresses the role of humans as participators, not as mere spectators, he is anxious to replace "reason" with a more suitable term. The term he selects is one that was also prominent in his idealistic phase: "intelligence."[19]

> There is thus involved more than a verbal shift if we say that the new scientific development effects an exchange of reason for intelligence. In saying this, "reason" has the technical meaning given to it in classic philosophic tradition, the *nous* of the Greeks, the *intellectus* of the scholastics. In this meaning, it designates both an inherent immutable order of nature, superempirical in character, and the organ of mind by which this universal order is grasped [QC 169–70].

"Reason," as far as Dewey is concerned, is a term that is just not suited for the experimental method of inquiry. Reason implies a fixed or "immutable" order of nature, whereas inquiry, as Dewey conceives it, requires that natural beings be amenable to the variations introduced by experimentation. Absolute rigidity is incompatible with this view. In fact, reason may be seen as a term which, along with *eidos*, summarizes the objectionable view of form analyzed in this chapter. By saying that reason carries with it the bag-

gage of an immutable "superempirical" order of nature, Dewey is arguing that it is allied to a philosophical tradition that is both outdated and erroneous.

If reason indicates fixity on the part of nature, and passivity on the part of the inquirer, then we can expect that Dewey will use "intelligence" to stress different characteristics. And indeed he does.

> Intelligence on the other hand is associated with *judgment*; that is, with selection and arrangement of means to effect consequences and with choice of what we take as our ends. A man is intelligent not in virtue of having reason which grasps first and indemonstrable truths about fixed principles, in order to reason deductively from them to the particulars which they govern, but in virtue of his capacity to estimate the possibilities of a situation and to act in accordance with his estimate [QC 170].

The two terms in this passage which are the best indications of Dewey's novel doctrine are "judgment" and "act." Knowledge, for Dewey, cannot be separated from action. The only way to resolve a problematic situation is to employ judgment, which is an estimation of the optimal method for a resolution, and then to act in accordance with that judgment.

Dewey wishes to emphasize that this is in no way a purely mentalistic endeavor. It involves active participation by the individual conducting the inquiry. It is in this sense, too, that the earlier terminological readjustment, that of "takens" for "givens," is connected with the use of intelligence. For if judgment involves "the selection and arrangement of means to effect consequences," then this selection involves "taking" from a complex whole those elements that are viewed as leading to a satisfactory resolution of the problematic situation. Dewey's choice of "intelligence" as a term to signify this procedure is well considered from an etymological point of view. The term means "selecting from among." The Latin *intellectus* from which it is derived is a compound of *inter* (among) and *legere* (to choose).[20] We can say, then, that the Deweyan process of inquiry involves different stages: judgment, selection (taking), and action, all of which are both summarized by the term "intelligence" and incompatible with the traditional theory of fixed forms.

But the use of a term such as "intelligence" leaves ample room for an alternative ontological theory. "Intelligence," by emphasizing "taking" or "selection," is outwardly directed, as is clear from Dew-

ey's argument, in the passage above, that intelligence involves the "capacity to estimate the possibilities of a situation." This means that it is the situation itself which to a degree will guide the solution. It also means that situations are not all alike, and that a limited amount of possibilities inheres in each situation. Limitation, as was pointed out in the Introduction, is usually a sign of structure or form. If not all situations offer the same grouping of possibilities, then it appears that they may be variously structured. Just how Dewey develops this line of thought will be the topic of the next chapters.

5. SUMMARY

Because Dewey is sensitive to the history of philosophy he seeks to situate his own philosophical orientation within that history. This chapter examined his critical evaluations of Greek thought, especially Aristotle's. The distinction between *techne* and *physis* prepared the ground for comparisons between Aristotle and Dewey. These two philosophers may be similar in many respects but they differ in a fundamental way: Aristotle's thought emphasizes *physis*; Dewey's stresses *techne*.

Dewey's criticisms of Greek metaphysics are in keeping with his appreciation of Darwin. He claims that the Greeks, as typified by Aristotle, underemphasized the role of change in their analyses of existence. He attempts to understand why this is so, and provides an explanation. The need for control in social life and knowledge, together with the use of art as an analogy for understanding nature, led them to stress permanence over change. Such one-sided analyses can be avoided, according to Dewey, if philosophers would simply remember that selections are constantly being made in a context and for a purpose. *Selective emphasis* is an unavoidable part of human life. What must be avoided is the tendency to disregard the context and purpose, recalling only those elements focused on as a result of selective emphasis.

Chapter 4 also brought an end to a *leitmotif* begun in Chapter 1 and continued in Chapters 2 and 3: the relationship of Dewey and Kant. Dewey's own analysis of the similarities and differences between his thought and that of Kant was examined. There is agreement between the two men that noetic activity involves both a pas-

sive and an active dimension, but the similarities end there. For Dewey, the process of inquiry which results in knowledge is experimental, hypothetical, and public, whereas for Kant the process is atemporal, apodictic, and internal.

In line with his criticisms of Kant, Dewey rejects two terms associated with a Kantian-type of analysis: "givens" and "reason." Dewey suggests that "takens" be used as a more appropriate term than "givens" and that "intelligence" replace "reason." The word "takens" has the advantage of keeping the selective nature of noetic activity clearly in focus. The temptation to hypostatize the results of inquiry, or to ignore the situation in which selections are made, is thus minimized. Dewey prefers the term "intelligence," a word that was prominent in his book on Leibniz, to "reason" because of the latter's association with passivity and fixity. "Intelligence," on the other hand, connotes the active participation of an inquirer selecting the means to resolve a problematic situation. It thus is better suited for expressing the novel philosophical orientation Dewey is beginning to formulate.

NOTES

1. See chap. 3, sect. 3.1.

2. The example concerning the production of metal from ore, cited later in this chapter, is typically Deweyan. See sect. 2. On the use of a physician as illustrative of his position, see chap. 3, sect. 3.1.

3. *Metaphysics* 1070A6–9, in *Basic Works of Aristotle*, ed. McKeon, pp. 873–74.

4. See chapt. 1, sect. 2.21.

5. *Metaphysics* 1032A19–20, in *Basic Works of Aristotle*, ed. McKeon, p. 791. A similar statement can be found in the *Categories* 1B27–28: "To sketch my meaning roughly, examples of substance are 'man' or 'the horse' . . ." (in ibid., p. 3).

6. *Metaphysics* 1025B19–27, in ibid., p. 778.

7. "If happiness is activity in accordance with virtue, it is reasonable that it should be in accordance with the highest virtue; and this will be that of the best thing in us. Whether it be reason or something else that is this element which is thought to be our natural ruler and guide and to take thought to things noble and divine, whether it be itself also divine or only the most divine element in us, the activity of this in accordance with its proper virtue will be perfect happiness. That this

activity is contemplative we have already said" (*Ethics* 1177A11–19, in ibid., p. 1104).

8. Dewey may not give to *theoria* the prominent place it held with earlier thinkers, but he is not so insensitive as to deny its value altogether. At *EN* 121, he argues that he has been misunderstood on this matter. "It is characteristic of the inevitable moral pre-possession of philosophy, together with the subjective turn of modern thought, that many critics take an 'instrumental' theory of knowledge to signify that the value of knowing is instrumental to the knower. This is a matter which is as it may be in particular cases; but certainly in many cases the pursuit of science is sport, carried on, like other sports, for its own satisfaction." A similar sentiment is voiced on page 304 where Dewey asserts that reflection "is a unique intrinsic good."

9. *Ethics* 1140A7–14, 16–17, in *Basic Works of Aristotle*, ed. McKeon, p. 1025.

10. "But in the practice of science, knowledge is an affair of *making* sure, not of grasping antecedently given sureties. What is already known, what is accepted as truth, is of immense importance; inquiry could not proceed a step without it. But it is held subject to use, and is at the mercy of the discoveries which it makes possible. It has to be adjusted to the latter and not the latter to it. When things are defined as instruments, their value and validity reside in what proceeds from them; consequences not antecedents supply meaning and verity" (EN 123). On this point, Dewey reveals himself to be a faithful disciple of Francis Bacon. "Of all signs there is none more certain or more noble than that taken from fruits. For fruits and works are as it were sponsors and sureties for the truth of philosophies" (*Novum Organum* 1.73, in *English Philosophers from Bacon to Mill*, ed. Burtt, p. 51).

11. "Dewey's Naturalistic Metaphysics," 687.

12. Alexander Marshak, who made the important discovery of prehistoric calendars, has suggested that agriculture is a "time-factored" activity. This implies that it depends on the ability of individuals to recognize the periodic or seasonal character of temporal flow. See his *The Roots of Civilization: The Cognitive Beginnings of Man's First Art, Symbol, and Notation* (New York: McGraw-Hill, 1972), pp. 14–15.

13. Concerning art, Dewey writes: "Resort to esthetic objects is the spontaneous human escape and consolation in a trying and difficult world" (EN 77).

14. "Yet it [Aristotle's theory] was a natural interpretation of things found in ordinary experience. The immediate qualitative differences of things cannot be recognized without noting that things possessed of

these qualitative traits fall into kinds, or families" (EN 163). Aristotle's classificatory scheme, however, is not as clear-cut as it is sometimes made out to be. W. D. Ross, for instance, claims that Aristotle was the first thinker systematically to classify living beings. But he qualifies this assertion by stating that "no cut-and-dried classification is to be found in his [Aristotle's] writing" (*Aristotle*, p. 115). D'Arcy Thompson, who was both a biologist and an Aristotelian translator, emphasizes this point even more strenuously: "Many commentators have sought for Aristotle's 'classification of animals'; for my part I have never found it, and, in our sense of the word, I am certain it is not there" ("Natural Science," in *The Legacy of Greece*, ed. R. W. Livingstone [Oxford: Clarendon, 1929], p. 158).

15. "The Path of the Law," in *Law and Philosophy*, ed. E. A. Kent (New York: Appleton-Century-Crofts, 1970), p. 6.

16. See chap. 3, sects. 3.2 and 3.3.

17. We saw in chap. 2. sect. 3 that two recent commentators, Richard Rorty and Robert Dewey, made just this sort of analysis.

18. A more accurately Deweyan version of Kant's perception/conception statement comes from Claude Bernard, the famous physiologist and theoretician of the experimental method. " 'A skilled hand without the head to direct it is a blind instrument; the head without the hand to carry out an idea remains impotent.' " Bernard's quotation is more Deweyan because of its emphasis on the "hand" which must manipulate and bring changes into the material being investigated. It stresses the public, external aspect of the experimental method. The quotation from Bernard is found in Mirko D. Grmek, "Bernard, Claude," *The Dictionary of Scientific Biography* II, ed. Charles C. Gillispie (New York: Scribner's, 1970), p. 32.

19. This term was discussed in chap. 1, sect. 2.242.

20. See *Oxford Latin Dictionary*, ed. P. G. W. Glare (Oxford: Clarendon, 1982), p. 936.

5

Metaphysics and Evolutionary Biology

1. CONTINUITY WITH THE CLASSICAL TRADITION

DEWEY'S NATURALISTIC PERIOD is characterized by the substitution of ontological issues for the methodological ones that dominated the experimentalist phase. This change in emphasis resulted from his continued preoccupation with certain concerns that had marked his idealistic period, two of which are relevant here: (*a*) the recognition that consciousness must be viewed as *active* as well as passive; and (*b*) *organicism*. From Morris, Dewey had come to appreciate the active role of intelligence in the acquisition of knowledge; and in Hegel, he had found a well–worked-out expression of organicism, a doctrine that had attracted him since his undergraduate years at the University of Vermont.

Each of these themes dominates in one or another of the subsequent periods of Dewey's development. The activity of intelligence is transformed, in his new logic, into the activity of the inquiring individual, with experimentation now playing the active role previously reserved for intelligence. Thus Dewey preserves a doctrine from his earliest phase by reformulating it in a non-idealistic manner.

His naturalistic period may be viewed as an attempt to make a similar reformulation of the notion of organicism. In this chapter, I shall begin to explore the positive aspects of this attempt. The previous chapter also dealt with Dewey's naturalistic phase, but the analysis presented there so concentrated on the objections to traditional theories found in his writings of this period that it could easily lead to a misrepresentation of his actual thought. Many of the ontological doctrines Dewey rejected were identified with Greek thought, often specifically with the philosophy of Aristotle. It may thus appear that the relationship between Dewey and these ear-

lier philosophers can be described only in terms of discontinuity.

But such an interpretation, though understandable, would be one-sided. John Herman Randall has argued for a different thesis, pointing out that if there is any philosopher whom Dewey most resembles, it is Aristotle.[1] The relationship of Dewey to Greek thought must be looked at in terms of both continuity and discontinuity. The previous chapter stressed the latter; these next chapters will redress the balance.

They will deal with the same books as Chapter 4, *Experience and Nature, Art as Experience,* and *The Quest for Certainty,* and will show how Dewey fits into the tradition of the great classical thinkers who concerned themselves with ontological issues. His solution to those problems will bear the stamp of his unique genius, of course, but this difference should not completely overshadow the similarity of concerns. The most important indication of continuity can be found in his understanding of what the metaphysical enterprise entails.

One reason that Dewey comes to face the same issues as a classical metaphysician such as Aristotle did is that they share a common understanding of metaphysics. The traditional ontological language of "being" was one that Dewey never found very congenial.[2] As a result, his definition of metaphysics may not appear, at first glance, to be similar to Aristotle's description of it as the study of "being *qua* being." Nonetheless, if Dewey's formulations are studied carefully, it is clear that he is indicating a field of study like the one presented in Aristotle's *Metaphysics.* Aristotle explains, at the beginning of Book Gamma, that what differentiates metaphysics from other studies is the breadth of its subject matter. Other disciplines "cut off a part of being and investigate the attribute of this part," whereas metaphysics "treats universally of being as being."[3] By contrast, biology, for example, does not treat of being as being, but only of living being. Mathematics, Aristotle's own example, deals with being in its quantitative dimension. Since no other discipline studies being as being, a separate field of study is needed which will dedicate itself to this task. That field, which Aristotle calls "first philosophy," has come to be known as "metaphysics."

Dewey's characterization of metaphysics is that it involves the "cognizance of the generic traits of existence" (EN 50). When he explains what he means by this phrase, the similarity with Aristotle

is manifest. Dewey argues that metaphysics has a subject matter of its own which is genuine and worthy of exploration. "This genuine subject matter is the fact that the natural world has *generic* as well as specific traits, and that in one case as in the other experience is such as to enable us to arrive at their identification."[4] Whereas Aristotle distinguishes between a discipline that treats only a part of being and one that treats being universally, Dewey makes a distinction between specific and generic traits of existence. Although the terminology is different, both agree on fundamental issues. For each, (*a*) metaphysics is defined according to its unique subject matter; (*b*) that subject matter is described in the most general of terms as either "being as being" or the "generic traits of existence"; and (*c*) metaphysical knowledge is thought to be as much a possibility as knowledge in other disciplines.

That a parallel of this sort should exist between Dewey and Aristotle is not so surprising as it may at first seem. There was, after all, the influence of the German Aristotelian Trendelenburg in Dewey's training at Johns Hopkins. But perhaps the most prominent factor in bringing out his incipient Aristotelian leanings was his colleague at Columbia University F. J. E. Woodbridge, a devoted disciple of Aristotle. We have not only textual evidence to this effect but also the testimony of both Herbert Schneider and John Herman Randall. Dewey's definition of metaphysics is a virtual mirror image of Woodbridge's in his article "Metaphysics"; Schneider claims that it was Woodbridge who "encouraged Dewey to think naturalistically, to take metaphysics empirically, and to write *Experience and Nature*"; and Randall, addressing himself directly to the issue of continuity with the classical tradition, says: "Indeed, Dewey's own appreciation for the superiority of the Greeks to modern dualisms, so marked in his writings from *Experience and Nature* onward, seems to have been greatly extended and developed through his discussions with Woodbridge."[5]

Dewey himself came to realize that there was an affinity between his philosophy and that of the Greeks.[6] In the introductory piece he wrote for Sidney Hook's *The Metaphysics of Pragmatism*, he admits that the pairing of the words "metaphysics"[7] and "pragmatism" in the book's title might not appear at first sight to be an enlightened choice, and then goes on to explain how the two terms do indeed belong together.

• But the reader who permits his idea of the meaning of these words to grow with and from the actual subject-matter of the following pages will find in them, I am confident, a penetrating and illuminating union of the basic ideas in the newer movement with those of the classic philosophical tradition, a union in which equal justice is dealt to the truths which are carried over and completed in the new development and the transformations in them which the new ideas enact.[8]

This passage sets the boundaries of the next two chapters. On the one hand, the problems they will deal with are similar to those treated in the classic philosophical tradition. On the other, the actual subject matter discussed will undergo the "transformations" Dewey refers to in the last sentence.

2. EVOLUTION AND ONTOLOGY

In spite of texts such as these, questions could still be raised concerning the impact of evolution. Was it not this biological doctrine which drew Dewey and other thinkers away from ontology, tainted as the latter was with the aura of permanence and changelessness? Is a philosophy influenced by Darwin not bound to be critical rather than constructive in this area? One commentator personally familiar with Dewey does not think so. Sterling Lamprecht argues, in fact, that what the Darwinian theory pointed to was a felt need to construct a new metaphysics: "Darwin stressed the interaction of organism with environment. . . . Darwin also stressed the fact that the world is in constant flux, and that novelty appears on the occasion of many a natural change. Darwinism is not a system of metaphysics. But the truths which Darwin forced scientists, and then also philosophers, to acknowledge prepared the way for a metaphysics of a different caliber than that which ensued from the Newtonian formulations."[9] Lamprecht is arguing here that serious thinkers could not avoid metaphysics as a theory of existents in general, and that criticism of traditional ontologies alone was an insufficient response. The novel manner of interpreting reality suggested by evolutionary theory occasioned constructive philosophical thinking about the very nature of entities.

Lamprecht's quotation not only indicates the need for a renewed metaphysical effort; it also outlines the main themes of this chapter.

As he presents it, evolution brought with it two great lessons for philosophy: the emphasis on the interaction[10] of an organism with its environment and the recognition that flux, novelty, and change are real factors in the natural world.[11]

Dewey understood these lessons well. As we shall see, for him, formed entities are the result of the interaction of organism and environment. One consequence of viewing forms this way is that the conflict with the obvious fact of change, objected to in the previous chapter, no longer is a problem. Nor is the compatibility of flux and form. The issue becomes that of articulating the manner in which both are incorporated into a single doctrine.

To elicit Dewey's contribution to this issue, I shall begin by treating the question of organism/environment interaction itself. The manner in which he allies this issue to that of matter and form will be developed in some detail. The second section will examine the dynamic interpretation of form. Following this, two sections will be given over to the examination of what might be called categorial considerations. Although he does not present an explicit doctrine of categories, Dewey does provide an incipient categorial scheme.[12] The two prominent categories are "event," his transposition of the Aristotelian *ousia* or substance,[13] and "relation," which plays a major and crucial role in his thought. Section 3 will deal with "event"; section 4, with "relation." Once this preliminary work is completed, the status of forms in Dewey's thought as *objectively relative* will be discussed. "Objective relativism" is an expression that A. E. Murphy coined, and a singularly successful one in encapsulating the Deweyan position.

2.1. Interaction and the Separation of Matter and Form

In *Art as Experience,* as he reaches back into history to discuss the problem of matter and form, Dewey uses the very terminology that is of interest to us. The passages in question offer some instances of his growing willingness to speak of form in a positive rather than a pejorative manner, and thus present an appropriate point of departure for investigating his reconstructed view of forms.

The inherent limitation of the context in which the discussion occurs is that it is concerned with artistic experience, or *techne*. But, as we shall see immediately, the manner in which Dewey's analysis

is presented could apply to *physis* as well; we shall see later that Dewey himself considers a generalized application of this sort defensible. The sections of central concern to my investigation deal with the separation of matter and form. According to Dewey, this separation is a serious error, whose roots can be traced to an improper understanding of the relationship of a creature and its environment. This is true both for those who emphasize form at the expense of matter and for those who stress matter at the expense of form.

> The sum of the whole discussion is that theories which separate matter and form, theories that strive to find a special locus in experience for each, are, in spite of their oppositions to one another, cases of the same fundamental fallacy. They rest upon separation of the live creature from the environment in which it lives. One school, one which becomes the "idealistic" school in philosophy when its implications are formulated, makes the separation in the interest of meanings or relations. The other school, the sensational-empiricist, makes the separation in behalf of the primacy of sense qualities [AE 136].

In an earlier chapter, we reviewed at length Dewey's analysis and criticism of these two schools.[14] What concerns us now is the elaboration of the doctrine of interaction which Dewey claims these other thinkers ignored.

2.2. Three Characterizations of Forms

In characterizing forms in Dewey's thought, there are three interconnected, somewhat overlapping points to be made, each of which simply emphasizes a different dimension of the analysis he has formulated. The first is that the failure to accept the primordial nature of the organism/environment interaction is the major cause of the mistaken isolation of form from matter. Dewey, in contrast to this view, holds that forms do not exist separately. They cannot have existence apart from the interaction of organism and environment. Secondly, forms are viewed as *results*, not as pre-existing givens. Finally, another way of stating this is to say that forms and materials are correlative.

A. If Dewey believes that the separation of form and matter is erroneous, and rests on a single fallacy, then we can expect a state-

ment that if the fallacy is recognized and overcome, the source of the union of form and matter will be made manifest. Dewey does not disappoint us. He explicitly connects the inseparability of form and matter with the organism/environment interaction:

> Since the ultimate cause of the union of form and matter in experience is the intimate relation of undergoing and doing in interaction of a live creature with the world of nature and man, the theories, which separate matter and form, have their ultimate source in neglect of this relation. . . . There *are* enemies of the union of form and matter. But they proceed from our own limitations; they are not intrinsic [AE 137–38].

With this quotation, we begin the reconstruction of the positive elements in Dewey's doctrine. The focus out of which it grows is the interaction emphasized in evolutionary thought. This interaction is the "cause" of the "union" of form and matter. But what exactly does Dewey mean by this union? We get a significant clue elsewhere in *Art as Experience* when he argues that the connection of form and matter does not mean that they are "identical." "It signifies that in the work of art they do not offer themselves as two distinct things: the work is formed matter" (AE 118–19). As is customary with him, Dewey is trying to avoid extremes here. If the isolation of form from matter is a mistake, the alternative is not their identification. Recalling the context out of which an analysis develops has significant implications in this instance. We have already seen how he criticized previous philosophers for isolating the results of analyses from the contexts which occasioned them.[15]

Dewey realizes that to speak intelligently about a work of art one has to deal with both the material out of which it is constructed and the way in which that material is arranged. Matter and form are distinguishable facets of an artwork. They are not identical because dealing with one alone would provide an insufficient, incomplete analysis. Yet if the context out of which discussion about art grows, the actual concrete works themselves, is always kept in mind, the temptation to treat the two aspects, separated in consciousness, as actually separate things will be minimized. Form and matter can be distinguished, but they are not distinct, separately existing things.

This description is, of course, simply a beginning, and one restricted to works of art. Yet in its essentials it can be transferred to

the realm of *physis* as well. That is to say, the position can be viewed as one of truly ontological generality, applying to all beings. It is possible to recognize all entities as formed entities in the sense just indicated by Dewey. This extension is supported by the fundamental assumption he is working with, the interaction of organism and environment. This is a model which came originally from nature, and which Dewey extended to the aesthetic realm. But the influence of the environment as Dewey describes it above is more readily understandable if it is viewed in terms of natural beings.

This is especially so if we consider the embryological model which I am offering as complementary to Dewey's emphasis on *techne*. In this case, the manner in which an entity organizes itself by using the materials of its surroundings gives rise to an organized, formed entity. An existent cannot develop in isolation from its environment. What a particular organism becomes is a product of a variety of factors including its own energies and the possibilities and limitations of its surroundings. It does not, it cannot, become what it is in isolation from what goes on around it. The occasion for novelty resides precisely in this fact.[16] Because of this, Dewey's stress on the union of form and matter within the context of organism/environment interaction is as well illustrated in *physis* as in Dewey's own selection from *techne*.

B. The second point, that forms must be seen as results, is fully consistent with an analysis that regards the interaction of organism and environment as a fundamental ontological fact. Individual forms are not given as pre-existent data which antedate the actual growth and development of a particular entity. Form is the product of the kind of interaction Dewey wishes to make a central concern of philosophy. "Interaction of environment with organism is the source, direct or indirect, of all experience and from the environment come those checks, resistances, furtherances, equilibria, which, when they meet with the energies of the organism in appropriate ways, constitute form" (AE 152). Let us underscore some of the more significant terminology in this passage. There is, in the first place, the emphasis on environment/organism interaction, which is said to be the source of all experience. Form is then described as flowing from this source; it is said to be *constituted* or *arrived at*. Dewey does not admit any essence hidden behind or within the accidental qualities of an entity. That is the static view of reality.

On this view, a being "really" is of a certain kind despite the vicissitudes and alterations it may suffer. Dewey is arguing, on the other hand, that what something "really is" is a function of the changes, alterations, and reactions to surroundings that it undergoes. It is what it is because of them, not in spite of them.

With form now the result of environment/organism interaction, the untenability of the separation of form and matter becomes clearer. Forms cannot be treated in isolation from the material constituents of beings. The material becomes formed in a certain way as the result of a variety of circumstances. Form is not independent of the being's activities. It is also not independent of human intervention, which may elicit a variety of forms from certain materials. This was the procedure undertaken by the professional breeders with whom Darwin was so impressed.

c. If forms are to be treated neither as identical to nor as isolated from the materials they qualify, then form and material should be treated as a correlative pairing. In other words, there is no theory of "forms," strictly speaking, in Dewey. They do not exist, do not make sense, apart from entities. This kind of analysis results from Dewey's elimination of other possibilities. We have already seen that he rejects the hypostatization and isolation of form and matter. We have also seen that he does not consider them to be identical. This leaves only the middle path of treating them in a bipolar fashion.

Dewey's explicit recognition of this fact comes in a different context, that of *physis*. While discussing "structure" in *Experience and Nature*, Dewey provides an analysis which is helpful to us here. His aim is a familiar one: the rejection of analyses in which a structure is dealt with in isolation from the being whose structure it is.

> Structure is constancy of means, of things used for consequences, not of things taken by themselves or absolutely. Structure is what makes construction possible and cannot be discovered or defined except in some realized construction, construction being, of course, an evident order of changes. The isolation of structure from the changes whose stable ordering it is, renders it mysterious—something that is metaphysical in the popular sense of the word, a kind of ghostly queerness [EN 64–65].

What Dewey says here about structure can also be said of form. Form is always to be interpreted as "form of," as an integral factor to be recognized in an ever-fluctuating individual. Only when this

analysis is overlooked do structures and forms become "metaphysical" in the negative, pejorative sense of the word. On this kind of analysis, if form were to be described grammatically, it would be a verb rather than a noun. Entities are formed, but form itself does not exist as a separate being. Form, therefore, is viewed as having a relational or complementary kind of existence. That is to say, there must always be an existent whose formation is actually going on. The error of previous philosophers had been to isolate the material constituents of a being from its form. This is but an instance of the fallacy of selective emphasis, discussed in the previous chapter.[17]

2.3. The Dynamic Interpretation of Beings

If form is unreservedly identified with a static view of existence, then it is futile to attempt any reconstruction of a doctrine of forms in Dewey. But form is not necessarily wedded to a static view, and the doctrine of interaction provides the context in which a dynamic interpretation of form can be developed.

Dewey's position, in more traditional metaphysical terminology, is that beings are beings-in-interaction. This is a fundamental, primordial datum of existence. In other words, whatever is is somehow in interaction with other beings. This interaction, Dewey has argued specifically in a passage quoted earlier, "constitutes" form.[18] Since form is always form-of something, and since that something is part of an organism/environment interaction, form will be dependent on the continued interactivity exhibited therein. Formation, in this context, is an ongoing process. The entity continuously sustains itself by means of the environment. If the organism proper were the sole source of form, if being were not being-in-interaction, then the static view would be comprehensible, and accepting form as a static, inherent, unchangeable factor of organization would be possible. By developing an ontology of being-in-interaction, Dewey is able with great consistency to suggest a view in which due attention is paid to both process and form.

Dewey also approaches this issue from the perspective of "order," a term he uses to express the formative activity of beings. Order, he argues, needs to be continually constructed and is constantly being built up in the external world, in a process he calls "admirable in a world constantly threatened with disorder." Natural beings, he goes

on to say, "can go on living only by taking advantage of whatever order exists about them, incorporating it into themselves" (AE 20). Dewey may be using different terminology here, but the thrust of his remarks remains the same. The aspects of change (disorder) and permanence (order) are blended together in such a way that both must be considered fundamental. There is order, but its source is not to be found outside the processes of existence. It results from the synthesizing capacities of each being.

Process, change, activity, and flux are very real in the universe that surrounds us. But Dewey is careful to qualify this recognition as only a partial view of the way things are. As fundamental as those dynamic elements may be, the presence of stabilizing factors (forms) must not be overlooked:

> There is in nature, even below the level of life, something more than mere flux and change. Form is arrived at whenever a stable, even though moving, equilibrium is reached. Changes interlock and sustain one another. Wherever there is this coherence there is endurance. Order is not imposed from without but is made out of the relations of harmonious interactions that energies bear to one another [AE 20].

There is no way of telling how much time Dewey spent drafting these sentences, but they are a masterly example of balance in illustrating the point I am making. Each of them incorporates and successfully illustrates the tensional, resonating aspect of form as Dewey conceives it. When he employs a term connoting stability, "equilibrium," he qualifies it with a dynamic adjective, "moving." When, on the other hand, he makes use of a term with connotations of fluidity, "change," he qualifies it with the stabilizing verb "interlock." "Coherence" and "endurance" imply continuity through change. In the last sentence, "order," implying stability, is coupled with "energies," a term connoting change and process.

In *Experience and Nature* Dewey fastens on the term "stable" to express the structured, ordered dimensions of existence. Chapter 2 of that text is entitled "Nature as Precarious and as Stable," and its intent is to emphasize the importance of recognizing both dimensions as "fundamentally significant for the formation of a naturalistic metaphysics" (EN 47). In choosing "stable" as his technical term, Dewey is emphasizing endurance in tension with change, and

expressing his position that regularity and equilibrium are facts of existence, but that they are not rigid, fixed, and eternal. For Dewey everything that exists is temporally conditioned.

One indication of this is his qualification of the term "stable" with the adverb "relatively." The idealist's doctrine of Absolute Experience may be erroneous, he asserts, but it is a symbol of two facts, one of which is pertinent to the point I am trying to make. "One is the ineradicable union in nature of the relatively stable and the relatively contingent" (EN 56). If, for some readers, "stable" implies that which is absolutely unchangeable, rigidly unalterable, even through the course of history, then Dewey's position would be misunderstood. To lessen the chance of this, Dewey explicitly qualifies "stable" in the above manner.

In another instance, he provides an analysis that can leave no doubt as to his intentions.

> The stablest thing we can speak of is not free from conditions set to it by other things. That even the solid earth mountains, the emblems of constancy, appear and disappear like the clouds is an old theme of moralists and poets. . . . A thing may endure *secula seculorum* and yet not be everlasting; it will crumble before the gnawing tooth of time, as it exceeds a certain measure. Every existence is an event [EN 63].

Time and change are factors that must be considered as integrally implicated in all existences. This does not mean that stabilities of all kinds are to be denied. But it does mean that they must be reinterpreted accordingly. Other terms besides "stable" might have served Dewey just as well. I can think of "enduring" and "persisting," both of which indicate a temporally qualified permanence. Whatever term is preferred, the important fact to keep in mind is that, for Dewey, the "stable" is always conditioned by temporality. Because of this he refers to entities as "events." Just exactly what he means by this term, and how it relates to the question of forms, is the next topic to be considered.

3. CATEGORIAL ANALYSIS

Events are, as Santayana called them, Dewey's "metaphysical elements."[19] Dewey has not provided us with a text that explicitly sets forth his categories. Nonetheless, every serious ontological thinker

possesses a categorial schema, and Dewey is no exception. The vocabulary in which philosophers choose to carry on their discourse reveals to a great degree their ontological assumptions. And the most general term used to describe beings, or existences, is of the highest significance in this respect.

Aristotle appears to have been the first philosopher to list explicitly his categories.[20] An Aristotelian category, as Sterling Lamprecht has expressed it, "is a basic concept which the world around us forces us to use in our analysis of it."[21] This means that a strong ontological dimension suffuses the doctrine of categories. If we wish to deal accurately, truthfully, with the world of our experience, then we must employ concepts consistent with the kind of world it is, not ones arbitrarily chosen. The most basic of these concepts are the categories.[22] Lamprecht expands his explanation:

> Among the terms of discourse we use about the world, some are more basic than others. The term *man*, for example, is not a category; for we do not need to use such a term in analyzing the stars. Nor is the term *star* a category; for we do not need to use it in analyzing man. But some terms are requisite to any and every analysis of any and every existing subject-matter. Men and stars are both substances, that is, concrete, individual things. And substance is a category; for every investigation we make of the world about us proves to be an investigation, if not about a man or a star, about some such concrete individual thing or things.[23]

Dewey, like Aristotle, elects a fundamental category, one that is requisite for "any and every analysis of any and every existing subject-matter." Unlike Aristotle, however, Dewey does not believe it to be "substance." He chooses, rather, "event." As we saw earlier, Dewey argues that "every existence is an event," and this means that, whereas star and man are both substances for Aristotle, they are both events for Dewey.

3.1. Events

Three questions immediately present themselves. Why does Dewey select this particular term? What does it mean? What relationship does this fundamental category bear to the doctrine of formed entities?

The discussion of Dewey's dynamic interpretation of forms in the

previous section provides the kind of context in which his use of "event" can be understood. We saw there that Dewey is eager to portray nature as an inextricably blended array of the stable and the precarious. To emphasize his recognition that both aspects must be taken into account Dewey chooses to describe existences as events. The crucial factor conditioning all existences, making them both stable and precarious, is *time*. By using "event" Dewey wishes to indicate that, in more traditional terminology, beings are beings-in-time. The temporal dimension does not merely provide a neutral medium in which events occur. It enters into their very constitution.

> Since existence is historic it can be known or understood only as each portion is distinguished and related. For knowledge "cause" and "effect" alike have a partial and truncated being. It is as much a part of the real being of atoms that they give rise in time, under increasing complication of relationships, to qualities of blue and sweet, pain and beauty, as that they have at a cross-section of time extension, mass, or weight.
>
> The problem is neither psychological nor epistemological. It is metaphysical or existential. It is whether existence consists of events, or is possessed of temporal quality, characterized by beginning, process and ending [EN 91–92].

What Dewey is arguing here is the insufficiency of a strictly synchronic analysis for fully understanding the complex characteristics of existents. New properties, traits, or efficacies may eventuate as results of processes of development or through acquisition of new relationships, and Dewey wants to emphasize that they are every bit as real as the antecedent conditions that made them possible. Because existents are events—that is, because they are "characterized by beginning, process and ending"[24]—to understand them properly both synchronic and diachronic approaches are necessary.

For Dewey, events are the real existents of the world.[25] If forms are to be discussed, they will have to be spoken of in the context of the metaphysical elements, the events, not as metaphysical elements themselves. This would then reduce the temptation to describe forms in terms implying the rigidly static or fixed.

If we take each of the three traits of forms mentioned earlier, we can indicate how the category of events both reinforces Dewey's

analysis and lessens the possibility of the view he rejects. The first and third points are simply the negative and positive ways of saying the same thing: forms must not be treated in isolation; they must be viewed as correlative to materials. Just as Dewey had argued with respect to works of art that form and matter were not distinct things, but rather that the work was formed matter, so we may now say that, on a more generalized level, events are formed matter. An event, whether it be a bridge, a battle, or a flower, involves both material constituents and an organization of those constituents. Events are the fundamental existents. Forms have meaning only in reference to them. They do not possess any ontological status in isolation from the event.

The category of event also dovetails nicely with Dewey's conviction that forms result from, or are constituted by, the organism/environment interaction. We saw that "event" is meant to emphasize the diachronic dimension in existence. Events are eventuations, things which come about through the process of interactions in time. Events that are living, or conscious, for example, have not existed *ab initio*. New species and variations of species have been produced in nature. These novel productions are, in a very real sense, formed. The forms are elicited from the events; they are not given prior to them. Since events are conditioned by evolutionary developments, so are forms. By stressing the ontological priority of events, we can grasp more clearly what Dewey's understanding of forms entails. An event is a concrete existent conditioned by temporal processes, and developed in the context of environment/organism interactions. Event thus epitomizes two essential Deweyan assumptions. It is the events which, in the Deweyan scheme, can be spoken of as formed. Forms do not, in the strictest sense, exist. Events do, but they are formed.

As I have interpreted it, event is Dewey's version, duly revised in terms of scientific progress, of Aristotle's category of substance. He also fastens on another of Aristotle's categories, one whose prominence can be traced back to Dewey's Hegelian phase: the category of relations. During his idealistic period, Dewey had emphasized the importance of relations as a weapon in his opposition to the empiricist tradition. The prominence of relations remains evident throughout his naturalistic writings.

3.2. Relations

There are two areas in which the topic of relations has a special
bearing on forms. One, obviously, is the organism/environment
relationship; the other, the particular relationship of parts in a
single entity. When the topic of form was introduced, I pointed out
that such a philosophical position usually depends on an empirical
fact: namely, that entities are complex.[26] In one crucial sense, form
requires this sort of complexity. It implies the organization of the
multiplicity in some uniquely ordered manner. One of Dewey's
definitions of form in *Art as Experience* indicates explicitly the importance of relations in understanding forms. "No material can be
adapted to an end, be it that of use as spoon or carpet, until raw
material has undergone a change that shapes the parts and that
arranges these parts with reference to one another with a view to the
purpose of the whole. Hence the object has form in a definitive
sense" (AE 121). Taking an artwork as a particular kind of event,
Dewey is saying that it is formed in a certain way because its constituent parts are *related* in a definite manner. This relationship,
Dewey asserts, is a directional one. The parts are related in view of
an *end* or purpose.

The quotation just cited is narrowly situated in the realm of
techne. This prompts the question whether the analysis of forms in
terms of end and relations can be extended to *physis* as well. Certainly, the term "purpose," implying an outside planning agent, is
not at all congenial to Dewey's understanding of nature. But relation is a topic that can more readily be spoken of in a generalized
sense, one applicable to both *techne* and *physis*. We have just seen
how one explanation of form is based on the recognition of relations. The first point to be noted in this respect is that even though
the discussion applies to art, Dewey's analysis is fully consistent with
his dynamic view of forms. In describing relations, he is careful to
distinguish between a static, non-relational positing of parts or individuals and a dynamic, energetic relationship.

> There is an old formula for beauty in nature and art: Unity in
> variety. Everything depends on how the preposition "in" is under-
> stood. There may be many articles in a box, many figures in a
> single painting, many coins in one pocket, and many documents in
> a safe. The unity is extraneous and the many are unrelated. The

significant point is that unity and manyness are always of this sort or approximate it when the unity of the object or scene is morphological and static. The formula has meaning only when its terms are understood to concern a relation of energies [AE 166].

There are several topics of interest in this passage. The general context for the discussion is, first of all, the subject of art. Nonetheless, Dewey makes clear from the outset that his analysis is of a formula that applies to both nature and art. This is significant if we are in search of an ontological position, one that applies to beings as such, and not to a restricted kind of existent. Secondly, we get a definitive statement that relations have significance only where there is activity. Real relations occur, Dewey is suggesting, not when there is a merely static or geometrical coordination, but when there is a coordination or cooperation of energies.

A pattern in Dewey's thinking is beginning to emerge at this point. The negative impact the doctrine of evolution had on the static world-view has already been discussed, and the association of the doctrine of form with this static view has been touched on. Earlier in this chapter we studied some of the indications that Dewey has provided concerning a revised doctrine of forms. The fact that this view has to stress flux and change was emphasized at that time. What may not have been stressed, but is equally important, is that the path from a dynamic interpretation of reality to a doctrine of formed entities is not all that difficult to travel. The movements and interactions of elements and energies, their fusion into some kind of order, are the continuous creation of formed events. In discussing the question of substance and form, Dewey speaks of "the inherent tendency of sense to expand, to come into intimate relations with other things than itself, and thus to take on form because of its own movement—instead of passively waiting to have form imposed on it" (AE 129).

Nowhere is this emphasis on the connection between form and process more distinctly stated than in his description of relations. In dealing with these, as we have seen, he is explicit about the inherent necessity of energies, of activities.

Form was defined in terms of relations and esthetic form in terms of completeness of relations within a chosen medium. But "relation" is an ambiguous word. In philosophic discourse it is used to

designate a connection instituted in thought. It then signifies
something indirect, something purely intellectual, even logical.
But "relation" in its idiomatic usage denotes something direct and
active, something dynamic and energetic. It fixes attention upon
the way things bear upon one another, their clashes and unitings,
the way they fulfill and frustrate, promote and retard, excite and
inhibit one another.

Intellectual relations subsist in propositions; they state the connection of terms with one another. In art, as in nature and in life,
relations are modes of interaction [AE 139].

In the earlier passage dealing with relations, Dewey had contrasted
his active interpretation with the static view. Here he contrasts the
dynamic position with another foe, a mentalistic interpretation of
relations. Dewey is explicitly extending his understanding of relations beyond what had been prevalent since the time of the empiricists. Relations, he is claiming, are not merely mental. They are real
because entities do actually "bear upon one another." They exist
wherever there is actual interaction; and this interaction, Dewey is
careful to insist, exists in nature and life as well as in art. This last
point is one of the reasons why the discussion of relations has been
focused on. For in this passage as in the earlier one, Dewey quite
clearly admits that his analysis can be extended beyond the realm
of art. If this is so, if, as Dewey says, relations are analogous in art,
life, and nature, then his position has ontological significance.

3.3. Categories Apply to Both *Techne* and *Physis*

In the three books which now concern us, Dewey appears to have
been attempting to do what has always been the aim of metaphysicians. He was developing a terminology (experience, organism/
environment interaction, events, energies, relations) generalized
enough to be applicable to the different kinds of beings. Such a
procedure is controversial, of course. Critics who have little understanding of metaphysics, and thus no sympathy for the discipline,
are quick to reject this kind of undertaking. Richard Rorty, for
instance, judges Dewey's endeavor to be a futile one. "Again, only
someone who thought that a proper account of the 'generic traits'
of existence could cross the line between physiology and sociology—
between causal processes and the self-conscious beliefs they make

possible—would have written the chapter in *Experience and Nature* called 'Nature, Life, and Body-Mind,' or have attempted to develop a jargon that would apply equally to plants, nervous systems, and physicists." Rorty goes on to say that this "return to Lockean modes of thought" ignores an established philosophical insight: "that nothing is to be gained from running together the vocabularies in which we describe the causal antecedents of knowledge with those in which we offer justifications of our claims to knowledge."[27]

Dewey would surely stand justifiably accused if he were seeking in physiology or even in psychology justifications for knowledge claims. But is this what Dewey is attempting? Is the enterprise of metaphysics, as the cognizance of the generic traits of existence, meant to provide the sort of justification for knowledge claims Rorty refers to? The answer is an unequivocal "no." Rorty's complaint is based on a misreading of what Dewey is trying to do. Dewey is not trying to develop a formula that would allow a clear-cut manner for justifying knowledge claims. He is certainly not engaging in a "Lockean" type of genetic explanation. Ever since his studies with George Morris, Dewey had incessantly criticized those thinkers who attempted the very sort of justification Rorty accuses him of seeking. Dewey ridiculed those thinkers who thought it important to ask and answer the question "Is knowledge possible?" Dewey's own interests in this area were confined to a descriptive analysis of *How We Think* (the title he gave to one of his books). Dewey wrote extensively on education because he was concerned that experimental methods of inquiry be acquired on a widespread basis. The existence and effectiveness of knowledge is a fact for Dewey. He does not share the Kantian assumptions which, by making the very existence of knowledge claims problematic, require the elaboration of justifications. He simply seeks to describe and secure the most appropriate method for gaining knowledge. He calls this method, as we have already seen, an "experimental logic."

The "jargon" Rorty criticizes has little to do with traditional epistemological issues that dominated philosophical discussions in the modern (post-Cartesian) era. Indeed, Dewey's significance as a living philosophical presence lies precisely in the manner in which his metaphysics undermines, and thus overcomes, the assumptions of modernity. Dewey's formulation of a novel terminology is part of this attempt to revise the metaphysical description of nature in

light of scientific discoveries, especially evolution. When he claims, for example, that "existence consists of events," he is arguing that temporality is an important factor for the "plants, nervous systems, and physicists" Rorty mentioned. He needs to emphasize this point because it accurately describes natural existence and had been widely overlooked in earlier philosophies.

Dewey does develop a terminology (not a "jargon") which is applicable both to *techne* and to *physis*. Such a procedure is indeed "metaphysical," but not in the sense of striving to identify what is beyond the physical. Like Heidegger, Dewey realized that only by a radical reworking of the tradition could philosophy break away from the now sterile generative ideas of modernity. Such a radical reworking involves addressing questions about the nature of existence which have always been the province of metaphysics.

Art as Experience can be considered a crucial text for understanding Dewey's metaphysics precisely because in it he developed analyses of this general sort, which can be transposed and applied to natural beings with little or no modification. Yet there are statements conflicting with this view which must be considered if an accurate interpretation of Dewey is to be presented. Essentially, these statements have Dewey asserting that the Greeks, as well as the objective idealists, transferred the traits of aesthetic experience to cognitive experience, in a mistaken procedure that limited not only the success but the very possibility of the experimental method. If the beings of nature are seen as fixed, final, and consummatory, then cognition is limited to contemplation, and experimentation is viewed as a violation of the fixed structures of existence.

In "Experience, Knowledge and Value: A Rejoinder," Dewey with great clarity exposes the error in question: "With respect to these issues, I call attention to the fact that in earlier writings I pointed out that the very type of philosophy Mr. Pepper attributes to me arose historically precisely from the fact that Greek thinkers took categories which *are* applicable to works of art and to their enjoyed perception and then extended them to the whole universe where they are not applicable."[28] *Experience and Nature* makes the same point in a more succinct manner. "In the classic philosophy of Greece the picture of the world that was constructed on an artistic model proffered itself as being the result of intellectual study" (EN 76). What implications for the present study are to be drawn from

statements like these? Is Dewey arguing in one instance something he denies in another? I do not think so. If we understand properly what Dewey is saying here, we can accept it as valid, without, at the same time, sacrificing a belief that certain characteristics apply to all beings, whether natural or artistic.

To grasp the real force of the objection exemplified in the two passages just quoted, we have to recall a topic discussed in the third chapter, the ubiquity of the knowledge relation.[29] Dewey has called this one of the major errors in philosophy. It involves taking the results of one kind of experience and believing that this gives us true knowledge of *the* real. As far as he is concerned, the scientifically based view of mechanistic materialism is an example of an erroneous position based on just this fallacy. The results of classical physics are thought to provide a privileged knowledge of the world as it *really* is. The results of refined noetic experience are interpreted as exhausting the characteristics of the natural world.

Dewey states that whereas our interests are dominated by scientific and economic concerns, the Greeks were "as much dominated by the esthetic characters of experienced objects" (EN 75). Because of this, the Greek version of the extension of mechanics to the whole of reality was the extension of aesthetic characters—wholeness, finality, completeness, stability—to the natural realm. Just as Dewey identified the ubiquity of the knowledge relation as a basic error of modern philosophy, he could have suggested that a ubiquity of the aesthetic relation was a special error in Greek thought. What he objects to in this instance is the *wholesale* transference of characters recognized as valid in art to the entire realm of beings. The result, as he perceives it, is the fixed world, unsuitable to experimentation, against which he so vehemently argues. The stability of natural beings is not identical to the stability of a statue. It would obviously be a mistake to confuse the two realms. But it is still possible to see, as Dewey does, that stability has a place in both.

Just as nature, though not wholly a machine, possesses a mechanical dimension, so nature is not a product of art, but has an aesthetic dimension. Dewey sets this position down in the early pages of *Experience and Nature*. "If experience actually presents esthetic and moral traits, then these traits may also be supposed to reach down into nature, and to testify to something that belongs to nature as truly as does the mechanical structure attributed to it in physical

science" (EN 13).[30] In light of such a direct assertion, the statements that could be used to contradict my interpretation must be read carefully in terms of their contexts, especially the position Dewey is arguing against.[31] It is true that he objects to the Greek extension of aesthetic traits to the natural realm. But it is the identification of the natural and the aesthetic which Dewey judges to be improper. There is nothing in his criticism of the Greek view to suggest that certain generic traits cannot apply to both natural and artistic entities.

All this is significant because I have thus far based my reading of Dewey to a great degree on his book *Art as Experience*. Because the remarks made there about forms can be generalized into a defensible ontological position, I have attempted to blend the discussion found in that text with an analysis of two ontological categories central to Dewey's presentation of his philosophical outlook: event and relation.

4. OBJECTIVE RELATIVISM AND FORMS

The previous discussion has given indications justifying the extension of some aspects of aesthetic experience to nature. In other words, there are continuities between the two realms, and Dewey freely admits them. I have concentrated in particular on his descriptions of forms in *techne*, and have argued that these descriptions can be extended to *physis*. The objection might legitimately be raised that, although Dewey admits continuities between *techne* and *physis*, there is no solid documentation that forms are among them. The present section will provide the textual justification for such an extension.

I shall undertake this discussion in the context of "objective relativism," an expression Arthur E. Murphy suggested to illustrate the originality of Dewey's approach. Murphy wanted to point out that in Dewey's novel orientation the old opposition of subjectivity and objectivity no longer successfully describes the actual situation of the natural world. The view that held to this opposition was another of the traditional philosophical commonplaces Dewey described as being dissolved as a result of scientific advances, especially Darwinism.[32]

Since Dewey describes forms in terms of the arrangement of parts

or means in light of an end or purpose,[33] there would appear to be some justification for arguing that his discussion of forms applies only to *techne* and not to *physis*: namely, that the introduction of the term "purpose" might seem to indicate that he considers forms subject-dependent. Since this factor, the artist fabricating according to a preconceived aim, is absent from nature, could it not be said that forms too are absent from nature? Murphy's doctrine of "objective relativism" is particularly helpful in seeing why this analysis is mistaken and how Dewey explicitly admits form in both nature and art. For if the very framework of subjective *vs.* objective no longer holds, then it is doubtful that Dewey will assert the subjectivity of forms even in *techne*.

Let us begin by understanding just what Murphy means by "objective relativism." The expression was chosen precisely because it combines two terms traditionally thought to be incompatible. According to previous philosophical analyses, either beings and their properties existed objectively or their existence was relative to the observing subject. Thus, in one tradition, primary qualities were interpreted as being objective, but secondary ones were relative. An unbridgeable gap separated the two. The originality of Dewey's position, according to Murphy, is that it cannot be restricted to the traditional framework.

> Its [the expression "objective relativism"] constituent terms have unpleasant and seemingly misleading associations, but their union in a single doctrine does seem to indicate fairly well what is most original and most controversial in the theories to be considered. It attempts to unite two propositions which have uniformly been taken to be incompatible. (a) The objective facts of the world of nature and of reality are the very "apparent" and relative happenings directly disclosed to us in perception. (b) In spite (or because) of such objectivity such happenings remain ultimately and inescapably relative.[34]

Murphy is offering here an analysis analogous to the one I undertook in my discussion of "events." Events, I argued, do not exist apart from a context or outside of the temporal sequence. Their emergence and character are relative to both their environment and the manner in which they alter through time.

What Murphy wishes to stress is that objectivity does not imply a substance of the Lockean kind, changeless and timeless.[35] Events are

both relative and objective. The only way to understand this position accurately is to recall the primacy of the organism/environment interaction for Dewey. All events are thus relational. This is what Murphy wants to emphasize by the term "relative." "The fact of relativity is here no other than the fact of relatedness."[36] An event is never a separate, autonomous existent. It is not objective in this sense. It is always context-dependent. "As an event, the situation is caught up in a whole network of interactions and circumstances, without which it would not be what it is."[37]

A similar analysis holds with regard to temporal relationships. Murphy argues that, for Dewey, time *makes a difference*. "If time is to be real, it must make a difference to existences themselves."[38] Events are thus seen to be fully context-dependent and so, in Murphy's term, "relative." But they are not subject- or mind-dependent. They are then, in traditional terminology, "objective." Within the older framework either objects were "objective" or they were relative to a knower or perceiver. In the new analysis, events are both objective and relative. They are relative to their environment, an environment that may or may not include a percipient.

In the new Deweyan framework, the terms "subject" and "object," legacies from epistemology-centered philosophy, have to be abandoned or radically redefined. In Dewey's metaphysics of existence, there are no "subjects" defined as exclusively rational beings that confront "objects" with the aim of reflecting them accurately. When Dewey entitled his Carus lectures "Experience and Nature," he was seeking a terminology which would allow him to break away from a universe of discourse dominated by "subject" and "object." He was trying, as Murphy indeed recognized, to develop a metaphysics of objective relativism.

4.1. Forms as Objectively Relative in *Techne* and *Physis*

If Murphy's analysis is accurate, then we should find passages in Dewey in which form is described as objectively relative. This should be true even in the field of *techne* where the subjective/objective dichotomy would no longer apply. Thus, the possible objection that the description of forms in art is subjective, and so not applicable to nature, would be circumvented. *Art as Experience*

provides a statement framed in traditional terminology that quite decisively shows that for Dewey forms are not subjective.

> Many tangled problems, multifarious ambiguities, and historic controversies are involved in the question of the subjective and objective in art. Yet if the position that has been taken regarding form and substance is correct, there is at least one important sense in which form must be as objective as the material which it qualifies. If form emerges when raw materials are selectively arranged with reference to rendering an experience unified in movement to its intrinsic fulfillment, then surely objective conditions are controlling forces in the production of a work of art [AE 151].

This position is consistent with Dewey's attitude of recognizing the importance of the environment/organism interaction. No artist creates in the theological sense of *ex nihilo*. All artworks are conditioned by the plasticity, resiliency, and recalcitrance of the raw materials with which the artist begins. The resultant product is forged from these materials, and its form is thus dependent to some extent on the elements of construction. Form cannot be haphazardly imposed upon materials; it must be consistent with the possibilities of those materials.[39]

This kind of analysis serves at once as a convenient backdrop for the present discussion and as a bridge to the discussion of forms outside works of art. It prepares the way for an acceptance of forms in the sphere of *physis* where there can be no question of a subject-dependent origin. Since Dewey does recognize the objectively relative character of forms in works of art, it is not surprising to find that he extends this objective relativism to the realm of *physis*. In so doing, he provides us with a more thorough characterization of what he means by "form."

> In a word, form is not found exclusively in objects labeled works of art. Wherever perception has not been blunted and perverted, there is an inevitable tendency to arrange events and objects with reference to the demands of complete and unified perception. Form is a character of every experience that is *an* experience. Art in its specific sense enacts more deliberately and fully the conditions that effect this unity. *Form may then be defined as the operation of forces that carry the experience of an event, object, scene, and situation to its own integral fulfillment.* The connection of

form with substance is thus inherent, not imposed from without. It marks the matter of an experience that is carried to consummation [AE 142].

Obviously, the most crucial dimension of this citation is the expanded and explicit definition of form. Since it comes after his admission that forms are not discovered exclusively in art, we expect a definition that is generalized enough to find application in all beings and not in conflict with the more restricted one presented earlier.[40] Yet there are some differences between the two. The earlier definition argued that objects are formed when "raw material has undergone a change that shapes the parts and arranges these parts with reference to one another with a view to the purpose of the whole." The emphasis in this description of forms fell on the "raw material," the part-to-whole relationship, and the purpose for that relationship. This definition is especially conducive to application within *techne* as the examples Dewey used, a rug and a spoon, indicate.

In the passage now under discussion, none of these elements is explicitly mentioned. They have not been abandoned, but an alteration in emphasis has meant a more generalized expression on Dewey's part. Instead of dealing with raw materials, Dewey prefers in this instance to mention items that imply a material constituent of some sort, "events," "objects," "scene," and "situation." By dealing with the "operation of forces," Dewey has shifted the emphasis to process and activity. We must keep in mind that Dewey is constantly refuting the static view of reality, and since form is often associated with this view, he is careful to point out that his is a dynamic doctrine of forms. Form has to be seen as an outcome, a result.

By using the term "experience" Dewey has introduced the importance of the environment/organism interaction to the understanding of form. Experience is a pivotal term in this quotation, and to understand it fully, we have to be clear on how Dewey himself understands this word. *Experience and Nature* quite appropriately is the source for Dewey's clearest characterizations of experience. "It is not experience which is experienced, but nature—stones, plants, animals, diseases, health, temperature, electricity, and so on. Things interacting in certain ways *are* experience; they are what is experienced. Linked in certain other ways with another natural ob-

ject—the human organism—they are *how* things are experienced as well" (EN 12–13). The most important portion of this passage is the clause asserting that "things interacting in certain ways *are* experience," for it indicates that in using the word "experience" in defining forms, Dewey wishes to stress the contextual situation of "event," "object," "scene," and "situation." Each is involved in a process of activity in its environment. None is an isolated existent.

Finally, there is the consideration of the telic dimension. In the earlier quotation, this was described in anthropomorphic terms as "purpose." This word has now been abandoned. In its place is another anthropomorphic, but less mentalistic, expression, "integral fulfillment." The change is significant. "Purpose" is still caught somewhat in the subjective–objective bifurcation. "Integral fulfillment" points rather to an objectively relative situation. The subject-dependent orientation of "purpose" has disappeared. At the same time, "integral fulfillment" indicates a procedure of synthesizing which can occur only in relation to the context in which an existent finds itself.

Each of these key terms, "forces," "experience," and "fulfillment," is linked in the quotation by the verb "carry." This is used to indicate the spatial and the temporal relationships integral to an experience, relationships on which the fulfillment ultimately depends. By using "carry" Dewey emphasizes at once activity and directionality, both central to his understanding of form. This passage not only incorporates all we have thus far learned about Dewey's thoughts on form, but expands the notion to a level of ontological generality.

5. SUMMARY

"Events" are the basic ontological elements in Dewey's thought. If forms are to be discussed, they are to be considered, not as events, but as implicated in the events. "Relation" is another ontological category of importance for Dewey. All events are involved in relations with their environments, and varied relationships can lead to real novelty. Forms result whenever relationships lead to an end or fulfillment. Implicated in all beings, forms can be spoken of both in *techne* and in *physis*. There is no conflict between an ontology

that recognizes forms and one that stresses the reality of change. Forms can be defined in terms of process and activity; they are "objectively relative."

NOTES

1. "In his naturalism, his pluralism, his logical and social empiricism, his realism, his natural teleology, his ideas of potentiality and actuality, contingency and regularity, qualitatively diverse individuality—above all, in his thoroughgoing functionalism, his Aristotelian translation of all the problems of matter and form into a functional context, to say nothing of his basic social and ethical concepts—in countless vital matters he is nearer to the Stagirite than to any other philosopher" ("Dewey's Interpretation of the History of Philosophy," *Philosophy After Darwin: Chapters for* THE CAREER OF PHILOSOPHY, *Volume III, and Other Essays,* ed. Beth J. Singer (New York: Columbia University Press, 1977), p. 326. This essay was originally published in *Philosophy of John Dewey,* ed. Schilpp, pp. 77–102.

2. Randall, "Epilogue: The Nature of Naturalism," p. 366.

3. *Metaphysics* 1003A24–25, in *Basic Works of Aristotle,* ed. McKeon, p. 731.

4. "Experience and Existence: A Comment," *Philosophy and Phenomenological Research,* 9 (1948–1949), 713.

5. Woodbridge's article "Metaphysics," originally published in 1908, was reprinted in a collection of his essays entitled *Nature and Mind,* published by Columbia University Press in 1937. Schneider's comment is from his *History of American Philosophy,* p. 474; and the passage from Randall can be found in "Epilogue: The Nature of Naturalism," p. 365.

6. Walter Veazie recalls that while he was doing graduate study at Columbia, some of his fellow-students were trying to draw up a classification of recent philosophers. The philosopher closest to them, Dewey, was also the most difficult to categorize. Someone suggested asking him where he ought to be placed. " 'That is easy,' " replied Dewey, " 'with the revival of Greek philosophy' " ("John Dewey and the Revival of Greek Philosophy," 3).

7. In "Experience and Existence: A Comment," 713, where Dewey describes what he means by "metaphysics," he also admits that he has despaired of rescuing the term from its many untenable meanings. As a result, he resolved never to use the word "metaphysics" again. Nonetheless, he is careful to qualify this assertion by stating that even though the words "metaphysics" and "metaphysical" proved to be unfortunate choices "that which they were used to name is genuine and important."

8. (Chicago: Open Court, 1927), p. 5.

9. *Metaphysics of Naturalism*, p. 75.

10. In the 1940s, Dewey sought to restructure his technical terminology. It was during this time that he vowed to stop using the word "metaphysics" (see note 7 above). During this period, also, he suggested that "interaction" should be replaced by "transaction." See John Dewey and Arthur Bentley, "Interaction and Transaction," *The Journal of Philosophy*, 43 (1946), 505–17.

11. See chap. 2, sect. 2.

12. A category is interpreted here in the Aristotelian sense of fundamental predicate. The word κατηγορία means "predicate," and, as W. D. Ross explains it, "The categories are a list of the widest predicates which are predicable essentially of the various nameable entities, i.e. which tell us what kinds of entity at bottom they are." So, as Ross tells us, if we ask what Socrates is, "the ultimate, i.e. the most general, answer is 'a substance', just as, if we ask what red is, the ultimate answer is 'a quality'" (*Aristotle*, p. 23). This issue will be treated at greater length later on in this chapter.

13. See chap. 2, sect. 3.

14. See chap. 3, sects. 3.2 and 3.3.

15. See chap. 4, sect. 3.4.

16. As a support for his argument of descent with modification, Darwin emphasized the similarity of embryos within a group whose adult forms would be considered distinct species. If the embryos are similar, this was because, at one time, the varied species observable at present were part of a unique original stock. Through modification and variation, novel species arose. "As we have conclusive evidence that the breeds of the Pigeon are descended from a single wild species, I compared the young within twelve hours after being hatched; I carefully measured the proportions (but will not here give the details) of the beak, width of mouth, length of nostril and of eyelid, size of feet and length of leg, in the wild parent-species, in pouters, fantails, runts, barbs, dragons, carriers, and tumblers. Now some of these birds, when mature, differ in so extraordinary a manner in the length and form of beak, and in other characters, that they would certainly have been ranked as distinct genera if found in a state of nature. But when the nestling birds of these several breeds were placed in a row, though most of them could just be distinguished, the proportional differences in the above specified points were incomparably less than in the full-grown birds" (*Origin of Species*, p. 342).

17. See chap. 4, sect. 3.4.

18. See the quotation from AE 152.

19. "Dewey's Naturalistic Metaphysics," 677.

20. Ross, *Aristotle*, pp. 22–23.

21. *Our Philosophical Traditions: A Brief History of Philosophy in Western Civilization* (New York: Appleton-Century-Crofts, 1955), p. 59.

22. Dewey, however, uses the actual word "category" in a manner different from the one explained in the text. His understanding of the term is much broader than the sense in which I am using it. For him, "category" designates "the conceptions which are formulated in universal propositions." Any kind of universal concept, such as "machine" or "criminal law," is a category, providing, of course, that the classifications are understood operationally and not statically. See LTI 271–72. My own intentions in the present section are to seek out Dewey's "categories" as that term was understood by Aristotle. I am not investigating the manner in which Dewey uses the *word* "category."

23. *Philosophical Traditions*, p. 58.

24. Dewey has expressed this quite decisively in an article entitled "Time and Individuality." In so doing, he also emphasizes that process does not preclude form. "The conclusion which most naturally follows, without indulging in premature speculations, is that the principle of a developing career applies to all things in nature, as well as to human beings—that they are born, undergo qualitative changes, and finally die, giving place to other individuals. The idea of development applied to nature involves differences of forms and qualities as surely as it rules out breaches of continuity. The differences between the amoeba and the human organism are genuinely there even if we accept the idea of organic evolution of species. Indeed, to deny the reality of differences and their immense significance would be to deny the very idea of development" (ENF 236). This article was originally delivered as a lecture in 1938.

25. Dewey selected the term "event" not only for its temporal implications, but also because it encompasses "situations" as well as individuals.

26. See Introduction, sect. 1.

27. CP 81.

28. P. 550.

29. See chap. 3, sect. 3.2.

30. This position is reinforced in a later chapter. "If we take advantage of the word esthetic in a wider sense than that of application to the beautiful and ugly, esthetic quality, immediate, final or self-enclosed, indubitably characterizes natural situations as they empirically occur" (EN 82).

31. In a note appended to "Experience, Knowledge and Value: A Rejoinder" (p. 550*n*33), Dewey argues that biologists are now using, with justification, the kinds of terms common in aesthetic discourse: "It may be pointed out that a large group of biologists have reached, on what they take to be experimental scientific grounds, conclusions they

call *organismic,* as over against previous 'cellular' conceptions comparable in biology to old views of atomism in physics. I do not know whether Mr. Pepper would bring against them the kind of charge he brings against me [idealism], since they also use with great freedom words like *whole, integration,* etc. There is, it seems to me, as much warrant in the one case as in the other" (in *Philosophy of John Dewey,* ed. Schillp, p. 550n33).

32. See the discussion in chap. 2, sect. 2.1.

33. See above, sect. 3.2. The quotation in which the synonym "structure" is used also accentuates this relationship. See the sect. 2.2. quotation from EN 64–65.

34. *Reason and the Common Good: Selected Essays of Arthur E. Murphy,* edd. William H. Hay, Marcus G. Singer, and Arthur E. Murphy (Englewood Cliffs, N.J.: Prentice-Hall, 1963), p. 50. The article from which this quotation and the following ones are taken originally appeared as "Objective Relativism in Dewey and Whitehead," *The Philosophical Review,* 36 (1927), 121–44.

35. By making "substance" that unknown subject in which properties inhere, Locke effectively rules out the possibility that it can be understood relationally. "It is by such combinations of simple ideas, and nothing else, that we represent particular sorts of substances to ourselves; such are the ideas we have of their several species in our minds; and such only do we, by their specific names, signify to others v. g., man, horse, sun, water, iron; upon hearing which words everyone who understands the language, frames in his mind a combination of those several simple ideas which he has usually observed or fancied to exist together under that denomination; all which he supposes to rest in, and be, as it were, adherent to, that unknown common subject, which inheres not in anything else" (*An Essay Concerning Human Understanding* 23.5, in *English Philosophers from Bacon to Mill,* ed. Burtt, pp. 296–97).

36. *Reason and the Common Good,* p. 58.

37. Ibid., p. 53.

38. Ibid., p. 56.

39. Joan Miró has gone so far as to suggest that the forms sometimes come from the material. " 'Nowadays, I rarely start a picture from hallucinations as I did in the twenties, or as later, about 1933, from forms suggested by collages. What is more interesting to me today is the materials I am working with. They very frequently supply the shock which suggests my forms much as the cracks in the wall suggested form to Leonardo. I start a canvas, without a thought of what it may eventually become' " (quoted in Étienne Gilson, *Painting and Reality* [Cleveland: Meridian Books, 1959], p. 360).

40. See sect. 3.2, the quotation from AE 121.

6

Dewey's Reconstruction of Traditional Metaphysics

1. INTRODUCTION

THE LAST TWO CHAPTERS have provided the necessary foundations for a proper understanding of the place of forms in Dewey's philosophy. By stressing his polemics against traditional views, Chapter 4 allowed us to recognize what direction the Deweyan analysis would not take. Chapter 5 then began outlining the positive alternative to the traditional doctrine which Dewey was attempting to work out. The present chapter continues that effort, expanding the analysis of two topics already touched upon and introducing some further dimensions of Dewey's philosophy. The two areas which will receive more extended treatment are the close association of forms and ends, and the particular manner in which form, though not possessed of a Platonic kind of separate existence, may still be distinguished and discussed independently. The new material falls under the general heading of the relationship between forms and knowledge in Dewey's thought and encompasses three topics: his defense of the thesis that knowledge grasps forms, not matter; the status of forms as possibilities for knowledge; and the pluralistic understanding of forms in his thought.

2. FORMS AND ENDS

The significant part the teleological dimension plays in Dewey's understanding of forms was underscored in the two definitions of form given in *Art as Experience*.[1] *Experience and Nature* allows us to probe this dimension more fully and to articulate more accurately the way in which form and end collapse together in a dynamic interpretation of existents. We know from "The Influence of Darwinism on Philosophy" that Dewey saw the affiliation of form and *fixed*

end as a trait of an outdated and erroneous philosophical attitude.[2] The Darwinian theory, in allowing a flexibility of ends and the possibility for real novelty, removed the scientific support for the earlier analysis and provided an alternative way to view ends. What evolutionary thought did was to eliminate the justification for fixed ends in nature. It did not reject the recognition that natural processes have endings and culminations. What it did reject was the inflexibility of ends and the impossibility of changes significant enough to result in real novelty.

Although the altered scientific climate might no longer pose a threat to a properly understood recognition of ends, Dewey believed that a serious objection could come from an entirely different field, axiology. Teleological terminology, such as "end," "aim," "goal," "purpose," carries with it a value connotation from which Dewey is anxious to disassociate himself. He argues that a term like "end" should not automatically be interpreted in an honorific or eulogistic sense. There are also theological connotations surrounding such a term, but Dewey is concerned not so much with these as with the axiological: "Barring this [theological] connotation, the word has an almost inexpugnable honorific flavor, so that to assert that nature is characterized by ends, the most conspicuous of which is the life of mind, seems like engaging in an eulogistic, rather than an empirical account of nature" (EN 82). On such a view, one can easily understand the rigidly structured and fixed society of the Greeks. The professional thinkers in this society, utilizing as they do the highest end of nature, the mind, are to be given the highest social status. On the other hand, those individuals whose work involves manual labor are to be viewed as of a lesser worth than the philosophers. I have already noted Dewey's dislike of this sort of a static hierarchy.[3] In the honorific interpretation of ends, we have what Dewey considers a prime theoretical underpinning for such societal stratifications.

Dewey does not, on this account, reject the importance of recognizing ends altogether. He only seeks to ensure that ends be understood properly and, in contrast to the Greek view, not in an inherently eulogistic manner.

> Something much more neutral than any such implication is, however, meant. We constantly talk about things coming or drawing to a close; getting ended, finished, done with, over with. It is a commonplace that no *thing* lasts forever. . . . We may conceive the

end, the close, as due to fulfillment, perfect attainment, to satiety, or to exhaustion, to dissolution, to something having run down or given out. Being an end may be indifferently an ecstatic culmination, a matter-of-fact consummation, or a deplorable tragedy. Which of these things a closing or terminal object is, has nothing to do with the property of being an end [EN 82–83].

Here Dewey is arguing a position consistent with his description of existents as events. Since events are histories, that is, have beginnings, careers, and endings, the telic dimension cannot be ignored.[4] What Dewey wishes to emphasize is that although endings may be interpreted as praiseworthy, such an identification must not be made automatically. There are various kinds of ends, and philosophers would once again commit the fallacy of selective emphasis if they isolated one of them exclusively.[5]

Dewey is careful to present this kind of analysis because he wishes to avoid the errors of the past. He seeks to appropriate the positive insights of classical thought and to transform them into defensible and acceptable doctrines. Such acceptability is to be defined especially in terms of scientific advances. Dewey's inclination is rarely to engage in wholesale rejection, and the case of teleological considerations certainly bears this out. But what exactly do these considerations have to do with forms?

The decisive step worked out in *Experience and Nature*, with regard to this issue, is the view that in an analysis of events form and end to some degree overlap or coalesce. This position, in some respects, recapitulates a doctrine of Aristotle's.[6] Dewey's approach is not abstract and dialectical. He seeks to examine the actual state of experience and to isolate the factors necessary for an intelligible interpretation of that experience. One of these factors is end or, to use Dewey's own expression, "end-in-view."

To a person building a house, the end-in-view is not just a remote and final goal to be hit upon after a sufficiently great number of coerced motions have been duly performed. The end-in-view is a plan which is *contemporaneously* operative in selecting and arranging materials. The latter, brick, stone, wood and mortar, are means only as the end-in-view is actually incarnate in them, in forming them. Literally, they *are* the end in its present stage of realization. The end-in-view is present at each stage of the process; it is present as the *meaning* of the materials used and acts done;

without its informing presence, the latter are in no sense "means"; they are merely extrinsic causal conditions [EN 280].

The first point to note about this passage is that the example is of an artifact. Though such an approach is typical of Dewey's philosophical endeavor, in this particular citation it is significant because human consciousness is the explicit source of the telic dimension.

The portion of the passage I wish to highlight underscores the importance of the end-in-view for Dewey and its close relationship to form. The selection does not employ the actual term "form" although the words "forming" and "informing" are used. Nonetheless, Dewey's elucidation of end-in-view as a *contemporaneously operative plan* suggests a similar meaning. The contemporaneously operative plan is what will guide the organization of parts into a structured or formed whole. It will, in other words, set the pattern according to which the materials are to be related to one another, relation being the key ingredient in Dewey's understanding of form.[7] If we explore the implications of the identification of form and end, we will find, as I have previously suggested, some affinities between Dewey's position and Aristotle's.

What Dewey means by "plan" is clear in the next few lines. The materials mentioned, wood, bricks, stone, mortar, simply amassed in piles would have no significance outside of being just what they are. They take on a special significance as they become means to a certain end. They have "meaning," as Dewey says, in light of the goal to be reached. This goal is the plan which guides the *forming* of the materials into a certain shape. The plan is an arrangement of materials which, when undertaken, results in a certain end-state, the completed house. The completed house is, therefore, *both* the end of the activity and the embodiment of the particular plan. The mobilization of energies necessary for the undertaking is guided throughout by this end-in-view. Plan and end-in-view, on this analysis, are inextricably implicated in one another. Since Dewey's analysis of beings stresses their temporality, such a view should come as no surprise. Form is not given ready-made. It results from interactions in time. It is an end-product.

In this respect, Dewey's thought is not nearly so far removed from that of the Greeks, especially Aristotle, as Dewey himself at times indicates. Of course, the qualification with which I began this analysis—that for Dewey ends are neither fixed nor inherently honorific—

suggests the manner in which the Deweyan and Aristotelian positions are distinct. But similarities remain—similarities worth pointing out in a work attempting to show that Dewey is dealing with ontological issues, and dealing with them on the same level as the classical metaphysicians did.[8]

To make the comparison more exact, and because I am mainly interested in showing how these two thinkers make similar distinctions concerning the subject of forms and ends, I have selected an example from Aristotle in the field of *techne*. One of the basic and most famous distinctions in Aristotle's thought is that between matter and form. Beings or entities are organized, composite wholes, and any attempt at understanding them will have to include both what they are composed of, the matter, and the manner in which it is arranged, the form. "Since we must have the existence of the thing as something given, clearly the question is *why* the matter is some definite thing; e.g., why are these materials a house? Because that which was the essence of a house is present. And why is this individual thing, or this body having a form, a man? Therefore what we seek is the cause, i.e., the form, by reason of which the matter is some definite thing. . . ."[9] For Dewey, materials apart from a plan have no meaning. They are not yet means to be used toward the completion of a certain goal. For Aristotle, the materials apart from the form are only potentials to be distinguished from their actualization as, for instance, in the very building of a structure. "And so, of the people who go in for defining, those who define a house as stones, bricks, and timbers are speaking of the potential house, for these are the matter. . . ."[10]

Both philosophers employ a similar series of distinctions. The materials needed to construct the house are "without meaning" in and of themselves for Dewey; they are simply "potentials" for Aristotle. What gives them meaning for one thinker, or actualizes them for the other, is the plan or form which directs their organization into a completed edifice. For Dewey this plan is the end-in-view, just as for Aristotle form or shape is the end or goal aimed at. In Book Delta of the *Metaphysics*, this point is explicitly made, and once again the example used is a house. Aristotle is explaining the various senses in which something can be said to come from something else. One of these is "From the compound of matter and shape, as the

parts come from the whole, and the verse from the *Iliad*, and the stones from the house; [in every such case the whole is a compound of matter and shape,] for the shape is the end, and only that which attains an end is complete."[11]

That Dewey and Aristotle regard forms and ends as overlapping in a significant sense is not surprising from one point of view. Since both stress the energetic dimension of existence, the awareness of a process moving in a certain direction is prominent in each case. For both, the particular organization found in an event (thus far only events within *techne*) cannot be divorced from the end. The alignment of parts and their functions serves the end of producing a particular kind of entity. The parts thus subserve the whole and are arranged in light of it.

To indicate the kind of situation I have been describing, Dewey chooses the word "design." This is an appropriate term because, although he does not use the exact words, it combines the two factors of form and end.

> It is significant that the word "design" has a double meaning. It signifies purpose and it signifies arrangement, mode of composition. The design of a house is the plan upon which it is constructed to serve the purposes of those who live in it. The design of a painting or novel is the arrangement of its elements by means of which it becomes an expressive unity in direct perception. In both cases, there is an ordered relation of many constituent elements [AE 121].

The term "design" suggests both the plan according to which the finished product is to be constructed and the aim which the activity seeks to fulfill. Thus, the end for which diverse elements are arranged is, in a certain way, the finished product. It stands as the embodiment of a plan or form. The interpenetration of form and end, a position with Aristotelian roots, is thus restated in Dewey. Of course, we know that for Aristotle the above example taken from *techne* is but an extension of what can be articulated about *physis*. The problem is exactly reversed for Dewey. Can what is said in *techne* be applied to *physis*? We saw in the last chapter that there are strong indications that such an extension is indeed justified on the basis of Deweyan texts. The following section seeks to extend and deepen this analysis, with specific reference to the interrelationship of forms and ends.

3. From *Techne* to *Physis* in Dewey

For such texts we must turn to Dewey's great work on *physis*, *Experience and Nature*. I shall begin with a passage in which Dewey resumes his attack on the Greek interpretation of form. This both will allow me, by contrast, to emphasize Dewey's own position, and will serve as an introduction to a more generalized interpretation of forms and ends. The context for this quotation is a familiar Deweyan one: the uncritical application of aesthetic traits to the natural world.

> Further confirmation of this proposition is found in classic philosophy itself, in its theory that essential forms "make" things *what* they are, even though not causing them to occur. . . . The essences of Greek-medieval science were in short poetic objects, treated as objects of demonstrative science, used to explain and understand the inner and ultimate constitution of things [EN 289, 290].

Leaving aside the question whether this is an accurate characterization of classical ontology, we can reverse the terms and provide an accurate characterization of Deweyan ontology. Instead of the forms making the things what they are, in Dewey's view it is *what the things are that makes the forms.*

As we have seen, Dewey rejects the hypostatized interpretation of forms which would make of them an inner essence which is *really* "what" a thing is.[12] In spite of this rejection, the *what* remains a significant part of his analysis. If my interpretation is correct, in elaborating on this "whatness" we can find Dewey's alternative to the classical doctrine of form. By studying *Experience and Nature* we can, at the same time, recognize that the explanation of form as the end of a history, of a process of changes, is as applicable to the natural world as it is to the artistic.

Entities, as events, are active and dynamic. Nonetheless, this processive dimension is not to be interpreted as haphazard and undirected. In fact, entities exhibit a "characteristic pattern" which, when disturbed, attempts to restore itself.

> By need is meant a condition of tensional distribution of energies such that the body is in a condition of uneasy or unstable equilibrium. By demand or effort is meant the fact that this state is manifested in movements which modify environing bodies in ways

which react upon the body, so that its characteristic pattern of active equilibrium is restored. By satisfaction is meant this recovery of equilibrium pattern, consequent upon the changes of environment due to interactions with the active demands of the organism [EN 194].

In this passage, which provides a sound basis for a Deweyan ontology of form, three elements are especially significant. First, beings are active or dynamic. This is the oft-repeated Deweyan theme, suggested by evolutionary theory. In other words, whatever exists is energetic. Second, this activity is not wholly random. It is directed toward a particular end, which is the development of what Dewey calls the "characteristic pattern of active equilibrium." Third, there is an element of continuity or stability in the entity, what Dewey calls "satisfaction." The pattern of which he speaks is not a wholly fragile one. Part of the activity of each entity involves the mobilization of energies in the direction of restoring the organization of parts if they are disrupted. Whatever is, then, tends to preserve its self-identity through the possibility of challenges or disturbances.

These latter two considerations apply directly to the description of forms in terms of ends. If each event is historical, and if historical change is interpreted as real and significant, then the form can only be the outcome or end of a process of development. Once an "equilibrium" is reached, it tends to become stabilized, and changes are ordered in a way that secures the stability. In other words, the interactions of organism and environment are conducted in light of an end, the preservation, "satisfaction," of a certain pattern. Dewey's expression "characteristic pattern of active equilibrium" is clumsier than the single word "form" but it is successful in emphasizing the dynamic character of events, an important concept in Dewey which the word "form" does not convey. Any doubts that this doctrine of Dewey's is less than fully ontological—that is, that it applies only to a restricted portion of beings, but not to all—are settled by other texts in *Experience and Nature,* in which Dewey extends his analysis not only to animate beings, but to inanimate ones as well.

We should not be surprised that in selecting examples to illustrate his analysis Dewey would consider the biological realm a primary source. "The interactions of the various constituent parts of a plant take place in such ways as to tend to continue a characteristically organized activity; they tend to utilize conserved consequences

of past activities so as to adapt subsequent changes to the needs of the integral system to which they belong. Organization is a fact, though it is not an original organizing force" (EN 195). This passage is a good summary of a variety of points I have been attempting to make in this study. To begin with, neither activity nor form (organization) is denied. Dewey has developed an analysis in which a doctrine of form need not be allied to a static ontology. Second, the three components of this dynamic interpretation of form, *activity*, *characteristic pattern*, and *satisfaction*, are well exemplified here. Third, although teleology is not explicitly mentioned, this passage reinforces the interpretation presented here of the relation between forms and ends. For Dewey argues that interactions in the plant "tend to continue a characteristically organized activity." In other words, the end of these interactions of parts is the constitution and preservation of a specific form. Finally, the last sentence is a strong indication that existents are in themselves formed, and that this formation is not due to the activity of percipients.

Yet Dewey does not rest his case on indications from the biological realm alone; he includes the inanimate world as well. The pattern of organization is always involved in activity and interaction with its environment. The environment is needed for sustenance, and the dangers to stability stemming from an altered or changing environment must be met in varying ways if the stability is to persist. This flexibility of reaction is not merely a characteristic of living things. "In this fact, taken by itself, there is nothing which marks off the plant from the physico-chemical activity of inanimate bodies. The latter also are subject to conditions of disturbed inner equilibrium, which lead to activity in relation to surrounding things, and which terminate after a cycle of changes—a terminus termed saturation, corresponding to satisfaction in organic bodies" (EN 195). The important terms in this quotation, "activity," "equilibrium," and "saturation," are offered as equivalents of the terminology used in dealing with organic beings, "activity," "characteristic pattern," and "satisfaction." Dewey is eager to stress the continuity of traits that he finds existing in nature, both organic and inorganic. Selective reaction, or bias in activity with respect to the end of establishing or restoring a relatively stable pattern (the form), is a truly ontological characterization of entities. In fact, if we recall the example that dealt with the end-in-view as a "contemporaneously op-

erative plan" in human construction,[13] we can grasp the way in which the analysis of beings from the threefold perspective of activity, form, and end applies to the artistic, as well as to the organic and inorganic, realms. For Dewey, all events are formed events, and these forms must be interpreted as the results or ends of developmental sequences.

This kind of formulation in more classical terms leads directly to our next field of investigation. The last chapter, together with the early sections in the present one, have established that there are both ample evidence of a reformed, not a rejected, doctrine of forms in Dewey's writings and sufficient textual justification for describing this doctrine as it is found in Dewey. These descriptions show it to be similar in some ways to that of at least one classical thinker, Aristotle. The question now is whether Dewey admits any recognition of the relationship between his doctrine and that set forth in classical philosophy. We know from Chapter 4 that he can be severely critical of Greek thought; nonetheless, there are texts in which he explicitly asserts the ways in which his own position recaptures the achievements of classical philosophy.

4. Dewey's Reformulation of Classical Insights

In the examination of these texts, four points stand out. The first is Dewey's somewhat surprising assertion that there is a very real sense in which forms can be considered *atemporal*. The second involves epistemology. Dewey claims that, when properly understood, the Greek teaching that form and not matter is grasped by the intellect can be accepted as an accurate and defensible doctrine. The third point builds on this analysis, and states that the ontological status of forms is that of possibilities. The fourth, in contrast to the previous three investigations, is a divergence from the Aristotelian tradition. Each event for Dewey is to be understood not primarily in terms of one form, as it is in the traditional doctrine of substantial forms, but from the perspective of a plurality of forms.

4.1. Forms as "Eternal"

The clearest statements about the way in which forms can be understood as outside the temporal dimension come from *The Quest for*

Certainty. Now, it is obvious from what we already know about Dewey's treatment of forms that, as he conceives them, they cannot be atemporal in every sense. Since they are not separate existents, Dewey cannot argue that they are atemporal in a Platonic sense of having always existed in a separate realm. Because they are dependent on the emergence of events, there is a sense in which forms will always be temporally conditioned. The relationship of part to whole (the form) in newly evolved species represents a real novelty that had no anterior existence. Despite these considerations, Dewey is still willing to admit that there is a justifiable manner in which forms can be treated as non-processive.

In the two quotations from *Art as Experience* which define it, form is identified with the characteristic pattern resulting from the part/whole and means/end relationships. In "The Influence of Darwinism on Philosophy," form is associated with the permanent aspects of reality. By aligning stability with relations, *The Quest for Certainty* bridges these two discussions. Dewey again stresses that nature is a mixture of the precarious and the stable, and goes on to argue that freedom depends on this blending of change and permanence. In so doing he explicitly states that stability is to be associated with relations: "Freedom is an actuality when the recognition of relations, the stable element, is combined with the uncertain element, in the knowledge which makes foresight possible and secures intentional preparation for probable consequences" (QC 199).

This quotation is another example of the interconnection in Dewey's thought of theoretical investigation and practical considerations. The moral dimension is always present in some sense, but it alternates between foreground and background. But for our purposes the significance of this quotation is Dewey's admission that relations represent the stable factor in existence. This is a stand already implicit in my interpretation, and its admission by Dewey reinforces the kind of analysis I am developing. It also indicates a consistency in his thought which runs at least from the article on Darwin (1909) through *The Quest for Certainty* (1929) to *Art as Experience* (1934). The common thread in each of these texts is the recognition that existence is characterized by precariousness and stability and that the stable aspects are what philosophers have called form. Form is the philosophical concept which traditionally

represents permanence, and Dewey understands form as allied to relations.

Once these kinds of identifications are understood and kept in mind, we will be able to grasp the sense in which forms are atemporal according to Dewey. The crucial element in this elaboration is the understanding of form in terms of relations. For, as Dewey explains, the kernel of truth found in the Greek claim of immutable forms can be located in the constancy of certain relations. Traditionally, as Dewey asserts, forms have been characterized in such terms as "ideality," "universality," and "immutability" (QC 129). His own theory, based on the importance of relations, offers an alternative that incorporates both the advances in science and the insights of classical philosophy. It does this by respecting change while recognizing how permanence is to be understood in a post-Darwinian world of flux and process.

> Operations as such, that is, as connective interactions, are uniform. Physically and sensibly, a machine changes through friction, exposure to weather, etc., while products vary in quality. Processes are local and temporal, particular. But the relation of means and consequence which defines an operation remains one and the same in spite of these variations. It is a universal. . . . Each process is individual and not exactly identical with others. But the *function* for which the machine is designed does not alter with these changes; an operation, being a relation, is not a process [QC 130].

This quotation is both a good summary of some issues that have been raised thus far and a statement by Dewey concerning just how the precarious and the stable are intermixed in existence. To begin with, there is the emphasis on interaction which we can now recognize as a familiar Deweyan theme. Secondly, there is a covert statement asserting the interpenetration of form and end. Dewey uses alternative terminology, but his point is the same. To reconstruct the argument, we must keep in mind once again that form is to be understood in terms of relations. This quotation then introduces a new term, "operation," an expression meaning the relation of means to consequences. This relation is spoken of as describing a function. The quotation thus restates the identification of form and end by associating operation (form) with function (end). Thus even though form is not mentioned the new doctrine does apply to an analysis

that recognizes forms. This novel doctrine concerns Dewey's admission that, although processes are temporal, there is a real sense in which *operations* are not. Although change and process are pervasive, the *function*, Dewey argues, "does not alter with these changes."

Dewey also states his position in traditional language, which he qualifies in accordance with his own orientation:

> The relation is thus invariant. It is eternal, not in the sense of enduring throughout all time, or being everlasting like an Aristotelian species or a Newtonian substance, but in the sense that an operation as a relation which is grasped in thought is independent of the instances in which it is overtly exemplified, although its meaning is found only in the *possibility* of these actualizations [QC 130].

Here then is Dewey's manner of explaining the integration of change and permanence. Relations supply the permanent or stable dimension. Stability means invariance through vicissitude. The particular entities in which an operation takes place may alter, wear down, break down, or run successfully. But none of this will have any effect on the relation of means to consequence which is the form. The function remains stable whether it is actually capable of being carried out or not. The human kidneys, for example, operate in such a way that they control the amount of salt in the blood. When they fail to accomplish this properly, discomfort results and help is sought. Help is needed in these cases because the function of the kidneys, although currently inoperative, remains the same. It is only because of this continuity of function that deficiencies, as lapses from a standard, can be identified. Because of considerations like this one, Dewey admits that there is an accurate sense in which forms can be spoken of as "eternal." They are eternal in that they are not affected by individual instantiations and temporal contingencies.

The word "eternal" may appear to be an unusual choice in view of the limited sense in which Dewey means it; nonetheless, it is a significant selection, insofar as it indicates Dewey's willingness to admit that traditional philosophy had grasped something of importance in its analyses. By giving it expression in a manner both justifiable and comprehensible, he seeks to restore that insight.

Dewey is also eager to re-emphasize another insight of classical thought, closely associated with this one: the doctrine that what the intellect grasps in cognition is form not matter.

4.2. Intelligence and Forms

Dewey asserts unambiguously in *Experience and Nature* that his own theory of knowledge recapitulates the Greek position that form rather than matter is seized in cognition. "In this respect, the view presented agrees with classic teaching, according to which perception, apprehension, lays hold of form, not of matter. I believe this view properly understood is inherently sound . . ." (EN 240). Because of our examination of Dewey's metaphysics we are now in a position to see in just what manner this teaching is to be "properly understood." When we speak of forms in Dewey, we are speaking of relations. *The Quest for Certainty* stresses the relation of means to consequences, whereas the books on art and nature tend to speak in terms of the relation of part to whole. These relations, as we know, account for whatever element of stability is present within entities.

This means that if Dewey were to argue that knowledge aims at the stable aspects of existence, he would be saying that it seeks out the relations (either of means to consequences or parts to whole)— in other words, the forms. In this way Dewey's teaching and that of traditional thinkers would agree in precisely the manner Dewey himself suggested. *The Quest for Certainty* provides exactly this sort of assertion:

> Nothing is more familiar than the standardized objects of reference designated by common nouns. Their distinction from proper names shows that they are not singular or individual, not existing things. Yet, *"the* table" is both more familiar and seemingly more substantial than *this* table, the individual. "This" undergoes change all the time. It is interacting with other things and with me, who am not exactly the same person as when I last wrote upon it. "This" is an indefinitely multiple and varied series of "thises."
>
> But save in extreme cases, these changes are indifferent, negligible, from the standpoint of means for consequences. *The* table is precisely the constancy among the serial "thises" of whatever serves as an instrument for a single end. *Knowledge* is concerned wholly with this constant, this standardized and averaged set of properties and relations . . . [QC 189].

The significance of this passage lies in its explanation of the connection between knowledge and forms. Dewey does not simply state here the relationship but rather builds up to it after introducing once again his teaching that relations account for the stable ("constant") aspects of existence. Epistemological considerations are thus consistent with ontological ones. If, as he says, knowledge is "wholly concerned" with the constant, then there must *be* constancy in existence. Just how this constancy, this permanence, is woven into the fabric of existence was the topic of the previous section. The atemporality of the relations which constitute forms is reiterated in this quotation by using a concrete example, that of a table.

The table, as opposed to *this* table, is, as Dewey asserts, not an "existing" thing. It is not, in other words, an event. It is not an event because alterations and changes are "indifferent" and "negligible" to it. *The* table, as a particular relationship of means to consequences, remains constant in spite of the fact that individual tables, as events, are constantly undergoing changes. This constancy is unaffected, even when the changes include those that lead to disrepair and decay. The relationship of means to consequences, which describes the *function*, remains the same for a table on which paint is chipping and wood rotting as for a brand new one. *The* table is a grouping together of various materials in a certain arrangement to serve a particular end. This fact remains constant in spite of the diversity of materials that may be used or the changes that may occur to those materials through time. Dewey has used various expressions to characterize this trait of existence. "Constant" is the one preferred in this quotation, but we have already seen that he also uses "stable" and "eternal."

Once Dewey has established how constancy or stability is a trait of existence, he reveals the importance of this fact for epistemology. A world of mere flux would be a world in which knowledge would be impossible. Knowledge depends on the fact of some stability. Dewey goes so far as to argue that it is *wholly* concerned with this constancy. Since we know that this constancy involves relations, and that relations define form for Dewey, we can understand how the connection between knowledge and forms is as firmly established in his doctrine as it was for the Platonic–Aristotelian tradition. Thus Dewey develops the ontological foundations for intelligibility in a coherent manner. Knowledge is possible because events are both

stable and precarious. Without the precariousness, problematic situations would not arise; without the stabilities, knowledge would be impossible. It is because events are formed that they are intelligible. Without the relations which constitute stability and define form, intelligibility would not be a trait of existence.

4.3. Forms as Possibilities

Forms are not events. They do not exist as things in the world or as entities in any other realm. Therefore Dewey is careful to stress the connotations of possibility in the term "intelligible." "Nature is intelligible and understandable. There are operations by means of which it becomes an object of knowledge, and is turned to human purposes, just as rivers provide conditions which may be utilized to promote human activities and to satisfy human need" (QC 168). Dewey's stress on the suffixes suggesting possibility and on the terms "may" and "becomes" offers decisive evidence of his view that forms have the status of possibilities in the events they characterize. They exist as possibilities[14] in relation to the inquirer whose task it is to seek them out.

We have already seen[15] how Dewey uses the term "intelligence" to indicate that some amount of activity on the part of the inquirer is requisite in coming to knowledge. This work can now be seen as uncovering, as analyzing in the literal sense of shaking loose, the possibilities (forms) inherent in events. "Nature is capable of being understood. But the possibility is realized not by a mind thinking about it from without but by operations conducted from within, operations which give it new relations summed up in production of a new individual object" (QC 172). Experimentation, Dewey is saying, is what allows the comprehensible to become the comprehended. It is important to note the stress once again on relations. Experimentation seeks certain stabilities (the relations) which have hitherto remained unknown. If it is successful, new "objects" are discovered and human knowledge is increased.

The famous physiologist Claude Bernard, for example, reveals the details of experiments undertaken to prove that secretions from the pancreas are responsible for breaking down fatty materials in an organic body. A chance observation during a dissection had suggested this possibility to him. An experiment had then to be con-

ducted to test this hypothesis, or "preconceived idea" as Bernard calls it. Since the pancreatic juices are not directly accessible from outside an organism (unlike urine and saliva, for instance) he had to construct a double experiment. The first was intended simply to extract a suitable sample of the fluid in question, and the second to test this liquid's effect on fats. After carefully carrying out both these steps, he was able to verify his hypothesis. "In fact pancreatic juice obtained in suitable conditions from dogs, rabbits and other animals, and mixed with oil or melted fat, always instantly emulsi-fied, and later split these fatty bodies into fatty acids, glycerine, etc., etc., by means of a specific ferment."[16]

I have used this illustration of an actual experimental discovery to emphasize the ingredients in Dewey's position. He claims that nature is intelligible and that intelligence, involving, as it does, di-rected operations, is the name given to the faculty that can elicit this intelligibility. Bernard did not come to recognize the function of the pancreas by sitting back and trying to deduce it from first principles. Rather, he engaged in operations that involved direct contact, interaction, and interference with the animal functions that were the subject of his study. Prior to the manipulations of inquiry, this function was operative but unknown. Its status in reference to a knower was that of a possibility. Actualization came about only as the result of intelligently directed operations.

We saw in our discussion of "intelligence" that its defining char-acteristic is the "capacity to estimate the possibilities of a situation and to act in accordance with [this] estimate."[17] This exactly de-scribes the procedure followed by Bernard and, Dewey would say, by all individuals who are engaged in the process of inquiry. There is, then, a real sense in which forms have the status of possibilities for Dewey. They are possibilities for knowledge which experimen-tation can actualize.

4.4. A Pluralistic Theory of Forms

If forms are indeed identified with the relations of means for con-sequences, and if events, engaged in interactions with humans, re-veal the possibilities for a variety of such relations, then Dewey must admit that each event embodies, not one form, but a cluster of them. Such indeed is his position. The Aristotelian tradition of the

Middle Ages began the movement in this direction by drawing a distinction between substantial and accidental forms. This distinction admitted that a plurality of forms must be taken into account, even in the analysis of a single being. However, this plurality is subjected to a rigid bifurcation of which Dewey would not approve. From a Deweyan perspective, the very labels "substantial" and "accidental" indicate but another case of philosophy's false search for *the* real, behind or beyond the transactions that actually characterize experience.[18] In spite of this, Dewey agrees that an accurate analysis must admit a plurality of forms for existents. He is even willing to accept some ordering of these, though not in a rigidly hierarchical fashion.

Perhaps the best way to get an accurate understanding of the Deweyan analysis is to compare it to the medieval view as exemplified in Thomas Aquinas. For Aquinas, the substantial form is responsible for the very being of an entity. Every entity is a material formed in a certain way. Without this substantial form, there can be no entity. Accidental form, on the other hand, presupposes an already existing entity, and simply qualifies it in some manner. On this analysis a being can be both determinate and indeterminate: determinate in that it is some definite thing (has a substantial form), but indeterminate in that it is potentially capable of taking on a variety of accidental forms. Aquinas explains it in this way. "But since the material that is joined to a substantial form nonetheless remains in potency to many accidental forms, what can be said to exist as finite in itself can be infinite in a relative way. Wood, for instance, is finite in accordance with its form, but is nonetheless infinite insofar as it is in potency with regard to the fact that it can be shaped or colored in an infinite number of ways."[19] A particular entity, then, according to this view, must be analyzed in terms of a plurality of forms. An entity presents itself both as something definite and as a capacity for a great number of alterations. This pluralistic approach is qualified by a sharp distinction between the substantial form, responsible for the very being of an entity, and the accidental forms which can accrue only if this other form is present.

Dewey, too, wishes to indicate that a thorough analysis of an event will involve a plurality of forms. However, he does not make the distinction into a kind of form absolutely requisite for existence, and one that must already take existence for granted. His is a much

more egalitarian view of forms. It is a mistake, he argues, to take *a* meaning for *the* meaning. "Essence, as has been intimated, is but a pronounced instance of meaning; to be partial, and to assign *a* meaning to a thing as *the* meaning is but to evince human subjection to bias" (EN 144). Once again we must return to the doctrine of interaction if we are to understand Dewey properly. As we know, the basic existential situation, as this thinker conceives it, is one of interaction of an organism with its environment. Philosophical issues must therefore be expressed in light of that fact.

Problematic situations arise within a context, and solutions are sought in terms of the possibilities inherent in that context. Because of this, a Deweyan doctrine of forms is bound to be context-dependent and thus to a degree relative. Since forms are defined as means for consequences, all the various means implicit in an event must be treated in an equal fashion. Different problems will occasion the discovery of different forms. None of these is to be judged as inherently superior to the others. They are to be evaluated individually only in their capacity for resolving each particular problematic situation. Wood, to use the example suggested by Aquinas, may take on a variety of forms depending on the context. A piece of wood may become a cane for a hiker with a twisted ankle, fuel for the same person's campfire, a weapon in case of danger, a unit of construction, or even an artwork in the hands of the right person. In each of these cases, a new possibility has been brought to realization. There is no manner, according to Dewey, in which one can be adjudicated as possessing a higher level of being than the others. Each is to be treated contextually.

Such a position, however, is not altogether unqualified in Dewey's writings. He does not argue that one kind of form is more real than another. He does admit, though, that certain forms become in practical ways the *standardized* forms of things. Because certain contexts remain relatively stable, a particular set of possibilities may continually be fastened upon as defining the event in question. In this sense, and in this sense alone, can one form be stressed at the expense of others.

> As habits form, action is stereotyped into a fairly constant series of acts having a common end in view; *the* table serves a single use, in spite of individual variations. A group of properties is set aside, corresponding to the abiding end and single mode of use which

form *the* object, in distinction from "this" of unique experiences. *The* object is an abstraction, but unless it is hypostatized it is not a vicious abstraction. It designates selected relations of things which, with respect to their mode of operation, are constant within the limits practically important [QC 190].

Obviously, this analysis is very closely related to the one, dealt with earlier in this chapter, concerning the manner in which forms could be understood as "eternal." In this case, as in the previous one, Dewey is attempting to salvage the truth of classical insights, without committing himself fully to a prescientific philosophy.

Dewey does not adhere to any doctrine of substantial forms, but he does realize how some forms can come, through reiteration, to be taken for the essential, as opposed to the accidental, characteristics of an event. Viewing a table as serving a particular and recurrent function is certainly a valid and common human response to a series of similar situations. It becomes invalid for Dewey only if it is seen as excluding other forms, or if the context within which this function is focused on is forgotten. In light of this analysis there are certain statements that accurately characterize the Deweyan position as regards the plurality of forms. To begin with, events are formed, but this must not be taken to imply that they have a single form. In fact, events possess a variety of forms. Secondly, none of these forms is to be treated as more real or as possessed of more being than any other. But, thirdly, since some contexts remain fairly stable, certain meanings through repetition may become standardized and may stand, for *practical* purposes, as embodiments of *the* object in question.

5. SUMMARY

The present chapter has dealt with two closely related concerns. The first, systematic in character, involved the continued elucidation and further discrimination of Dewey's teaching on forms. The second, of historical interest, analyzed the manner in which some traditional philosophical insights were preserved in his reconstructed philosophical position.

The following issues were especially prominent in this chapter. (*a*) It was argued that Dewey's dynamic view of existence leads him to express the relation of form and end as one of interpenetration,

of coalescence. Form, on this view, is the end of a temporal sequence. (*b*) Dewey's analysis is one of truly ontological generality. He always tends to emphasize *techne*, but he readily admits the viability of applying the same analysis to *physis*. (*c*) Dewey asserts that Greek thinkers such as Aristotle were not altogether mistaken when they spoke of forms in atemporal terms. Indeed, he is willing to characterize them as "eternal" as long as this label is properly understood. (*d*) Dewey also finds acceptable the teaching that form rather than matter is grasped in noetic inquiry. (*e*) This means that forms must be interpreted as possibilities. (*f*) Because each event offers a diverse range of functional possibilities, it would be incorrect to assign a single form to a single event. Dewey believes that an event involves not a unique form, but a multiplicity of them.

NOTES

1. See chap. 5, sects. 3.2 and 4.1.

2. See chap. 2, sect. 2.

3. See chap. 2, sect. 2. The same point is made in a somewhat different manner at EN 84: "Such a view may verbally distinguish between something called efficient causation and something else called final causation. But in effect the distinction is only between the causality of the master who contents himself with uttering an order and the efficacy of the servant who actually engages in the physical work of execution. It is only a way of attributing ultimate causality to what is ideal and mental—the directive order of the master—, while emancipating it from the supposed degradation of physical labor in carrying it out, as well as avoiding the difficulties of inserting an immaterial cause within the material realm."

4. See the discussion of "event" in chap. 5, sect. 3.1.

5. Dewey makes his displeasure over such an analysis quite plain, calling it a "Great Bad." "Classic metaphysics is a confused union of these two senses of ends, the primarily natural and the secondarily natural, or practical, moral. Each meaning is intelligible, grounded, legitimate in itself. But their mixture is one of the Great Bads of philosophy" (EN 88).

6. See chap. 2, sect. 2.

7. See chap. 5, sects. 3.2 and 4.1.

8. By suggesting this comparison, I signal my agreement with John Herman Randall, Jr., in reference to the important contributions of Dewey. "But Dewey's enduring contribution is to be found where he extends and broadens the classic tradition, by setting it in the context of the wider experience of modern knowledge" ("John Dewey, 1859–1952,"

in *Dewey and His Critics: Selected Essays from* THE JOURNAL OF PHI
LOSOPHY, ed. Sidney Morgenbesser [New York: The Journal of Philosophy, Inc., 1977], p. 4; the article from which this citation is taken was
originally published in *The Journal of Philosophy*, 50 [1953], 5–13).

9. *Metaphysics*, 1041B3–8, in *Basic Works of Aristotle*, ed. McKeon,
p. 811.

10. *Metaphysics* 1043A14–16, in ibid., p. 814.

11. *Metaphysics* 1023A32–35, in ibid., p. 773.

12. See chap. 4, sect. 3.4.

13. See above, sect. 2.

14. Dewey understands "possibility" in a very straightforward manner, as that which may result, or be made to result, from a set of factual
conditions. At QC 239, he explains "the possible" in this way: " 'The
actual' consists of given conditions; 'the possible' denotes ends or consequences not now existing but which the actual may through its use
bring into existence."

15. See chap. 4, sect. 4.2.

16. *An Introduction to the Study of Experimental Medicine*, trans.
Henry C. Green, repr. ed. (New York: Dover, 1957), p. 154.

17. See chap. 4, sect. 4.2.

18. Dewey's analysis of this issue is discussed in chap. 4, sect. 3.4.

19. Thomas Aquinas, *Summa theologiae* (Ottawa: Garden City Press,
1941), 1, 7, 2c. The translation is my own. Other references which explain Aquinas' position include the following: 1, 77, 6c; 1, 44, 2c; and
1, 76, 4c.

7

Logical Forms

Logic: The Theory of Inquiry holds a special prominence in regard to the issue of forms. This stems from two facts: (*a*) as a text on logic, it returns to the subject Dewey treated in 1916 when he published the *Essays in Experimental Logic*; and (*b*) as a late book in his career (it was published in 1938 when he was nearly seventy-nine), it follows those that were studied in the last three chapters. These two facts combine to make it a special work for my undertaking insofar as there appears to be an historical progression on Dewey's part concerning the topic of forms. My interpretation has revealed Dewey's growing appreciation of the need to situate properly the permanent or stable dimensions of existence. It is this dimension which, as we know, is encapsulated in the concept of form.

With respect to form, my interpretation has established the following stages of development. In the *Essays* of 1916, form or its equivalents are not denied, but they are not focused on as significant. Dewey is eager to establish his new logic, and doing so requires that the materials to be investigated exhibit an amenability to the kind of procedures involved in scientific research. Since these procedures necessitate experimentation, Dewey wishes to stress that entities are *not* so rigidly fixed as to resist the guided alterations involved in experimentation. It is not surprising, therefore, to find that this book accentuates change, process, and pliability rather than stability and fixity. The *Essays* do contain a significant passage in which Dewey denies the possibility of there being such a thing as *"mere* existence," that is, existence without qualification in terms of organization.[1] But this remark remains an isolated one, far outweighed by the stress on change.

In *Experience and Nature*, published in 1925, there is a discernible shift in emphasis. Stability and precariousness are given equal prominence. It is the mixture of the two, Dewey argues, which occa-

sions philosophical problems and allows for their solutions. The term "form," still allied in Dewey's mind with the absolutely static interpretation of reality, is not widely used. He relies instead on such synonyms as "structure" and "organization." Yet the term "form" is used non-pejoratively in one context. The Greeks, Dewey says, were correct in arguing that form and not matter is taken into account in knowledge. In 1929, *The Quest for Certainty* not only deepens the analysis of this point, but argues that there are other classical views which, if properly understood, are still acceptable. Outstanding among these is the teaching that the elements of stability may, in a sense, be called "eternal." But the term "form" still finds no general non-pejorative application in this text.

For the transition to the use of the actual word in a positive sense, it is necessary to advance a few years to 1934 and the famous book on art. Here, his task made easier no doubt by the context of art, Dewey engages in a significant analysis of what is meant by "form." The definitions articulated in this text were found to be consistent with his analysis of structure in *Experience and Nature* and with the explanation of relations in *The Quest for Certainty*. Dewey was reluctant to use "form" in the context of nature because of its association with a pre-Darwinian view. Nonetheless, when form is understood as it is presented in *Art as Experience*, it is found to be consistent and continuous with the analyses in the two other books published in the decade 1925–1935.

We are now brought, in our chronological sequence, to *Logic: The Theory of Inquiry*. Does this text also reveal the growing stress on form in Dewey's thought? The answer is an unequivocal "yes." Unlike the previous logic texts, which pay scant attention to this topic, and like the intervening books, in which forms gain more and more in prominence, *Logic* deals with its subject matter in the context of forms. The specific topic is *logical* forms, but his analysis builds on the more generalized interpretation that has been presented in the earlier chapters.

I am not suggesting that the *Logic* of 1938 is a radical departure from the *Essays* of 1916. Quite the contrary is the case. The texts exhibit astonishing similarity and consistency for books separated by twenty-two years of intense philosophical activity. What I am suggesting is that in those twenty-two years, Dewey has come to understand forms in an original sense, one that is justifiable and

defensible with regard to contemporary scientific discoveries. As a result, he is no longer hesitant to frame his analyses in terms of "forms."

Dewey's own explanation of the relationship between the logical books indicates this difference.

> This book is a development of ideas regarding the nature of logical theory that were first presented, some forty years ago, in *Studies in Logical Theory*; that were somewhat expanded in *Essays in Experimental Logic* and were briefly summarized with special reference to education in *How We Think*. While basic ideas remain the same, there has naturally been considerable modification during the intervening years. While connection with the problematic is unchanged, express identification of reflective thought with objective inquiry makes possible, I think, a mode of statement less open to misapprehension than were the previous ones. The present work is marked in particular by application of the earlier ideas to interpretation of the forms and formal relations that constitute the standard material of logical tradition [LTI 3].

Dewey's quotation emphasizes three points. First, there has remained, over forty years, an essential similarity with regard to the basic conception of logic. Second, whereas earlier he spoke of "reflective thought," he is now going to describe logic in terms of "inquiry," not because of any repudiation of earlier positions, but because of a need to clarify earlier doctrines. Finally, in the one significant change in the new text, he will be dealing with *logical* forms. Here, too, the continuity with the earlier texts is to be maintained, but a new "application" of these ideas to logical forms is to be undertaken. What these forms are and how they can be integrated with what we already know about Dewey's treatment of forms in general will be investigated in this chapter.

To set the context for this analysis, two preliminary issues must be discussed. One is important for understanding Dewey's logical theory; the other, for the line of inquiry I have been presenting. The first involves a clarification of just what Dewey means by the term "logic," since he uses the word in a manner that differs from generally recognized usage. The second deals with his unfortunate overstatement about the absolute separation of logic and ontology. As we shall see, because of the particular manner in which Dewey conceives of logic, he is unable to uphold this separation consistently.

2. Logic as Methodology

To explain what Dewey understands by "logic" I shall begin by presenting a commonly accepted division of branches within the field, and then indicate Dewey's meaning by reference to this standard classification. According to one historian of logic, I. M. Bocheński, this term is one of the most ambiguous in all of philosophy.[2] Even when most of the sources of ambiguity are removed, there remains an irreducible threefold division of disciplines covered by the term: "Logic, as the science of inference, comprises three disciplines which should be kept sharply distinct"[3]—(a) formal logic, (b) methodology, and (c) philosophy of logic. Formal logic deals with the laws of valid inference; methodology concerns itself with the application of these laws; and the philosophy of logic asks fundamental questions about the nature of logic and its laws.[4]

Dewey makes no distinction between the first two disciplines mentioned, arguing that formal logic and methodology should not be viewed as separate fields. Inquiry, the actual application of methodology, is, on Dewey's interpretation, what provides the *forms* of logic. Because of this, the continuity between the methodology of investigation and the formal canons that guide investigation must be maintained.

> The plausibility of the view that sets up a dualism between logic and the methodology of inquiry, between logic and scientific method, is due to a fact that is not denied. Inquiry in order to reach valid conclusions must itself satisfy logical requirements. It is an easy inference from this fact to the idea that the logical requirements are imposed upon methods of inquiry from without.... How, it will be asked, can inquiry which has to be evaluated by reference to a standard be itself the source of the standard? How can inquiry originate logical forms (as it has been stated that it does) and yet be subject to the requirements of these forms? The question is one that must be met. It can be adequately answered only in the course of the entire discussion that follows [LTI 13].

That Dewey would argue in such a manner should come as no surprise. This is a theme that can be traced back to his Hegelianism, and to the disdain he had inherited from Morris for any logic that was purely formal.[5] This outlook first manifested itself negatively, in his criticisms of Leibniz,[6] but by the turn of the century, he was

able to provide a positive manifestation of it in his attempt to develop a logic that assiduously avoided the radical separation of logic and methodology.

Fully in line with these considerations is Dewey's assertion that the fallacy of selective emphasis was an especially tempting one for philosophers.[7] The sharp separation of formal logic and methodology is but another manner in which this fallacy manifests itself. Dewey is clear to point out in the passage above that the use of logical laws as a norm for valid inquiry is not denied. The point he is trying to make is that these logical forms do not come from a higher realm of being or from an *"Intellectus Purus"* (LTI 18). They have been developed, rather, within the very processes of inquiry. Gradually they were arranged and codified so that they could be effectively employed. But the fact that they are capable of separate use does not mean that they originated from any source other than actual human attempts to resolve problematic situations. They are the results which have been selectively isolated from the context which gave rise to them. This latter point is the one Dewey wants to stress. Logical forms should not be separated from the situation which occasioned them. This is the reason he calls his text *Logic: The Theory of Inquiry,* combining two terms which traditionalists like Bocheński would want decisively separated.[8]

Dewey is not saying that formal logic cannot be studied as a distinct branch of logic or that the validity of its laws is to be questioned. What he is saying is that this fact of being capable of separate study should not lead to the belief that its *source* is independent of experience. For the purposes of my study, two issues arising out of this discussion must be noted. First of all, there is an indication that logical forms will be treated in a manner consistent with my interpretation of forms in Dewey's earlier writings. Logical forms are said to "originate" in inquiry. This is merely another way of arguing that forms result in an organism/environment interaction. Secondly, this stress on *inquiry* is an indication of a fact that becomes evident as one reads Dewey's *Logic.* He is concerned much more with methodology, with the process of inquiry, which is the source of logical forms, than with the formalism itself. This position is typical of Dewey's general emphasis on "context" and "tensional situations." Inquiry, as the activity which applies the proper methodology for resolving these situations, receives extensive treatment

in this text.[9] Formal logic is treated only incidentally. There is no symbolic notation in the entire book.

3. LOGIC AND ONTOLOGY

The stress on methodology is important for dealing with Dewey's outright assertion that logic is independent of ontology. Were this assertion true, *Logic: The Theory of Inquiry* would be of only marginal significance for my investigation. Since I am concerned to interpret Dewey's ontology, a book that was irrelevant to ontological issues would not merit much attention.

But this claim is erroneous. Dewey himself, as we shall see, does not succeed in keeping the two fields apart. His arguments for separating them are closely related to his arguments for uniting the two disciplines of formal logic and methodology. Dewey claims that this latter, and incorrect, separation is based on some version of a dualistic ontology. On such a scheme, two realms of being lead to two sources of knowledge, *a priori* and *a posteriori*. These, in turn, lead to two branches of logic, formal and methodological. Those who come to logic with a preconceived ontology and epistemology, Dewey argues, impose a dualistic interpretation upon it. The corrective is to treat logic in isolation from metaphysics.

> Logic as inquiry into inquiry is, if you please, a circular process; it does not depend upon anything extraneous to inquiry. The force of this proposition may perhaps be most readily understood by noting what it precludes. It precludes the determination and selection of logical first principles by an *a priori* intuitional act, even when the intuition in question is said to be that of *Intellectus Purus*. It precludes resting logic upon metaphysical and epistemological assumptions and presuppositions [LTI 28].

To get an accurate picture of what Dewey means, it is necessary to keep two things in mind: (*a*) Dewey is using "metaphysics" in the popular, pejorative sense of that which is beyond empirical verification;[10] and (*b*) metaphysics refers here to the various controversial systems, the various *isms* which are endemic to philosophy. A logical theory, Dewey is saying, should be operative no matter what particular philosophical system holds one's allegiance.[11]

I find Dewey's analysis not only incorrect but ironic in a special sense. If he held for the strict separation of formal logic and meth-

odology, then he might be able to argue that formal logic is independent of ontology. But since he insists on negating this distinction, and especially since his text is mostly concerned with methodology, ontological considerations will of necessity intervene. To explain my claims in a somewhat more complete manner, I shall begin by referring to the great development of this century in the field, mathematical or symbolic logic. If a case could be made for the independence of logic and ontology, in the sense Dewey articulates, it would apply directly to this formalization. The founders of the discipline were mostly Platonists (Frege, the early Russell, Whitehead), yet the most aggressive application of this technique was at the hands of the neo-positivists.[12] Here we are confronted with widely diverging ontological positions which yet utilize an identical logical procedure. The fact that most schools of philosophy now use this technique indicates even more strongly the basis on which a Deweyan claim could be erected.[13]

If by "logic" Dewey meant formal logic, it would appear that his argument for the separation of logic and ontology might have some merit. The problem with his analysis lies precisely in the fact that when he uses "logic" he means primarily methodology. This peculiar usage entirely alters the possibility that logic can proceed in isolation from ontology since the methodology is not formalistic; it involves the specific character of the subject matters being dealt with.

This, in turn, leads directly to ontological considerations. For the entities that become the subject matters of inquiry must exhibit at least one generic trait: amenability to investigation.[14] If beings were opaque to the experimental method of inquiry Dewey suggests, then a new methodology (a new "logic") would have to be developed because of ontological considerations. Methodological prescriptions and ontological descriptions must work in concert if success in inquiry is to be achieved. Dewey's own "experimental logic" was a response to the new ontological situation introduced by evolutionary thinking, and by the scientific movement in general. Because the new ontology describes beings as changeable, and not as fixed, a methodology which emphasizes experimentation and manipulation can be successful.

If we understand metaphysics as the study of beings as beings or, in Deweyan terminology, as the study of the generic traits of exist-

ence,[15] then methodological analyses will reveal their interconnections with ontological considerations. The ontology may be only implicit, but it will be present. Indeed, Dewey's *Logic* addresses this very issue. He admits that subject matters must *be* of a certain sort if the operations of inquiry are to be successful, and he does this by reverting to venerable ontological considerations, by returning to themes that Trendelenburg had emphasized: potentiality and actuality.

Dewey asserts, after summarizing the main tenets of his position, that "It is important, in this connection, not to confuse the categories of potentiality and actuality. Crude materials must possess qualities such as permit and promote the performance of the specific operations which result in formed-matter as means to end" (LTI 385–86). On the following page, we find a similar statement framed expressly in ontological language: "Existence in general must be such as to be *capable* of taking on logical form, and existences in particular must be capable of taking on *differential* logical forms. But the operations which constitute controlled inquiry are necessary in order to give actuality to these capacities or potentialities" (LTI 387).

Both passages deal with questions of ontology since both describe *existences as such*, indicating something about them in reference to inquiry. Dewey thus appears to be admitting here in practice what he has previously denied in theory. When he says that "existence in general must be such as to be *capable* of taking on logical form," he is admitting that his logic is not independent of ontological assumptions. Indeed, his logic *depends* on an important ontological fact: that beings are suited to the kinds of inquiries he suggests.

In the last chapter, the understanding of forms was seen to be tied closely to the notion of possibility. The position is restated here in a manner consistent with the texts previously studied. The previous chapter also claimed that forms possess the status of potentials until they are actualized in experience.[16] Events possess certain possibilities, but it takes the work of inquiry to realize them. In the *Logic*, Dewey describes his position in similar terms. The above quotations assert that, in relation to existences, logical forms are possibilities until these existences undergo the operations of guided inquiry.

This indication of a coherent position in regard to forms lends support to my interpretation. I am claiming that an ontology of

formed beings can be found in Dewey's texts; I am arguing, in other words, that Dewey develops a revised version of a position with Greek roots. Thus far, we have seen that his comments concerning form fall together in a defensible and consistent pattern through three of his major works. The above quotations suggest that this analysis is continued and expanded in *Logic: The Theory of Inquiry*. What we must turn to now is a further analysis of this text to see just how the topic of forms is treated there.

4. LOGICAL FORMS

Various considerations will guide this investigation. First of all, I shall examine Dewey's statement that forms accrue to subject matter. Second, I shall show that Dewey's meaning for "logical form" is not a rigidly univocal one, and that there are two senses in which this expression can be understood. Third, I shall show how the doctrine which is presented in this text is both consistent and continuous with the analyses I have presented of Dewey's other writings.

The position which Dewey defends has been adumbrated in the discussion of method and ontology:

> The theory, in summary form, is that all logical forms (with their characteristic properties) arise within the operation of inquiry and are concerned with control of inquiry so that it may yield warranted assertions. This conception implies much more than that logical forms are disclosed or come to light when we reflect upon processes of inquiry that are in use. Of course it means that; but it also means that the forms *originate* in operations of inquiry. To employ a convenient expression, it means that while inquiry into inquiry is the *causa cognoscendi* of logical forms, primary inquiry is itself *causa essendi* of the forms which inquiry into inquiry discloses [LTI 11–12].

Several typical Deweyan themes are recapitulated in this citation. His insistence, for example, that forms are not given ready-made but originate in inquiry is simply another version of a continuing polemic against presentative realism.[17] This polemic, secondly, is based on Dewey's theory of transactions with an environment. Forms result from interactions. They are not immediate givens, merely to be espied by a knower/spectator.[18] This means, thirdly,

that the kind of activity termed inquiry is a necessary element in the origination of forms.

We have already discussed Dewey's insistence that the independence of formal logic as a norm in inquiry does not imply a transcendent origin for logical forms.[19] The argument that these forms are innate or *a priori* Dewey considers erroneous. His text seeks to refute this position by developing a doctrine of logical forms which is based on the kinds of analyses presented in his earlier books. The arguments against presentative realism, his teachings on the centrality of interactions, and his doctrine of experimental inquiry receive a new focus in logical theory. But the aim remains the same as in those texts: to stress the active as well as the passive character of inquiry, and to indicate that novelty, in the sense of new discoveries, becomes a real possibility. In this respect, logical theory is no different from any other kind of inquiry. Logic has had a history in which it has not remained unaltered. New forms have resulted in its development through time.

What are these forms? Using the expression in two distinct senses, without acknowledging their difference, Dewey provides both a restricted and a generalized meaning for "logical forms." The narrow sense refers specifically to the canons of logic, while the wider one extends to events in general. I shall begin by treating the narrow sense. This is the new meaning Dewey introduces in the *Logic*, and his alternative to other logical theories is based on it. The more generalized meaning will be discussed afterward.

Dewey identifies logical forms with *"proximate logical* subject-matter" (LTI 19), and explains the latter in the following way: "Proximate subject-matter is the domain of the relations of propositions to one another, such as affirmation-negation, inclusion-exclusion, particular-general, etc. No one doubts that the relations expressed by such words as *is, is-not, if-then, only (none but), and, or, some-all,* belong to the subject-matter of logic in a way so distinctive as to mark off a special field" (LTI 9). Given Dewey's intentions in this text, this kind of explanation is exactly what one would expect. Logical forms are the relations of propositions to one another which have been standardized in the procedures of formal logic. It is these forms—*modus ponens,* for example—that Dewey wishes to claim arose within the context of actual inquiries.

Dewey argues that these forms, much like legal and artistic forms, can be isolated from the context in which they occur. They can then be applied to new situations. But, as he reminds his readers time and again, the context may be abstracted from for practical purposes, but it must never be forgotten. "Just as art-forms and legal forms are capable of independent discussion and development, so are logical forms, even though the 'independence' in question is intermediate, not final and complete. As in the case of these other forms, they originate *out of* experiential material, and when constituted introduce new ways of operating with prior materials, which ways modify the material out of which they develop" (LTI 107).

When the logical forms are isolated, they can help guide reasoning to valid conclusions. In this way, they resemble formal legal descriptions, such as the statutes dealing with contracts. People have always engaged in making mutual promises, but the growing complexity and variety of these promises led to the necessity for codifying the conditions under which they must be kept. This formal codification could then be applied to the situations in which various individuals are involved in this kind of mutually dependent relationship. If properly applied, they lead to settlements of disputes concerning just when a valid contract has been made.[20]

The important fact for Dewey is that the formal conditions, once codified, may then be applied to the very kinds of situations which occasioned them, and may even "modify" those situations. In the same manner, logical forms may act as normative guidelines for inquiry, even though they were ultimately developed out of just those kinds of situations. Contractual forms guide the validity of mutual promises, and logical forms ensure the accuracy of reasoning processes. Yet neither comes from a separate realm of absolute certainty. Both, Dewey argues, have developed temporally.

Given the kind of endeavor Dewey undertook, that of providing a new explanation for logical forms, it would seem that the meaning just explained would have been fully satisfactory for his purposes. Indeed, so astute a commentator on Dewey's logic as Ernest Nagel explains logical forms in just this manner. He gives no indication that Dewey may have employed the expression in another, wider sense.[21] Yet there is sufficient textual evidence to suggest that, for Dewey, the label "logical form" has two clearly distinguishable meanings, both of which have to do with inquiry. The first, as we

have already seen, results from inquiry into inquiry itself, and refers to the different ways in which propositions may be related to each other as means to consequences.

The second deals with inquiry into situations in general. It also offers some confirmation for the type of interpretation I have been suggesting. Logical forms in this sense are presented by Dewey as alternatives to the fixed ontological forms of traditional thought. These logical forms are those forms that have arisen, not as a result of inquiry into inquiry, but within the process of inquiry into events. Logical forms are not restricted therefore to the relations of inference that a formal logician would discuss, but apply wherever inquiry has been successful.

Dewey's own manner of introducing the novelty of his approach to logical theory allows both the restricted and the generalized interpretations. "The differential trait of the variety of this type of theory expounded in this Part is that logical forms accrue to subject-matter in virtue of subjection of the latter in inquiry to the conditions determined by its end—institution of a warranted conclusion" (LTI 370). The importance of this characterization is that its scope is wide enough to allow the inclusion of natural and artistic forms under the heading "logical form." This is fully consistent with the Deweyan position as it has been explained thus far. Forms in general exist originally as possibilities, and the only manner in which they are realized is the experimental method. Inquiry is the name for the activity which employs this method, and for Dewey inquiry is identified with logic. Thus, all inquiries can in a sense be labeled logical, and all results called logical forms.

Dewey provides examples which explicitly illustrate this extended sense.

> Form and matter may become so integrally related to one another that a chair seems to be a chair and a hammer a hammer, in the same sense in which a stone is a stone and a tree is a tree. The instance is then similar to that of the cases in which prior inquiries have so standardized meanings that the form is taken to be inherent in matter apart from the function of the latter. . . .
>
> These instances exemplify the principle stated in the first part of this chapter; namely, that forms regularly accrue to matter in virtue of the adaptation of materials and operations to one another in the service of specified ends [LTI 383].

Dewey is stating here that the examples he has provided are illustrations of his teaching concerning logical forms. Yet the examples chosen are not the sort that deal with the formal processes of inference. Instead, he chooses items from *techne* and *physis*, arguing that their formed character must not be interpreted as *a priori* or pre-existent, but be viewed as having accrued during a temporal process.

Chairs, hammers, stones, and trees do possess standardized meanings. As we saw in the last chapter, Dewey is willing to admit that certain meanings may be focused on somewhat exclusively.[22] But what Dewey wants to suggest is that even such standardized meanings do not indicate the presence of eternal essences. Other forms, other meanings, are possible. This is why he extends the notion of logical forms to cover such instances not directly related to formal logic. Other inquiries, he is saying, would result in the accrual of other forms. Since logic is the theory of inquiry, these resultant forms can appropriately be called "logical." On a Deweyan interpretation, forms primarily indicate the relationship of means to consequences and of parts to wholes. Since these relationships can become realized only in the methodological procedure of inquiries, and since method for Dewey is logic, then all forms are in a very real sense logical forms, not just those relating specifically to the subject matter of formal logic.

A similar analysis is presented elsewhere in the *Logic* as the contrast between the ontological and the logical. In this instance as well, the clearly generalized thrust of "logical" becomes manifest. Dewey is discussing "substance," and he argues that this is not an ontological (i.e., fixed, eternal) determination, but a logical one.

> It [substantiality] is a form that accrues to original existence when the latter operates in a specified functional way as a consequence of operations of inquiry. It is not postulated that certain qualities always cohere in existence. It is postulated that they cohere as dependable evidential signs. The conjoined properties that mark off and identify a chair, a piece of granite, a meteor, are not sets of qualities given existentially as such and such. They are certain qualities which constitute in their ordered conjunction with one another valid signs of what will ensue when certain operations are performed. An object, in other words, is a set of qualities treated as *potentialities* for specified existential con-

sequences. Powder is what will explode under certain conditions; water as a substantial object is that group of connected qualities which will quench thirst, and so on [LTI 132].[23]

We find in this lengthy passage strong confirmation that the expression "logical forms" possesses a significance for Dewey much wider than either he openly admits or commentators like Nagel will allow. The substantiality that accrues as a result of inquiry is that of a chair, meteor, water, or powder. These are logical forms, ordered complexities exhibiting characteristic behaviors which have been realized in the process of inquiry.

At this point, we are in a position to ascertain the significance of *Logic: The Theory of Inquiry* for the present investigation. I mentioned at the beginning of this chapter that the *Logic* could be viewed as exemplifying the continuation of the growing prominence of forms in Dewey's thought. Because of this, it reinforces the interpretation I have been presenting of Dewey's philosophical endeavor. It has been my intention to demonstrate that, when Dewey is read carefully and interpreted properly, he can be viewed as presenting a coherent doctrine concerning the manner in which permanence is integrated with change. By concentrating on permanence, which few commentators have done, and especially on form, which no commentators have dealt with, I undertook to reconstruct a significant aspect of Dewey's ontology.

My interpretation that there is a revised doctrine of forms in Dewey's writings seems to be successfully established in three of his major works, but not yet in an important logical text. The topic of forms was conspicuous by its absence in the last book on the subject, *Essays in Experimental Logic,* published in 1916. Would a logical text written after the books on art and nature reflect the doctrinal developments that I had traced? Specifically, would a positive, reconstructed outlook on forms take a prominent place in a new exposition of logical theory? Such questions are the reasons why Dewey's *Logic* is in major respects a test of my interpretation.

Were these questions answered in the negative, then my interpretation would not have been automatically rejected, but it would certainly have been mitigated. For this would have meant that the *seeming* recognition on Dewey's part that forms are significant would have been just that, an appearance. Had forms been ignored in his *Logic,* this would have meant that Dewey did not consider

them to be of any special significance. The interpretation of the three books in which constructive analyses regarding form were found would remain valid, but truncated. Dewey's logical theory would have to be seen as standing apart from these texts, rather than as being continuous with them.

Of course, the two questions mentioned above are not to be answered in the negative. As a result, the *Logic* provides support for my interpretation in three ways. First of all, by choosing to deal with logical issues from the perspective of forms, Dewey reveals a conscious recognition that such a doctrine is present in his writings. Second, the manner in which he presents his discussion of logical forms is quite in accord with his positions in the previous books. Third, by using the expression "logical form" in a general sense, he explicitly recapitulates and retroactively validates the interpretive position that I have been developing.

5. SUMMARY

The significant issues raised in this chapter can be summarized by examining one of the few neologisms Dewey coined. His career was one great effort to overcome the fixed oppositions of modernity. The realists were wrong to assume an order of natural entities which simply needed to be reflected by the human mind. The idealists were mistaken in assuming either that "mere existence" had to be structured by mind, or that a higher Reason or Absolute Spirit had to be posited to mediate the oppositions of subject and object.

The Deweyan alternative to this position is that forms accrue to subject matters in the process of inquiry. This means, to use his neologism, that nature is "logiscible."[24] "Logiscible" signifies the possibilities that can be determined or realized through inquiry (which Dewey links to logic), and indicates the fact that nature will allow elucidation if the methodology of experimental logic is properly applied. "Logiscible" preserves the positive sense of "intelligible," but allows Dewey to stress the need for activity on the part of the inquiring individual. Otherwise the possibilities will remain unrealized. The term indicates a situation in which certain possibilities can be actualized if the appropriate procedures are utilized.

The main issues that have been raised in this chapter can be clustered around this technical term "logiscible." The first topic

attended to was the exact meaning that Dewey attached to the word "logic." We saw that, for Dewey, logic means primarily methodology. The experimental method, which he articulated at the beginning of the century and restated in the *Logic*, is still adhered to and held to be the main avenue for resolving tensional situations. The second topic discussed dealt with Dewey's claim that logic is independent of metaphysics. But "logiscible" refers to a trait of beings. It is an ontological assertion. This means that Dewey's insistence on the separation of logic from ontology cannot be supported even by his own approach to logical issues. There may be a sense in which the isolation Dewey suggested is valid, but his categorical assertion was shown to be untenable.

Third, "logical forms" were revealed to be what results when the logiscible becomes actualized in inquiry. Logical forms are neither innate nor uncovered by any means other than the empirical. They are actualized, realized counterparts of the possibilities described by the term "logiscible." We then came to understand that Dewey used the expression "logical form" in two senses. The first refers specifically to the procedures of formal logic; the second, to the results of any inquiry whatsoever. This generalized application led to the final issue discussed, a defense of the thesis I have been arguing. *Logic: The Theory of Inquiry* reinforces my ontological interpretation of the place of forms in Dewey's thought. To argue that events in general are formed is but another way of saying that they are logiscible. The forms are possibilities in relation to the inquiring, logical consciousness.

NOTES

1. See chap. 3, sect. 3.3.
2. *The Methods of Contemporary Thought,* trans. Peter Caws (Dordrecht: Reidel, 1965), p. 8.
3. Ibid.
4. Ibid., pp. 8–9.
5. Dewey's daughters have commented on this in the biography of their father prepared for the Schillp volume. "The influence of Professor Morris was undoubtedly one source of Dewey's later interest in logical theory. Morris was given to contrasting what he called 'real' logic, and associated with Aristotle and Hegel, with formal logic of which he had a low opinion. Dewey, in his years of association with Morris in Ann

Arbor, developed the idea that there was an intermediate kind of logic that was neither merely formal nor a logic of inherent 'truth' of the constitution of things: a logic of the processes by which knowledge is reached" ("Biography of John Dewey," ed. Jane M. Dewey, in *Philosophy of John Dewey*, ed. Schillp, p. 18).

6. As we saw in chap. 1, Dewey's only real criticism of Leibniz was that he had steadfastly adhered to a formal logic that was inconsistent with the overall tenor of his philosophy. See chap. 1, sect. 2.243.

7. See chap. 4, sect. 3.4.

8. Speaking of all three disciplines within logic, formal logic, methodology, and philosophy of logic, Bocheński has the following to say: "The most important thing is to maintain a strict separation between the three fields. Much mischief has been caused by their not being kept sufficiently apart" (*Methods*, p. 9).

9. H. S. Thayer, explaining what Dewey means by logic, indicates this stress on inquiry and method. "The scope of logic, according to Dewey, may be described in a general sense as the articulation and explicit formulation of the controlling instrumentalities and operations that function when problems are being inquired into and warranted solutions are arrived at. The theory of inquiry is a descriptive explanation of what happens when problems are investigated and solved logically or methodically and deliberately, with respect to the means taken to reach solutions. . . . What usually passes for logic and scientific method are not contrasted as two kinds of rational techniques for dealing with certain kinds of problems, but are incorporated as designating procedural and material means within the general movement of inquiry" (*Logic of Pragmatism*, pp. 9–10).

10. He uses the term explicitly in this sense later in the text. "The theory criticized holds that there is a cognitive subject antecedent to and independent of inquiry, a subject which is inherently a knowing being. *Since it is impossible to verify this assumption by any empirical means, it is a metaphysical preconception* which is then mixed with logical conditions to create a mode of 'epistemology' " (LTI 518; emphasis added).

11. "On the face of the matter, it does not seem fitting that logical theory should be determined by philosophical realism or idealism, rationalism or empiricism, dualism or monism, atomistic or organic metaphysics" (LTI 10).

12. I. M. Bocheński, *Contemporary European Philosophy*, trans. Donald Nicholl and Karl Aschenbrenner (Berkeley: University of California Press, 1957), p. 252.

13. Ibid.

14. Similar considerations were discussed in chap. 3, sect. 4.2.

15. I have already discussed Dewey's understanding of metaphysics in chap. 5, sect. 1.

16. See chap. 6, sect. 4.3.

17. Dewey's arguments against realism were discussed in chap. 3, sect. 3.2.

18. Dewey finds the Aristotelian logic to be an example of this procedure. "Traditional theory, however, takes the propositions as given ready-made and hence as independent and complete in themselves. They are just there to be noticed, with description of whatever properties they present. This mode of treatment becomes intelligible when it is viewed in conjunction with its derivation from the ontological logic of Aristotle, whence it ultimately derives. In the latter logic, species or kinds are the ultimate qualitative wholes or real individuals. Some of these species are by nature, or by inherent essence, exclusive of others" (LTI 182).

19. See above, sect. 3.

20. Dewey uses the example of contractual agreements at LTI 371.

21. Nagel explains what Dewey means by "logical form" in the following way. "According to him, things and qualities acquire *functions* in inquiry which they did not have antecedently to it, and the specifically distinct *ways* in which things function in this context is just what he understands by logical form. For example, perceptual material in its sheer existential status does not have the logical form of being evidence, nor does the occurrence of an idea in revery have the status of a hypothesis—any more than a bear is always a target—except on the occasions when these items enter appropriate contexts involving specific types of activity" ("Dewey's Reconstruction of Logical Theory," in *The Philosopher of the Common Man: Essays in Honor of John Dewey to Celebrate His Eightieth Birthday*, ed. Sidney Ratner (New York: Putnam's, 1940; repr. New York: Greenwood, 1966), p. 73.

22. See chap. 6, sect. 4.4.

23. There are echoes in this discussion concerning substance of the earliest, Kantian, phase in Dewey's development. He had struggled, at that time, with the distinction between "substance" and "mere succession of phenomena." (See chap. 1, sect. 2.1.) In the *Logic*, Dewey distinguishes between "substance" and "original existence." But the particular way in which he treats this distinction is indicative of the direction in which his development has moved since his earliest writings. Two points especially stand out in this regard: (*a*) Substance is determined no longer by a mind separate from the phenomena, but by an experimenter who actively engages in purposefully directed transactions with the subject matter; and (*b*) "original existence" must not be interpreted as an amorphous, unknowable "x." Since his Hegelian phase, Dewey has

been quite clear on the fact that there is no such thing as *mere* existence. "Original existence" means simply the subject matter as it exists at the beginning of inquiry. It may and probably does possess some standardized meanings that are susceptible of being transformed in a new inquiry.

24. The word "logiscible" is not found in many Deweyan texts, but Randall has focused on it as an important and accurate expression of what Dewey wanted to say. "Frederick J. E. Woodbridge, speaking as a structuralist, holds, 'Nature has a logical structure.' Dewey the functionalist preferred to say, "Nature has a 'logiscible' structure" ("T. H. Green and Liberal Idealism," *Philosophy After Darwin*, ed. Singer, pp. 68–69). He also refers to the word "logiscibility." See *Nature and Historical Experience: Essays in Naturalism and in the Theory of History* (New York: Columbia University Press, 1958), p. 134. One of the few places in which Dewey uses the term is in the article "The Applicability of Logic to Existence," *The Journal of Philosophy*, 27 (1930), 179.

CONCLUSION

Some Implications of the Study

1. DEWEY AND THE
FOUNDATIONALIST/ANTI-FOUNDATIONALIST CONTROVERSY

THE INTERPRETATION OF DEWEY'S METAPHYSICS presented in the preceding chapters has a direct bearing on a much-discussed topic in contemporary philosophical literature. I am referring to the dispute between foundationalists and anti-foundationalists, especially as it has been articulated in the works of Richard Rorty. Rorty is a prominent defender of the anti-foundationalist side of this issue, of course, but he is particularly important with respect to my analyses because he enlists Dewey's support in his enterprise. Rorty admires Dewey as someone who encouraged the promulgation of "a non-epistemological sort of philosophy" (MN 381)[1] by undermining "philosophical realism" (MN 382). A list of "the richest and most original philosophers of our time" (CP 51) would include Dewey along with Heidegger and Wittgenstein. These thinkers are praised as forward-looking individuals who were effective at criticizing the tradition (CP 35), while helping philosophy to break free from its "outworn" (MN 12) past.

Such high praise is counterbalanced by the admission that there are weaknesses in Dewey's philosophy, the most significant of which speaks directly to the line of interpretation I have been defending in this book. Dewey did well, according to Rorty, until he was "side-tracked into doing 'metaphysics'" (CP 82). The very expression "naturalistic metaphysics" (CP 81) is a contradiction in terms because it seeks to combine the empirical with the ahistorical. This "bad ('metaphysical')" (CP 214) side of Dewey is most evident when he seeks to redescribe *nature* and *experience* (CP 85). Dewey failed here to carry his criticism of the tradition to its proper conclusion. By attempting to provide descriptive characteristics of experience and nature he was backsliding and engendering conflict "according to the old rules" (CP 35). On this view Dewey did not realize that

197

his criticisms of the philosophical tradition opened the way to what Rorty calls a "post-Philosophical" (CP xxi) culture. Disappointingly, Dewey went about doing what philosophers have always done, providing formulations of experience, nature, and value which are thought to be more accurate than the erroneous views of their predecessors (CP 79–80). Rorty wants to claim Dewey as an "edifying" non-foundationalist philosopher, but "Dewey's mistake" (CP 85), his wrongheaded excursion into metaphysics, is a great embarrassment to such an interpretation. Rorty thus dimisses it as a lapse on Dewey's part. The *real* Dewey, covered over by such expendable texts as *Experience and Nature*,[2] has no need for such an undertaking. Indeed, metaphysics is something that "Dewey's own view of the nature and function of philosophy precludes" (CP 77).

To sort out the confusions, misunderstandings, and misrepresentations Dewey suffers at the hands of Rorty, I shall review some of the main lines of my interpretation in light of his claims. The proper understanding of what metaphysics involves along with Rorty's views on this matter were taken up in the Introduction. I shall not repeat them here. My remarks will be limited to a commentary on the attempted appropriation of Dewey to the anti-foundationalist camp.

We must begin by recognizing that the foundationalist/anti-foundationalist split is not a *problem* that can be *solved* on Deweyan lines. The very formulation of the antithesis is foreign to the spirit of what Dewey sought to accomplish. We saw in Chapter 3 how he refused to align himself with either the realist or the idealist schools. We also saw how the influence of Darwin led Dewey to realize that the very phrasing of controversies such as that of mechanism *vs.* teleology prevented a satisfactory resolution of them. Dewey was a naturalist who stressed the interaction of existents with their environments as a primordial trait of existence. Those polarized oppositions which resulted from an alternative (usually dualistic) ontology had to be restated in light of the more accurate ontological analysis. They were, as we saw, not so much solved as dissolved.

The foundationalist and the non-foundationalist positions offer another instance of the same procedure. They arise in the context of "epistemology," in the derisive sense Dewey gave to that term. The foundationalist viewpoint is constructed on assumptions derived

from Plato and Kant. The Platonic division into two realms of being and two subsequent levels of cognition, when combined with
the Kantian endeavor to certify the adequacy of knowledge claims,
provides the background against which foundationalists operate.
They ask the Platonic question "What differentiates knowledge
from mere belief?" and go off in search of foundations that will
provide the criteria for categorizing certain claims as real knowledge. One response common to foundationalists, according to Rorty,
is that the criteria involve "reference to an object" (MN 156). The
image best exemplifying this view is that of a mirror that accurately
reflects objects. Such a mirror containing the correct reflections becomes the "touchstone for choice between justified and unjustified
claims" (MN 212). Rorty summarizes the foundationalist position
in the following way: (a) The original impulse is that of "having
our beliefs determined by being brought face-to-face with the object
of the belief" (MN 163); (b) improvements in knowing result from
improvements in the accuracy of representations within the mirror
of nature (MN 163); (c) "Then comes the idea that the way to have
accurate representations is to find, within the Mirror, a special class
of representations so compelling that their accuracy cannot be
doubted" (MN 163). These representations, innate ideas, sense data,
the structure of language, or Platonic forms, and the like, provide
the boundaries of knowledge. They act, Rorty says, as "constraints,"
imposing "frameworks beyond which one must not stray, objects
which impose themselves, representations which cannot be gain-
said" (MN 315).

Without the dualistic assumption of a knowing subject that is both
distinct and separate from a known object there would be no context within which such questions as "Is knowledge possible?" "How
are knowledge claims to be justified?" or "What are the most accurate representations?" would make sense. If there is no separate substance called "mind" to which objects are "presented" or "given,"
then the issue of providing justifications for asserting that certain
representations are more accurate reflections of a disparate object
than others does not arise. Such questions, indeed, do not interest
Dewey in the least. The whole vocabulary in which such topics are
phrased has been revised by what he called his "Copernican Revolution," which he described as:

The old centre was mind knowing by means of an equipment of powers complete within itself, and merely exercised upon an antecedent external material equally complete in itself. The new centre is indefinite interactions taking place within a course of nature which is not fixed and complete, but which is capable of direction to new and different results through the mediation of intentional operations [QC 232].

By suggesting this Copernican Revolution Dewey has completely altered the context in which gnoseological questions are raised. The whole vocabulary in which such topics have been phrased under the influence of Cartesian and Kantian philosophies now has to be revised. After Dewey, philosophical questions have to be reformulated in the same way as astronomical questions had to be reformulated after Copernicus.

This is not to say that Dewey ignores reflection, inquiry, and cognition. His novel ontological orientation simply leads him to a concern with different questions in relation to knowing. Consistent with his recognition that events are temporal is his rejection of the textbook notion that there are rigidly fixed philosophical problems that have plagued thinkers from Thales to the present. The very formulation of questions depends on an ontological orientation. Dewey has opened the door to post-modern philosophy by revealing the ways in which the modern map of generative ideas was flawed, sterile, and truncated. His metaphysics, as I have interpreted it, articulates the lineaments of existence in a manner which transforms the very manner in which philosophical questions are to be posed.

Dewey is not interested, for example, in ascertaining whether knowledge is possible. Intelligence in the service of modifying the environment/organism interaction is an ongoing and obvious fact. What he seeks to discover is the manner in which human beings can increase, improve, and manipulate what is known in order to attain more security, harmony, and satisfaction. Dewey wants to examine "how we think" so that we may better attain this kind of security, harmony, and satisfaction. The question of justifying knowledge claims by suggesting that they are grounded, or have their foundations, in something like the "directly evident" or the "self-presenting"[3] is a relic of a previous and outmoded philosophical era. It is not a relic because he supports the kind of anti-

foundationalist view Rorty espouses. Rather, the entire controversy must be viewed as artificial because it is based on an erroneous metaphysics, one that separates matter and mind.

Rorty's claims notwithstanding, Dewey's own orientation cannot be properly understood apart from his new metaphysics as I have described it in this book. Any attempt at understanding Dewey while not appreciating the ontology he worked out in his writings from 1925 onward will lead to the claim that there are two Deweys: one who is a foundationalist, and one who is not. There exist many Deweyan texts which if taken in isolation can provide solace to both the foundationalist and the anti-foundationalist. The only avenue left open for Rorty, if he wishes Dewey as an ally, is to dismiss as unimportant those texts that do not support his view. This is of course exactly what he does. Such a procedure, the selective appropriation of an earlier thinker's writings, is entirely defensible as a later thinker weaves the strands of a new synthesis. But what is not defensible is the coupling of this selective appropriation with the claim that the *real* Dewey is being brought out. It is one thing for a scholar to say "there are many aspects of Dewey's thought that I find accurate and enlightening." It is another matter entirely for the same scholar to claim that "those aspects with which I agree represent Dewey more accurately than he represented himself." Yet it is an assertion like the latter, absolutely unjustified as an historical or interpretive statement, which Rorty makes.

A thorough reading of Dewey would lead to a different conclusion: that his great achievement was to reformulate entirely the philosophical orientation within which such controversies as that between the foundationalists and the anti-foundationalists could take place. Dewey's importance for subsequent thinkers resides in this very attempt at reformulating philosophical problems. He does indeed criticize the tradition in the manner for which Rorty praises him, but he does so in order to *reconstruct* not *deconstruct* the philosophical heritage. Chapters 5 and 6 of the present book reveal this with special clarity.

If we ask how exactly it is that Dewey reconstructs the tradition, three major prongs of his analysis must be re-emphasized. (*a*) Interaction of existents within situations is the basal descriptive fact that philosophers must recognize. Situations are not constructed out of separate, disconnected, individual elements that somehow have re-

lations superimposed on them. Relations are a primary or archaic (in its etymological sense) factor. This is a constant Deweyan theme from his Hegelian period onward. (*b*) Vital experience[4] is neither wholly nor primarily cognitive. Dewey denied the ubiquity of the knowledge relation from his experimental phase onward and, like his younger contemporary Heidegger, rejected the identification of οὐσία with ἰδέα.[5] Ordinary experience is wider than cognition, including, as it does, moral and aesthetic dimensions. Dewey's criticisms of realism and idealism, discussed in Chapter 3, are based on the recognition of this fact. (*c*) Forms must be understood in terms of possibility. The possibility/realization or logiscibility/accrual distinction worked out in his naturalistic period is what allowed Dewey to reconstruct traditional views in light of scientific achievements. If these three doctrines are properly appreciated, it will be possible to understand how Dewey was able to avoid the excesses of the earlier realistic philosophies, while not succumbing to the reactive excesses of abandoning the connectedness or grounding of ideas in nature. The articulation of the contribution Dewey can make to the foundationalist/non-foundationalist dispute will evolve as an outgrowth of these three points.

Rorty's writings on this issue are fertile, exciting, and provocative. He is especially to be praised for delivering one more (perhaps final) blow to the edifice of epistemology-centered philosophies that have been dominant since the time of Descartes. But his own response to foundationalism, a blend of historicism and coherentism, offers only one, and perhaps not the most suitable, alternative to the Cartesian and Kantian traditions he is seeking to overcome. His suggestion that "conversation" and social practice replace the confrontation with objects suggested by previous philosophers does offer a viable alternative to foundationalism. Still, it is only one alternative. More important, given the line of research undertaken in this book, it has little in common with the philosophy of John Dewey. This is significant because Rorty, as I have already made clear, claims to be carrying on the type of endeavor Dewey began. That endeavor, properly understood, opens a path that allows philosophers to avoid the errors of past epistemologies while preserving the integrity and connection of humans with the natural world. This view cannot be properly grasped, however, if certain central doctrines within his philosophy are excised.

Rorty claims that Dewey was a leader in the undermining of philosophical realism, and he goes on to build an interpretation of Dewey as an unmitigated non-realist. But such an interpretation is not at all sensitive to the nuances in Dewey's thought. The argument in Chapter 3 describing the objections Dewey marshaled against both realism and idealism must be recalled if he is to be interpreted correctly. What must be kept in mind in relation to realism is that only certain versions of that doctrine were criticized. He was careful to single out "presentative," "analytic," and "epistemological" realisms as discredited positions. These three varieties of realism share one untenable assumption: in a knowledge situation an antecedently existing object is simply presented to a knower. A knower, Dewey well realized, is no simple spectator, taking in (or mirroring) the entities that make up the natural world. The "metaphysics of presence," that *bête noire* of the deconstructionists, Dewey had already disposed of in the early decades of this century. Knowing involves an objective that can be attained only by means of some manipulation or experimentation with the antecedently existent situation. The knower has to *do* something to attain knowledge. This was what Dewey meant to emphasize by the label "instrumentalism." Knowing and doing must not be interpreted as antithetical activities. In Chapters 2 and 3, I explained this view and indicated how a careful appreciation of the idiosyncratic manner in which Dewey uses the term "object" is necessary for a proper grasp of what he is saying. Nonetheless, it is clear that, as far as Dewey is concerned, knowing does not simply mirror beings.

Dewey could be aligned with the anti-foundationalists *if* this represented his position in its entirety. But it does not. Dewey's view cannot be classified as supporting either foundationalism or Rorty's brand of non-foundationalism. If any term describes his orientation, it is "eventualist." Events themselves set the boundaries of reflection and inquiry for Dewey. The direction and effectiveness of inquiry are guided by the situation out of which the need for inquiry arises. The outcomes or eventuations of inquiry must then be examined and adjudicated by reference to the situations out of which they arose. The link between nature and human nature is not severed in Dewey's thought from his Hegelian period onward. He could never have written an article with the title which Rorty gave to one of his efforts, "The World Well Lost" (CP 3–18). Indeed, he spent his

whole philosophical life trying to articulate properly the manner in which humans and the natural world are related.

The importance of *experience, interaction,* and *possibility* can be ascertained at this point. Dewey is difficult to understand because he articulates a novel metaphysics. Commentators on his works who overlook the centrality of these three doctrines cannot gain a proper understanding of his thought. I shall begin with some remarks on experience and interaction while pursuing the topic of possibility later on.

Readers who persist in seeing subject and object or individual and environment as primordial data will misinterpret Dewey badly. The primal, basal situation involves complex multirelational *circumstances*[6] (if I may use this word in its etymological sense as the totality of surrounding things). Ingredients within the circumstances, such as individuals, qualities, hindrances, activities, whatever someone might consider to be "simple" or "self-evident," can be focused on by choice. They are, Dewey says, "selected for a purpose" (EN 35). Cognition involves this kind of refined, selective activity. Life experiences, those interactions which comprise most of our lives, are to a great degree non-cognitive. They concern use and enjoyment. It is only when problematic situations arise that reflection and inquiry are brought to bear on experience. Such problematic situations can come about for any number of reasons: changes might occur which upset the usual rhythm of use and enjoyment; questions arise out of curiosity as to what things are like or how they work; people seek ways to avoid certain aspects of experience while extending and securing others. Warranted assertibility results when the appropriate method for resolving problematic situations is employed. Dewey had learned from Morris to avoid the vices of epistemology-centered idealisms. Thus he does not consider the questions "How is knowledge justified?" and "Is anything antecedently given or directly evident or self-presenting?" to be especially burning issues. The significant question is, rather, how do we go about "bettering and enriching the subject-matters of crude experience" (EN 29). How, starting from life experience in its complexity, do we go about securing the "possibility of intelligent administration of the elements of doing and suffering" (EN 29)?

Rorty asserts that the non-foundationalist seeks an "airtight case," not an "unshakeable foundation" (MN 157). Dewey does not seek

an unshakeable foundation; nor does he consider the appropriate-
ness of his approach to be judged on the basis of "conversation between persons, rather than a matter of interaction with non-human
reality" (MN 157). Dewey could never assent to such a claim because of the manner in which interaction with environment is
denigrated. While Dewey does not consider warranted assertibility
to be the outcome of scrutinizing, examining, or otherwise interacting with non-human reality as represented for example by a
Platonic realm of Forms, he nonetheless emphasizes forcefully that
interactions within a situation are the *sources* of inquiry and the
touchstones of its success or failure. Dewey does not spend his philosophical time examining such issues as the structure of "mind," or
engaging in "conceptual analysis," but he does assert the need for
awareness of the context, limitations, and direction provided by the
natural world. "The exacting conditions imposed by nature, that
have to be observed in order that work be carried through to success, are the source of all noting and recording of nature's doings.
They supply the discipline that chastens exuberant fancy into respect for the operation of events, and that effects the subjection of
thought to a pertinent order of space and time" (EN 100).

There are no foundations in Dewey if by foundations we mean
some form of a self-evident given. But inquiry is not self-enclosed.
It reaches beyond itself and is to be judged on how well the eventuations, objects, of inquiry have resolved problematic situations.
For Dewey, the forms which accrue as the outcomes of inquiries have
come out of a particular set of circumstances, and they are to be
judged in relation to that context. There are no unshakable, *a priori*, or apodictic foundations, but knowledge can be considered
meaningful only by referring to the *interactions* with the natural
world of which humans form a part.

Interaction is thus a term which points beyond inquiry for Dewey.
It is both what occasions reflection and what adjudicates it. Such a
teaching would appear to bring Dewey dangerously close to the
realisms he so steadfastly opposed in his career. The next dimension
of Dewey's metaphysics that I wish to discuss, "possibility," reveals
the manner in which he is able to distance himself from those realisms. Trendelenburg, as I indicated in Chapter 1, had sought to
overcome the polarities in modern philosophy by reintroducing the
Aristotelian doctrine of potentiality and actuality. Dewey concen-

trated on this distinction in his favorable interpretation of Leibniz. This seed, planted during his idealistic period, reached full maturation during his naturalistic phase.

If the interpretation presented in this book is correct, forms are neither given (as some foundationalists might claim) nor denied (the Rortyan non-foundationalist view). There is no simple either/ or for Dewey. It is the doctrine of possibility which allows the actual complexity of existence to be delineated. Rorty appears to have oversimplified the options within philosophy. His depiction of the foundationalist/anti-foundationalist dispute embodies a false dilemma: either Plato or Protagoras. Dewey, on the other hand, embraces neither the correspondence theory nor the coherence theory. His view breaks out of these molds altogether. Rejecting correspondence to "objects" that existed prior to inquiry, he embraces in a significant sense "grounding" in the natural world. So prominent is this aspect in his thought that one leading Dewey scholar has claimed that "it is hard to imagine a theory of ideas more rigorously controlled by the nature of objects than this one [Dewey's]."[7]

To express accurately the way in which a proper understanding of possibility allows Dewey to overcome the constraints inherited from the modern tradition in philosophy, I shall not construct an imaginary community of Antipodeans but refer in a more mundane, concrete, and realistic manner to a famous contemporary of Dewey's, the plant breeder Luther Burbank. Here was an individual who worked marvels with his cross-breedings. The reflections he has left us on his work offer an opportunity for elucidating Dewey's teachings. The three elements of the Deweyan analysis mentioned above must be kept in mind as we examine Burbank's example: (*a*) primary experience is wider, more inclusive than cognitive reflection; (*b*) all experience grows out of interactions;[8] (*c*) forms are possibilities that are realized as a result of inquiry. These are familiar doctrines which have been exposed and commented on in the previous seven chapters. I am restating them here even at the risk of being repetitious because they are so crucial to a correct interpretation of Dewey's philosophical orientation.

The Burbank citation is one in which he describes how some of his "most important and valuable work" was with plums. The occasion for this effort was the fact that the plum, though consumed and

enjoyed, was, prior to his breeding experiments, "small, usually acidic, generally unfit for shipping, often with a large stone."

> I wanted to get a plum that would ship . . . a plum that would be beautiful and delicious, a plum that would be large, a plum for canning, a plum with a small pit or none at all, and so on. My designs were pretty carefully worked out. For instance, as regards the shipping plum. The plum developed to be picked from the tree and eaten right there, or within a few hours in the house, was quite a different thing from the plum that could be picked, packed, shipped, delivered maybe thousands of miles away, unpacked, sold, carried home, and finally eaten fresh. . . . And this couldn't be acquired by accident or chance—it had to be studied and the specifications pretty carefully written.[9]

All the ingredients for an accurate interpretation of naturalistic metaphysics and inquiry as Dewey conceives them are included in this passage. There is, to begin with, the original situation of primary, vital, ordinary experience. This provides the milieu which occasions Burbank's efforts. Use and enjoyment predominate in this milieu. Humans find themselves in an environment which includes a certain fruit, the plum. This fruit is consumed and enjoyed. It provides sustenance and refreshment. The plum is thus a natural good which is selected, preferred by a number of individuals. Now, out of this original, not yet cognitive, experience there arise issues that call forth cognition. Change and improvement are important factors in human life. Direct, concrete experience gives way to a situation that is "tensional" or "problematic" when certain questions arise. The people enjoying the plum might, for example, wonder how they can go about enhancing the qualities of the plum while minimizing its deficiencies. They might, in addition, seek out ways to share the fruit with their fellow–human beings on a wider scale than is currently possible.

Questions like these transform an experience that was not primarily cognitive into one which seeks the direction and control that knowledge can bring. The concrete experience of use and enjoyment has been altered. The kinds of issues Burbank raised affect the rhythm and equilibrium of ordinary experience. Whereas the original plum was accepted as a fruit of a certain size, with a certain level of acidity, and a large pit, those characteristics are now brought

into question. Use and enjoyment within the direct, primary experience no longer suffice. An attempt is being made to improve
the ordinary experience. It would be preferable to enjoy a larger,
sweeter, seedless plum. Instead of the original plum enjoyed by a
limited number of people because it did not ship well, it would be
helpful to produce one that could travel thousands of miles, yet
remain attractive to the palate. Inquiry is, for Dewey, an attempt
to resolve problems such as these. The ends sought could not be
achieved, as Burbank remarked, "by accident or chance." The task
of this particular inquiry was well defined: to investigate by means
of experimentation whether certain varieties of plums satisfying the
new criteria could be brought into existence. Knowledge in this
case does not strive to ascertain antecedently existent reality, but
attempts to attain certain objectives. Burbank did not prejudge his
experiments as failures because of *a priori* constraints and limitations. He did not view his efforts as necessarily condemned to failure because there was a fixed form of plum which could not be
altered. He simply undertook, by experimenting with various par-
ent stocks, to select for the qualities he sought. He pressed the plum
species to reveal its possibilities and produce new forms of the fruit.
The varieties resulting from this endeavor were structured in certain ways. They possessed characteristic patterns of appearance and
behavior. They were, in other words, formed entities.

Once these had been produced, their "truth" and "value" could
be determined by examining in what ways they satisfied the aims set
forth at the beginning of the inquiry. There is only one sure way of
deciding whether a plum can travel a thousand miles, be stored on a
grocery shelf, brought home, and remain not merely edible but
tasteful: send some of the new varieties on just such a journey. The
problematic situation arose within a context, and the success or failure in resolving it will be judged by a return to that context. This
indicates one of the ways in which Dewey could be said to stand
with the foundationalists. For him, inquiry is indeed judged by
more than the Rortyan criterion of "what society lets us say" (MN
174). The new plum has restored equilibrium where there was tension if indeed it can be shipped thousands of miles, placed on a
supermarket shelf, brought home, and at that point reveal itself as
soft, juicy, and sweet. Success in inquiry is inextricably connected to
interactions between humans and their environments. No theory

which severs this connection can claim Dewey as one of its adherents.

Dewey's sensitivity to the nuances of possibility inherent in existential situations serves him particularly well in this respect. The forms, as he understands them, do not exist prior to their eventuation in natural beings. There can thus be no correspondence to antecedently existing forms as the touchstone of truth and certainty. At the same time the forms (as in the case of the plum varieties Burbank produced) are "logiscible," capable of being realized. On that account, all talk of structure and essence should not be abandoned. This is a position which Rorty suggests when he chides Sartre for not pushing further his insight that there is no human essence. Sartre, he says, should have "followed up his remark that man is the being whose essence is to have no essence by saying that this went for all other beings also" (MN 361–62*n*7). Dewey, true to his reconstructionist attitude, wishes to reject only what is untenable in older philosophies. That any pre-evolutionary doctrine of forms falsifies existence is a view Dewey accepts; that any doctrine of forms is false is an overreaction Dewey is careful to avoid.

By concentrating on contextually centered analyses, by focusing on problems of securing and enhancing values, and by recognizing the importance of formulating a metaphysics for such an endeavor, Dewey reconstructed in a large-scale manner the philosophical heritage that gave rise to problems such as the foundationalist/antifoundationalist controversy. He cannot, I must repeat once again, be allied to either side of this controversy. His whole endeavor, from the Hegelian period onward, was to reveal the manner in which such philosophical problems had been inaugurated and sustained by erroneous ontological assumptions. Dewey is significant in relation to the question of foundationalism *vs.* non-foundationalism, but it is as someone who restructured our very way of looking at this entire topic.

2. On Interpreting Dewey

The misrepresentation of Dewey by a sympathetic scholar like Rorty raises the question of how it could happen that Dewey would be so badly misunderstood. This topic deserves a few comments since Dewey is a thinker who can readily be misinterpreted. Because of the great variety of philosophical traditions that were

ingredients in his ultimate synthesis, Dewey's writings present special problems. It is possible on the basis of having read some of these texts to impute to him various positions that he did not hold at all. I have dealt at length in this book with critics who accuse him of being an idealist. He could also be misrepresented as a realist, a Lockean, an Hegelian, or, as I have mentioned, as both a foundationalist and a non-foundationalist. Such interpretations could all call on certain texts for support. Dewey interpretation cannot then be simply a matter of reading a substantial portion of his writings and selecting extracts that are said to typify his orientation. Views imputed to him on this basis are more than likely to be misleading, if not entirely false. Deweyan scholarship needs to make a special effort if it is to portray this thinker's positions accurately. That effort will involve both a strenuous philosophical reorientation and a sensitivity to certain factors in his writing style and evolution as a thinker.

Much of the difficulty surrounding a proper interpretation of Dewey rests on one important fact: he significantly altered the very assumptions according to which philosophers were accustomed to proceed. His interpreters must vigilantly seek to avoid reading their own assumptions into Dewey's texts. Anyone, for example, who claims to find a discussion of the is/ought or mind/body questions along typical (modern, dualistic) lines in Dewey's writings has failed badly to learn from the Deweyan corpus. The mind/body problem and the is/ought distinction are among the issues that a Deweyan philosophy regards as associated with an earlier, erroneous ontology. Admittedly, it is a difficult task to understand Dewey properly when our very language embodies polarities (subject/object, knowing/doing, individual/environment) as givens of experience which Dewey argues are "takens," selected for a particular purpose. Yet, until thinkers begin to conceive of situations and circumstances rather than individuals as primary, Dewey's insights will remain either hidden or distorted by the prism of earlier assumptions.

Unfortunately, this theoretical problem is compounded by the notorious difficulty of expression in Dewey's works. James Gouinlock, who knows Dewey's writings as well as anyone, admits quite readily that "Dewey never won any prizes for clarity." He goes on to say that there are many "obscure, ill-expressed, and confusing

passages in his works; and a scholar might read them in various ways." [10] There are, however, certain safeguards to maximize the chances of a correct interpretation of Dewey.

First of all, no interpreter can come to a proper understanding of Dewey's philosophy unless two crucial aspects of his career and writings are recognized. Dewey scholars must learn the lesson that Jaeger taught with regard to Aristotle: the philosophy in question is a *developmental* one. It is a position that has evolved through time. Dewey's thinking underwent a considerable amount of modification as his career progressed. Secondly, many of his writings are of a *polemical* nature. They cannot be read as texts conceived in isolation from burning philosophical controversies. Those same controversies may no longer arouse the passions they once did, but Dewey must be seen as a thinker engaged in active disputations with other philosophers. No serious analysis of Dewey's thought can afford to overlook these two considerations.

The *developmental* aspect is significant for critics and supporters alike. Both the critic wishing to accuse Dewey of error or inconsistency, and the supporter arguing that a particular position accurately reflects Dewey's thinking, must take account of the fact that his was an evolving, continually developing philosophy.[11] Only then can the criticism or exposition be justified. The polemical aspect is closely interwoven with the developmental. Dewey tends, as is not uncommon in the heat of controversy, to overstate his position. This means that if only selected texts are studied, with reference neither to their place in Dewey's career nor to the particular controversy occupying him, his position can easily be misunderstood. Would-be interpreters of Dewey should ask themselves two questions when confronting his texts: (*a*) At what stage in Dewey's evolution does this text occur? and (*b*) Has the controversial climate in which this text was prepared perhaps led Dewey to employ exaggerated formulations?

The care and work needed for an accurate reading of Dewey does, however, repay the effort. Here is a philosopher who touched, in an original and provocative way, a variety of significant philosophical disciplines from logic to the philosophy of culture, and whose writings are of such a nature that they tend to encourage further constructive effort rather than static satisfaction with the pronounce-

ments of a master. There are a few special characteristics of the Deweyan corpus that are especially significant in this regard. I should like to end by identifying them.

The most prominent among these is Dewey's attitude toward other disciplines. It is an attitude best described by the adjective *irenic*. Dewey sought to overcome the isolation of philosophy from the natural sciences, the social sciences, literature, and art. New discoveries or productions in these areas he did not fear as threats to an established and unchangeable philosophical system. They were, rather, welcomed as opportunities to increase meaning and understanding, to secure further goods, and to enhance the occasions for consummatory experiences.

Another characteristic is his *experiential* approach to philosophical problems. He did not begin with the pronouncements of previous philosophers. Instead, his procedure was to confront the experienced world directly. He never sought to fit the facts of experience into preconceived schemas (not even the ones he had set forth). The virtue which is required if such an orientation is to bear fruit, and which Dewey possessed, is *courage*: the courage to be honest in dealing with philosophical problems, even if this means modification of previously held positions. This is a trait which Dewey shared with one of his favorite philosophers, Plato. The only difference between the two men would appear to be that the Plato who wrote the *Sophist* and the *Parmenides* was more interested in retrogressive self-reflection than Dewey, whose main concern was to move forward.

Finally, in a more specific sense, Dewey is to be commended for his attempt to work out a metaphysics at the very time the anti-metaphysical propaganda of the logical positivists was beginning to have an effect on philosophy in English-speaking countries. To be sure, there are limitations that adhere to Dewey's formulated positions. But, in many respects, these result from the fact that, in important ways, Dewey was a pioneer breaking new ground. This willingness of his to explore new ontological ground stands as an example of his philosophical courage. He deserves recognition not only as someone whose ontological analyses reached a certain level of achievement, but, more significant, considering the neo-positivist impact on Anglo-American philosophy, as one who undertook ontological analyses at all.

NOTES

1. References to Rorty's *Philosophy and the Mirror of Nature* (MN) and *The Consequences of Pragmatism* (CP) will be given in parentheses in the text.

2. "I myself would join Reichenbach in dismissing classical Husserlian phenomenology, Bergson, Whitehead, the Dewey of *Experience and Nature*, the James of *Radical Empiricism*, neo-Thomist epistemological realism, and a variety of other late nineteenth- and early twentieth-century systems" (CP 213–14).

3. These two expressions are from a defender of the foundationalist position, Roderick Chisholm. The second is a later, emended version of the first. See *The Foundations of Knowing* (Minneapolis: The University of Minnesota Press, 1982), p. 26.

4. Many confusions engendered by Dewey's use of the term "experience" could have been avoided if commentators had paid attention to the adjectives with which Dewey qualifies this term. In the first chapter of EN the following are among the list of qualifiers used: "concrete" (p. 39), "direct" (p. 23), "primary" (p. 23), "gross" (p. 24), "ordinary" (p. 17), "crude but total" (p. 19). The original version of the first chapter also included "coarse and vital" (p. 367) as a way of expressing what Dewey intended.

5. Martin Heidegger, "Plato's Doctrine of Truth," trans. John Barlow, in *Philosophy in the Twentieth Century* III, edd. William Barrett and Henry Aiken (New York: Random House, 1962), p. 267.

6. Jose Ortega y Gasset has brought the word "circumstance" into the universe of philosophical discourse. "All life means finding oneself in 'circumstances' or in the world around us. For this is the fundamental meaning of the idea 'world.' The world is the sum total of our vital possibilities. It is not then something apart from and foreign to our existence; it is its actual periphery" (*The Revolt of the Masses* [New York: Norton, 1932], p. 44). Dewey, seeking an appropriate term to indicate his philosophical orientation, had attempted to introduce the Latin word *res* during his experimental phase: "Philosophers in their exclusively intellectual preoccupation with analytic knowing are only too much given to overlooking the primary import of the term 'thing': namely, *res*, an affair, an occupation, a 'cause'; something which is similar to having the grippe, or conducting a political campaign, or getting rid of an overstock of canned tomatoes, or going to school, or paying attention to a young woman:—in short, just what is meant in non-philosophic discourse by 'an experience' "(MW X 322–23).

7. James Gouinlock, "Pragmatism Reconsidered," the Roy Wood Sellars Lecture delivered at Bucknell University, April 18, 1983.

8. "In other words, in its ordinary human usage, the term 'experience' was invented and employed previously because of the necessity of having some way to refer peremptorily to what is indicated in only a round-about and divided way by such terms as 'organism' and 'environment,' 'subject' and 'object,' 'persons' and 'things,' 'mind' and 'nature,' and so on" (MW X 324).

9. *The Harvest of the Years* (Boston & New York: Houghton Mifflin, 1927), p. 81.

10. "Pragmatism Reconsidered."

11. The importance of recognizing this fact can be illustrated by the case of Stephen Pepper, who was at once a supporter and a critic of Dewey's. Pepper was a pragmatist who, in the early '30s, noting the lack of work in pragmatic aesthetics, had begun to research the topic in Dewey's writings. When AE appeared, Pepper read it avidly. He noted that Dewey had included the elements he had thought significant, but to his surprise he found him making many assertions "which I should have thought Dewey would rather have bitten his tongue than to have said." This side of Dewey's presentation, which Pepper had not foreseen at all, so predominated that Pepper finally concluded in favor of his own aesthetic theory as the truly pragmatic, whereas "it was Dewey who had here gone astray." Whether Pepper's harsh judgment is correct is not a point on which I am prepared to decide. What I do wish to point out is that we have here, in the very fact of comparing Dewey's positions at two stages, an indication of how important it is to recognize the developmental character of his philosophy. See Pepper's "Some Questions on Dewey's Aesthetics."

BIBLIOGRAPHY

Alexander, Thomas. *The Horizons of Feeling: John Dewey's Theory of Art, Experience, and Nature*. Albany: State University of New York Press, 1987.

Aquinas, Thomas. *Summa theologiae*. Ottawa: Garden City Press, 1941.

Aristotle. *The Basic Works of Aristotle*. Ed. Richard McKeon. New York: Random House, 1941.

——. *De partibus animalium I et De generatione animalium I*. Ed. D. M. Balme. Oxford: Clarendon, 1972.

Aspects of Form: A Symposium on Form in Nature and Art. Ed. Lancelot Law Whyte. Bloomington: Indiana University Press, 1951. Repr. 1961.

Bacon, Francis. *Novum Organum*. In *The English Philosophers from Bacon to Mill*. Ed. Edwin A. Burtt. New York: Modern Library, 1939. Pp. 24–123.

Bakewell, Charles. "The Issue Between Idealism and Immediate Empiricism." *The Journal of Philosophy*, 2 (1905), 687–91.

——. "An Open Letter to Professor Dewey Concerning Immediate Empiricism." *The Journal of Philosophy*, 2 (1905), 520–22.

Benda, Julien. *Trois Idoles romantiques: Le dynamisme, l'existentialisme, la dialectique matérialiste*. Paris: Mont-Blanc, 1948.

Bergson, Henri. *Oeuvres*. Paris: Presses Universitaires de France, 1959.

Bernard, Claude. *An Introduction to the Study of Experimental Medicine*. Trans. Henry C. Green. Repr. ed. New York: Dover, 1957.

Bernstein, Richard. "Dewey, John." In *Encyclopedia of Philosophy* II. Ed. Paul Edwards. New York: Macmillan, 1967.

——. "Dewey's Naturalism." *Review of Metaphysics*, 13 (1959), 340–53.

——. "John Dewey's Metaphysics of Experience." *The Journal of Philosophy*, 58 (1961), 5–14.

Bertrand Russell's Dictionary of Mind, Matter, and Morals. Ed. Lester E. Denonn. New York: Philosophical Library, 1952.

"Biography of John Dewey." Ed. Jane M. Dewey. In *The Philosophy of John Dewey*. Ed. Paul A. Schillp. The Library of Living Philosophers 1. New York: Tudor, 1939. Pp. 1–45.

Blau, Joseph L. *Men and Movements in American Philosophy*. New York: Prentice-Hall, 1952.

Bocheński, I. M. *Contemporary European Philosophy*. Trans. Donald Nicholl and Karl Aschenbrenner. Berkeley: University of California Press, 1957.

——. *A History of Formal Logic.* Trans. and ed. Ivo Thomas. Notre Dame: University of Notre Dame Press, 1961.

——. *The Methods of Contemporary Thought.* Trans. Peter Caws. Dordrecht: Reidel, 1965.

Bowers, David F. "Hegel, Darwin, and the American Tradition." In *Foreign Influences in American Life: Essays and Critical Bibliographies.* Ed. David F. Bowers. Princeton: Princeton University Press, 1944. Pp. 146–71.

Brentano, Franz. *Psychology from an Empirical Standpoint.* Trans. D. B. Terrell, Antos C. Rancurello, and Linda L. McAlister. Ed. Linda L. McAlister. London & New York: Humanities Press, 1973.

Brodsky, Garry M. "Absolute Idealism and John Dewey's Instrumentalism." *Transactions of the Charles S. Peirce Society,* 5 (1969), 44–62.

Burbank, Luther. *The Harvest of the Years.* Boston & New York: Houghton Mifflin, 1927.

Cassirer, Ernst. *The Logic of the Humanities.* Trans. Clarence Smith Howe. New Haven: Yale University Press, 1961.

Cohen, Morris R. *American Thought: A Critical Sketch.* Ed. Felix S. Cohen. Glencoe: Free Press, 1954.

——. "Some Difficulties in Dewey's Anthropocentric Naturalism." *The Philosophical Review,* 49 (1940), 196–228.

Chapters in Western Civilization II. Ed. Contemporary Civilization Staff of Columbia College. 2nd ed. New York: Columbia University Press, 1954.

Chisolm, Roderick. *The Foundations of Knowing.* Minneapolis: The University of Minnesota Press, 1982.

Copleston, Frederick, s.j. *A History of Philosophy.* VI. *Wolff to Kant.* London: Burns & Oates, 1960.

——. *A History of Philosophy.* VIII. *Bentham to Russell.* London: Burns & Oates, 1966.

Costello, Harry Todd. "Professor Dewey's 'Judgments of Practice.' " *The Journal of Philosophy,* 17 (1920), 449–55.

Croce, Benedetto. "On the Aesthetics of Dewey." Trans. Katharine Gilbert. *The Journal of Aesthetics and Art Criticism,* 6 (1948), 203–207.

Darwin, Charles. *The Life and Letters of Charles Darwin, Including an Autobiographical Chapter.* Ed. Francis Darwin. New York: Appleton, 1897.

——. *The Origin of Species and The Descent of Man.* New York: Modern Library, n.d.

Delaney, Cornelius F. *Mind and Nature: A Study of the Naturalistic Philosophies of Cohen, Woodbridge, and Sellars.* Notre Dame: University of Notre Dame Press, 1969.

Deledalle, Gérard. *L'Idée d'expérience dans la philosophie de John Dewey*. Paris: Presses Universitaires de France, 1967.

Dewey, Robert E. *The Philosophy of John Dewey: A Critical Exposition of His Method, Metaphysics, and Theory of Knowledge*. The Hague: Nijhoff, 1977.

Dykhuizen, George. *The Life and Mind of John Dewey*. Carbondale: Southern Illinois University Press, 1973.

Eiseley, Loren. *The Immense Journey*. Repr. ed. New York: Time, Inc., 1962.

Gilson, Étienne. *Painting and Reality*. Cleveland: Meridian Books, 1959.

Grmek, Mirko D. "Bernard, Claude." In *The Dictionary of Scientific Biography* II. Ed. Charles C. Gillispie. New York: Scribner's, 1970.

Gouinlock, James. *John Dewey's Philosophy of Value*. New York: Humanities Press, 1972.

——. "Pragmatism Reconsidered." The Roy Wood Sellars Lecture, Bucknell University, April 18, 1983.

Heidegger, Martin. "Plato's Doctrine of Truth." Trans. John Barlow. In *Philosophy in the Twentieth Century* III. Edd. William Barrett and Henry Aiken. New York: Random House, 1962. Pp. 251–70.

Hofstadter, Albert. "Concerning a Certain Deweyan Conception of Metaphysics." In *John Dewey, Philosopher of Science and Freedom: A Symposium*. Ed. Sidney Hook. New York: Dial, 1950. Pp. 249–70.

Holmes, Oliver Wendell, Jr. "The Path of the Law." In *Law and Philosophy: Readings in Legal Philosophy*. Ed. E. A. Kent. New York: Appleton-Century-Crofts, 1970.

Hook, Sidney. *John Dewey: An Intellectual Portrait*. New York: Day, 1939.

——. *The Metaphysics of Pragmatism*. Chicago: Open Court, 1927.

Intelligence in the Modern World: John Dewey's Philosophy. Ed. Joseph Ratner. New York: Modern Library, 1939.

Jones, Marc Edmund. *George Sylvester Morris: His Philosophical Career and Theistic Idealism*. Philadelphia: McKay, 1948.

Kant, Immanuel. *The Critique of Pure Reason*. Trans. Norman Kemp Smith. London: Macmillan, 1929.

——. *Prolegomena to Any Future Metaphysics*. Trans. Paul Carus. Chicago: Open Court, 1902.

Kestenbaum, Victor. *The Phenomenological Sense of John Dewey: Habit and Meaning*. Atlantic Highlands, N.J.: Humanities Press, 1977.

Laird, John. *Recent Philosophy*. London: Thornton Butterworth, 1936.

Lamprecht, Sterling. "An Idealistic Source of Instrumentalist Logic." *Mind*, 33 (1924), 415–27.

——. *The Metaphysics of Naturalism*. New York: Appleton-Century-Crofts, 1967.

——. *Our Philosophical Traditions: A Brief History of Philosophy in Western Civilization*. New York: Appleton-Century-Crofts, 1955.

Larrabee, Harold. "John Dewey as Teacher." *School and Society*, 86 (1959), 378–81.

Locke, John. *An Essay Concerning Human Understanding*. In *The English Philosophers from Bacon to Mill*. Ed. Edwin A. Burtt. New York: Modern Library, 1939. Pp. 238–402.

Lotze, Hermann. *Logic* I. Ed. and trans. Bernard Bosanquet. Oxford: Clarendon, 1888.

Maritain, Jacques. *Moral Philosophy: An Historical and Critical Survey of the Great Systems*. Trans. Marshall Suther et al. London: Bles; New York, Scribner's, 1964.

Marshak, Alexander. *The Roots of Civilization: The Cognitive Beginnings of Man's First Art, Symbol, and Notation*. New York: McGraw-Hill, 1972.

Mayr, Ernst. *Evolution and the Diversity of Life: Selected Essays*. Cambridge: The Belknap Press of Harvard University Press, 1976.

McGilvary, Evander Bradley. "The Chicago Idea and Idealism." *The Journal of Philosophy*, 5 (1908), 589–97.

——. "Professor Dewey: Logician–Ontologician." *The Journal of Philosophy*, 36 (1939), 561–65.

——. "Professor Dewey's 'Brief Studies in Realism.'" *The Journal of Philosophy*, 9 (1912), 344–49.

——. "Pure Experience and Reality." *The Philosophical Review*, 16 (1907), 266–84.

——. "Pure Experience and Reality: A Reassertion." *The Philosophical Review*, 16 (1907), 422–24.

Murphy, Arthur E. "Objective Relativism in Dewey and Whitehead." *Reason and the Common Good: Selected Essays of Arthur E. Murphy*. Edd. William H. May, Marcus G. Singer, and Arthur E. Murphy. Englewood Cliffs, N.J.: Prentice-Hall, 1963. Pp. 43–66. Orig. publ. in *The Philosophical Review*, 36 (1927), 121–44.

Nagel, Ernest. "Can Logic Be Divorced from Ontology?" *The Journal of Philosophy*, 26 (1929), 705–12.

——. "Dewey's Reconstruction of Logical Theory." In *The Philosopher of the Common Man: Essays in Honor of John Dewey to Celebrate His Eightieth Birthday*. Ed. Sidney Ratner. New York: Putnam's, 1940. Repr. New York: Greenwood, 1966. Pp. 56–86.

——. "Some Leading Principles of Professor Dewey's Logical Theory." *The Journal of Philosophy*, 36 (1939), 576–81.

New Studies in the Philosophy of John Dewey. Ed. Stephen M. Cahn. Hanover, N.H.: The University Press of New England, 1977.

Northrop, F. S. C. "Evolution in Its Relation to the Philosophy of Nature and the Philosophy of Culture." In *Evolutionary Thought in America.* Ed. Stow Person. New Haven: Yale University Press, 1950. Pp. 44–84.

Ortega y Gasset, Jose. *The Revolt of the Masses.* New York: Norton, 1932.

Oxford Latin Dictionary. Ed. P. G. W. Glare. Oxford: Clarendon, 1982.

Pepper, Stephen C. "Some Questions on Dewey's Esthetics." In *The Philosophy of John Dewey.* Ed. Paul A. Schillp. The Library of Living Philosophers 1. New York: Tudor, 1939. Pp. 369–89.

Popper, Karl. "The Rationality of Scientific Revolutions." In *Problems of Scientific Revolution: Progress and Obstacles to Progress in the Sciences.* Ed. Rom Harré. The Herbert Spencer Lectures for 1973. Oxford: Clarendon, 1975. Pp. 72–101.

Preus, Anthony. *Science and Philosophy in Aristotle's Biological Works.* Studien und Materialien zur Geschichte der Philosophie, kleine Reihe 1. Hildesheim & New York: Olms, 1975.

A Question of Physics: Conversations in Physics and Biology. Edd. Paul Buckley and David F. Peat. Toronto: University of Toronto Press, 1979.

Randall, John Herman, Jr. "The Changing Impact of Darwin on Philosophy." *The Journal of the History of Ideas,* 22 (1961), 435–62.

———. "Dewey's Interpretation of the History of Philosophy." *Philosophy After Darwin: Chapters for* THE CAREER OF PHILOSOPHY, *Volume III, and Other Essays.* Ed. Beth J. Singer. New York: Columbia University Press, 1977. Pp. 304–27. Orig. publ. in *The Philosophy of John Dewey.* Ed. Paul A. Schillp. The Library of Living Philosophers 1. New York: Tudor, 1939. Pp. 75–102.

———. "Epilogue: The Nature of Naturalism." In *Naturalism and the Human Spirit.* Ed. Yervant H. Krikorian. Columbia Studies in Philosophy 8. New York: Columbia University Press, 1944. Pp. 354–82.

———. "John Dewey, 1859–1952." In *Dewey and His Critics: Selected Essays from* THE JOURNAL OF PHILOSOPHY. Ed Sidney Morgenbesser. New York: The Journal of Philosophy, Inc., 1977. Pp. 1–9. Orig. publ. in *The Journal of Philosophy,* 50 (1953), 5–13.

———. *The Making of the Modern Mind: A Survey of the Intellectual Background of the Present Age.* Rev. ed. New York: Houghton Mifflin, 1940.

———. *Nature and Historical Experience: Essays in Naturalism and the Theory of History.* New York: Columbia University Press, 1958.

———. "T. H. Green and Liberal Idealism." *Philosophy After Darwin: Chapters for* THE CAREER OF PHILOSOPHY, *Volume III, and Other Essays.* Ed. Beth J. Singer. New York: Columbia University Press, 1977. Pp. 65–96.

Ratner, Joseph. "Introduction to John Dewey's Philosophy." In *Intelligence in the Modern World: John Dewey's Philosophy.* Ed. Joseph Ratner. New York: Modern Library, 1939. Pp. 3–241.

Ratner, Sidney A. "The Development of Dewey's Evolutionary Naturalism." *Social Research*, 20 (1953), 127–54.

———. "Evolution and the Rise of the Scientific Spirit in America." *Philosophy of Science*, 3 (1936), 104–22.

———. "The Evolutionary Naturalism of John Dewey." *Social Research*, 18 (1951), 435–48.

Riley, Woodbridge. *American Thought: From Puritanism to Pragmatism and Beyond.* New York: Smith, 1941.

Robinson, Arthur L. "High Energy Physics: A Proliferation of Quarks and Leptons." *Science*, November 4, 1977, pp. 478–81.

Rorty, Richard. *The Consequences of Pragmatism.* Minneapolis: The University of Minnesota Press, 1982.

———. *Philosophy and the Mirror of Nature.* Princeton: Princeton University Press, 1979.

Rosenstock, Gershon George. *F. A. Trendelenburg: Forerunner to John Dewey.* Carbondale: Southern Illinois University Press, 1964.

Ross, W. D. *Aristotle.* 5th ed. New York: Barnes & Noble, 1964.

Russell, Bertrand. "Dewey's New *Logic*." In *The Philosophy of John Dewey.* Ed. Paul A. Schillp. The Library of Living Philosophers 1. New York: Tudor, 1939. Pp. 135–56.

———. *A History of Western Philosophy.* New York: Simon & Schuster, 1945.

Russell, John Edward. "Objective Idealism and Revised Empiricism." *The Philosophical Review*, 15 (1905), 627–33.

Santayana, George. "Dewey's Naturalistic Metaphysics." *The Journal of Philosophy*, 22 (1925), 673–88. Repr. in *The Philosophy of John Dewey.* Ed. Paul A. Schillp. The Library of Living Philosophers 1. New York: Tudor, 1939. Pp. 243–61.

———. *Lotze's System of Philosophy.* Ed. Paul G. Kuntz. Bloomington: Indiana University Press, 1971.

Schneider, Herbert, W. "Historical Construction and Reconstruction." *Eranos*, 29 (1960), 243–64.

———. *A History of American Philosophy.* 2nd ed. New York: Columbia University Press, 1963.

———. "The Influence of Darwin and Spencer on American Philosophical Theology." *The Journal of the History of Ideas*, 6 (1954), 3–18.

——. *Sources of Contemporary Philosophical Realism in America.* Indianapolis: Bobbs-Merrill, 1964.

Simpson, George Gaylord. "Biology and the Nature of Science." *Science,* January 11, 1963, pp. 81–88.

Skolimowski, Henryk. "Problems of Rationality in Biology." In *Studies in the Philosophy of Biology: Reduction and Related Problems.* Edd. Francisco Jose Ayala and Theodosius Dobzhansky. Berkeley & Los Angeles: University of California Press, 1974. Pp. 205–24.

Sleeper, Ralph. *The Necessity of Pragmatism: John Dewey's Conception of Philosophy.* New Haven: Yale University Press, 1987.

Suppes, Patrick. "Nagel's Lectures on Dewey's Logic." In *Philosophy, Science, and Method: Essays in Honor of Ernest Nagel.* Edd. Sidney Morgenbesser, Patrick Suppes, and Morton White. New York: St. Martin's, 1969. Pp. 2–25.

Szent-Györgyi, Albert. *The Living State; with Observations on Cancer.* New York & London: Academic Press, 1972.

Thayer, H. S. *The Logic of Pragmatism: An Examination of John Dewey's Logic.* New York: Humanities Press, 1952.

——. *Meaning and Action: A Critical History of Pragmatism.* Indianapolis: Bobbs-Merrill, 1968.

Thompson, D'Arcy Wentworth. "Natural Science." In *The Legacy of Greece.* Ed. R. W. Livingstone. Oxford: Clarendon, 1929. Pp. 137–62.

——. *On Aristotle as a Biologist.* London: Oxford University Press, 1911.

——. *On Growth and Form.* 2nd ed. 2 vols. Cambridge: Cambridge University Press, 1942. Repr. 1952.

Ueberweg, Friedrich. *History of Philosophy.* II. *History of Modern Philosophy.* Trans. George S. Morris. New York: Scribner's, 1873.

Veazie, Walter B. "John Dewey and the Revival of Greek Philosophy." *University of Colorado Studies in Philosophy,* 2 (1961), 1–10.

Walsh, Paul. "Some Metaphysical Assumptions in Dewey's Philosophy." *The Journal of Philosophy,* 51 (1954), 861–67.

Ward, Leo. "John Dewey in Search of Himself." *The Review of Politics,* 19 (1957), 205–13.

Weiss, Paul. *The Science of Life: The Living System / A System for Living.* Mount Kisco, N.Y.: Futura, 1973.

White, Morton. *The Origin of Dewey's Instrumentalism.* New York: Columbia University Press, 1943.

Whitehead, Alfred North. *Science and the Modern World.* New York: Macmillan, 1926.

Woodbridge, F. J. E. "Metaphysics." *Nature and Mind.* New York: Columbia University Press, 1937. Repr. New York: Russell & Russell, 1965. Pp. 95–112.

Dewey, John.
"Antinaturalism *in Extremis.*" In *Naturalism and the Human Spirit.* Ed. Yervant H. Krikorian. Columbia Studies in Philosophy 8. New York: Columbia University Press, 1944. Pp. 1–39.

"The Applicability of Logic to Existence." *The Journal of Philosophy,* 27 (1930), 174–79.

Art as Experience. The Later Works. X. *1934.* Ed. Harriet Furst Simon. Carbondale & Edwardsville: Southern Illinois University Press, 1987.

The Early Works. I. *1882–1888.* Carbondale & Edwardsville: Southern Illinois University Press, 1969.

Essays in Experimental Logic. Chicago: The University of Chicago Press, 1916.

"Experience and Existence: A Comment." *Philosophy and Phenomenological Research,* 9 (1948–1949), 709–13.

Experience and Nature. The Later Works. I. *1925.* Edd. Patricia Baysinger and Barbara Levine. Carbondale & Edwardsville: Southern Illinois University Press, 1981.

"Experience, Knowledge and Value: A Rejoinder." In *The Philosophy of John Dewey.* Ed. Paul A. Schillp. The Library of Living Philosophers 1. New York: Tudor, 1939. Pp. 515–608.

Human Nature and Conduct. The Middle Works. XIV. *1922.* Ed. Patricia Baysinger. Carbondale & Edwardsville: Southern Illinois University Press, 1983.

"Introductory Word." In Sidney Hook. *The Metaphysics of Pragmatism.* Chicago: Open Court, 1927. Pp. 1–5.

The Later Works. V. *1929–1930.* Ed. Kathleen E. Poulos. Carbondale & Edwardsville: Southern Illinois University Press, 1984.

Logic: The Theory of Inquiry. The Later Works. XII. *1938.* Ed. Kathleen Poulos. Carbondale & Edwardsville: Southern Illinois University Press, 1986.

The Middle Works. II. *1902–1903.* Ed. Jo Ann Boydston. Carbondale & Edwardsville: Southern Illinois University Press, 1976.

The Middle Works. IV. *1907–1909.* Edd. Jo Ann Boydston and Barbara Levine. Carbondale & Edwardsville: Southern Illinois University Press, 1977.

The Middle Works. X. *1916–1917.* Edd. Jo Ann Boydston and Anne Sharpe. Carbondale & Edwardsville. Southern Illinois University Press, 1980.

On Experience, Nature, and Freedom. Ed. Richard Bernstein. The Library of Liberal Arts. Indianapolis: Bobbs-Merrill, 1960.

Psychology. The Early Works. II. *1887.* Ed. Jo Ann Boydston. Carbondale & Edwardsville: Southern Illinois University Press, 1967.

The Quest for Certainty. The Later Works. IV. *1929.* Ed. Harriet Furst Simon. Carbondale & Edwardsville: Southern Illinois University Press., 1984.

Reconstruction in Philosophy. The Middle Works. XII. *1920.* Ed. Bridget A. Walsh. Carbondale & Edwardsville: Southern Illinois University Press, 1982.

——, and Bentley, Arthur. "Interaction and Transaction." The *Journal of Philosophy,* 43 (1946), 505–17.

INDICES

INDEX RERUM